PLACE
POSTAGE
HERE

SAFARI PRESS
P.O. Box 3095
Long Beach, CA 90803-0095, USA

The African Diary of Bob Eastman

The African Diary of Bob Eastman

By Rick Sapp

Safari Press

Sapp, Rick

Second edition

Safari Press

2012, Long Beach, California

ISBN 978-1-57157-405-3

Library of Congress Catalog Card Number: 2012930998

10 9 8 7 6 5 4 3 2 1

Printed in China

Table of Contents

Introduction

When I began hunting in Africa nearly fifty years ago, I took a gross of arrows and came home with an empty quiver. Now, after thirty trips to hunt on that continent, I take two dozen arrows and return with most of them. It is a matter, I think, of success, seasoning, and maturity.

It was easy to fall in love with a place that, in the mid-twentieth century, we still thought of as the "Dark Continent." Of course, by then Africa had been thoroughly explored, mapped, and, in its own way, civilized. After all, Stanley found the elusive and fatally ill, but nevertheless determined, David Livingstone—"Dr. Livingstone, I presume?"—nearly a century before my first hunt.

Nevertheless, an image of high romance clung to Africa then, in part due to the imaginative storytelling of writers such as Ernest Hemingway *(The Snows of Kilimanjaro, The Green Hills of Africa)* and Robert Ruark *(Something of Value, Uhuru).* Muscular movie heroes Johnny Weissmuller and Buster Crabbe starred in *Tarzan the Ape Man,* based on the book by Edgar Rice Burroughs. The folksy, bringing-it-home-to-you style developed by Peter Capstick (*Death in the Long Grass, Death in the Silent Places)* captivated a later generation of hunters by selling them on danger in the bush.

Imaginative storytelling and exciting movies brought Africa to life. It was terribly exciting for an outdoorsman, and I was young and ready for adventure. I had the money to go see Africa, to experience it for myself—hence the gross of arrows.

Few modern archers had hunted in Africa in those days, and this became part of the allure. Howard Hill and Fred Bear were the most recognizable of that small club, but it also included Bob Swinehart, Bill Negley, and, of course, those earliest toxophilite entrepreneurs, Art Young and Saxton Pope.

Appearing in national magazines, Bear's stories were fresh and powerful. These stories were ultimately collected and rewritten for *Fred*

Bear's Field Notes, and the lanky businessman and outdoorsman, with his engaging "everyman" personality, set thousands of bow hunters on fire with longing to grab their bows, get the kids a job, and mortgage the house.

Of course, hunting whitetails, not lions, was then and remains the American bowhunter's bread and butter, and every fall we went into the field for deer. That was how I got started. Roy Colter and John Borg, my archery mentors from Westchester County, New York, were deer hunters, and good ones.

Years later I moved to California and discovered Catalina Island. I didn't literally discover it, of course, but for an Easterner, its dry Mediterranean landscape had an exotic and exciting feel. It was cheap, close enough for a weekend camp-out, and overrun by exotic sheep, goats, and feral hogs. Catalina also offered an occasional glimpse of a movie star letting his or her hair down. To a young man from the woods of New York via Michigan, the arid island was full of magic. That was half a century ago. Today, Catalina Island Conservancy owns all but a sliver of the island and has eliminated the goats and sheep.

By the late '60s, when I began flying to Africa with bows and arrows, the colonial regimes of Portugal, Britain, Spain, Germany, and France were on their way out. *Uhuru,* the Swahili word for "freedom," was all the rage. The European nations did not leave without a struggle, though, and they forced each fledgling tribal-bound state to fight for independence. Unfortunately, once these peoples attained their independence, they discovered that the twentieth century was inhospitable to the old ways of clan and tribe. The new nation-states faced a world of atomic weapons and economic integration in which they were ill prepared to participate.

Upon gaining independence, most Africans simply exchanged one harsh master for another, and the new ones proved to be equally terrifying, adept at graft and murder. Russia and America—my own country, and I love it deeply, with all of its majesty and flaws—fought one another, country by country, in sad, squalid wars across Africa. At home we remember it as the Cold War, but to most Africans it was anything but cold or distant. Mozambique, Rhodesia, Angola, the Congo, Namibia—each played a small but bloody part in the worldwide struggle.

Today China has established a presence in East Africa, Sudan, Ethiopia, the Congos, and Tanzania. The new colonial master exchanges boatloads of the cheapest baubles, everything from rubber flip flops and thin cotton shirts to shamefully produced tools, in exchange for Africa's precious natural resources. Unlike Africa's former colonial masters, the Chinese will not so easily be driven away, I fear.

A turbulent world in transition seemed unimportant to me in those days. I was obsessed with the bowhunting. After a few weeks abroad, I always returned home having had outlandish experiences and having met wonderful and occasionally bizarre people. The trophies followed a few months later: wildebeest, zebra, giraffe, Cape buffalo, and eventually lion, hippo, elephant, leopard, and much more. And I would not be home very long before the urge to return became overpowering, almost a physical necessity.

Since that first trip in 1968, I have returned thirty-two times, hunting in most subequatorial countries and not a few in the Northern Hemisphere. And I hope to go again soon. My sons, Rob and Erik, have accompanied me, as has my patient and thoughtful spouse, Ann.

From bongo in Cameroon to elephant in Angola, from ground blinds in South Africa to face-offs with Cape buffalo in Tanzania, I have drunk very deeply of the African experience. And always with the recurve bow. Never once have I pulled the trigger of a firearm to harvest a game animal, but I have no argument with those who prefer gunfire to the silent grace of a bow and arrow.

While I have been as dedicated to bringing trophies home as any American big-game hunter, including Theodore Roosevelt who took an eleven-month safari, I understand and accept archery's inherent limitations. The bow and arrow force one to hunt close to one's quarry, to be patient and observant. Whether one hunts smarter or harder with a bow is an open question. But one must accept the difficulty as part of its appeal and realize that danger is close. Always. In Africa.

For me, the bow is primal. It lets me experience leopards and zebras and hippos as close as is humanly possible in the wild without being killed. The bow is somehow necessary to me and expressive of my nature. Whatever that is, I like it.

I would like to claim that I can recall every hunt and hunting partner, every professional hunter, every trophy shot, but I cannot. I would like to sit back and laugh about each of the funny incidents in my long hunting career and to remember the few tragedies and numerous close calls, but I cannot. I would like to claim that I remember everything, exactly as it happened, but that is not true. The curtain of time slides quietly down, slowly but inexorably. It obscures the days and their events, even some of the participants. The trips run together in memory, merging like herds of wildebeests seeking water. So the urge to commit to paper this nearly half-century of visits to one of the last wild places in the world is important to me beyond the weight of any actual event.

Even though for me a trip to Africa still means wild places, unpredictable events, and, often, unusual companions, Africa has changed dramatically during the half-century since I first hunted there. It has changed more so, I believe, than in any half-century in human history or prehistory. During this era, human populations and their needs and desires have exploded, driving some of the continent's wildlife to the brink of desperation, if not outright extinction.

Bowhunting in Africa has changed as well. Half a century ago, no professional hunters understood the bow or the dynamics of hunting with it. Gradually and, I think, grudgingly, some of them have now accepted it.

With extreme pressure on the land and animals, the bowhunting equation has become less free-range and more confined to dark, silent hides near water holes on private ranches surrounded by high, game-proof fences. Such a hunt, usually in South Africa, is clearly more affordable than the traditional, old-style safari. It is more democratic as well, allowing thousands of bow hunters to experience that special thrill of being able to cast arrows in exotic environments. Still, I have often heard the argument that the same experience can be had at many a ranch in Texas without the arduous trauma of flying halfway around the globe, and at half the price. Don't believe it.

I have changed over the years as well. On many evenings in the past, we drank straight from the bottle of whatever potent brew we had brought with us and cursed when it was empty. Now, instead of carrying a spare bottle of Jack Daniels and sipping cocktails around the campfire, I find myself reading a business text by lantern. And, as I said in the beginning, the gross of arrows has become a mere two dozen, most of which I give to the guides and trackers before flying out of the bush.

All of this reaffirms that the quality, the estimation, and even the nature of change depend on one's point of view. For me, even as I write, I itch to plan the next adventure. Nearing seventy years old, I feel that familiar, persistent urge to test myself again, whether it be against a lion from a thornbush blind or from some shaky machan or against one more magnificent buffalo bull from a herd of hundreds, any one of which would be delighted to kill me.

Such an inner claim on my desire drives me to return to Africa time and again. And when I no longer have the muscle to draw a sixty-five-pound recurve bow and hold it steady, when my legs are no longer strong enough to stalk through the high grass while temperatures and humidity climb into the nineties, I will have a storehouse of memories. When that time comes, I will blow upon the coals of long-dead campfires. The dancing images that come to mind will carry me back to old friends and hot passions, spectacular visions and missed opportunities that will only live in an old man's memory and in this book.

* * *

Rick Sapp and I wrote several of the stories in this book together over six years. The chapters are presented roughly in sequence by year, beginning with my earliest adventure in Africa more than forty years ago, but there may be different perspectives on certain people and events in multiple chapters. Far from being a drawback, this gives the material a dimension it might otherwise lack because of the difficulty in contacting professional hunters who have retired or in sorting through my unorganized photo and memory files.

Several of the stories have been published in one form or another in U.S. periodicals such as *SAFARI* magazine and *Bowhunting World.* I thank the editors for publishing our stories and for supporting regulated hunting and scientific wildlife conservation around the world.

Bob Eastman
Flushing, Michigan
September 2011

Jerry Does a Back Flip

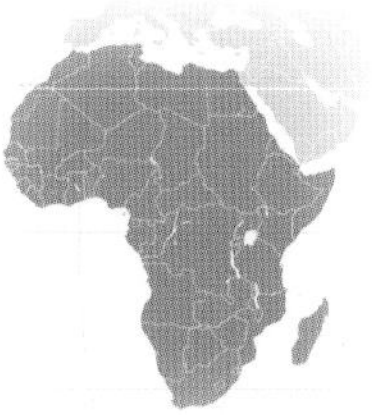

1968

Chapter 1

"All I wanted to do now was get back to Africa. We had not left it, yet, but when I would wake in the night I would lie, listening, homesick for it already."

Green Hills of Africa[1]

Ernest Hemingway

The hot breath of an elephant or a lion, or any of the Big Six—elephant, lion, leopard, Cape buffalo, rhino, or hippo—on one's neck can cause even the most courageous man to develop a tic. Hunting must be similar to combat, for no man knows how he will react when mortar rounds begin to burst in the trees, or when the first man in the squad collapses with a bullet in his belly. Does any man know how quickly or how capably he will respond when a mugger grabs his wife?

No matter how many videos you watch or how many books you read, no matter how many pounds you can bench press or how well you do in the half-marathon, no matter what your ability to maintain meditative inner balance, when the moment arrives to stand up to the charge of a screaming elephant—a massive animal that can barely distinguish a man from a chicken—only then, at that instant, can you possibly know how you will react.

Just as animal handlers train for confrontations with caged lions and police officers learn to defuse violent situations, it is theoretically

[1]Page 72.

possible for hunters to practice suppressing their emotions during life-altering situations. People are not born to be cool under fire, though Kipling advises one who would be a real man to "keep your head when all about you are losing theirs and blaming it on you. . . ."[2] After all, being a cop or a circus performer is a vocation. Such people are paid to yawn at danger. Statistics suggest that the adrenaline rush, the thrill of danger, is one reason a person becomes a cop or a firefighter, a soldier or a racecar driver.

Call it a passion or an obsession, hunting is a hobby. Hunters are first of all teachers and businessmen, fathers and husbands. The days when a community of bushmen could feed themselves by hunting and gathering are lost. So no one is going to pay a hunter to master his fear, unless he becomes one of the handful of professional hunting guides in the world. No one is going to create training opportunities with a leopard, and the cost of facing an elephant or a lion on one's own is virtually prohibitive, so it has always been an event that occurs only once or twice in a lifetime.

Few recreational hunters will ever be steady enough to disregard the PH when a Cape buffalo whirls and begins its rush, the menace in its tiny black eyes reflecting the hunter's imminent dismemberment, the width of its boss and the sweep of its horn shifting instantly from trophy to weapon. In this life, coping with danger is a learn-by-doing experience for hunters, and every instance of peril carries with it the real possibility that something unique and painful will occur.

Fateful Times, Fateful Places

The year 1967 was turbulent, and 1968 would be even more so. In 1967 China exploded its first hydrogen bomb. America's youth

[2]Rudyard Kipling's poem *If* was published in 1909.

A first elephant is a terrific accomplishment, especially with the bow and arrow because a hunter must be close and must place his arrow precisely between the ribs. Bob Eastman's initial elephant hunt in the '60s in Mozambique resulted in the trophy above; it was just not one for the record book.

challenged the civil war that Lyndon Johnson and Robert McNamara were prolonging in Indochina. Racial violence hammered Detroit, and Israel hammered its Arab neighbors in the Six-Day War. The United States edged close to two hundred million residents, and NASA astronauts Grissom, White, and Chaffee died in a flash fire inside their Apollo space capsule at Cape Canaveral. *The Graduate, Bonnie and Clyde,* and *Cool Hand Luke* swamped movie theaters, while The Beatles released their *Sgt. Pepper's Lonely Hearts Club Band* album.

That year the tiniest building blocks of nature, quarks, were discovered, and Communist revolutionary Ché Guevara was killed in Bolivia. Mankind examined its world through a microscope, and the eye of a lunatic reflected in the lens.

In 1967 Bob Eastman took the first of his half-century of African safaris, and his friend Jerry Gentellalli, quite literally beneath the tusks of a charging elephant, turned a perfect backflip.

Jerry Gentellalli owned La Mesa Archery in San Diego. The sporting goods store was part of the House of Gentellalli, Jerry's hair salon. Although he began his working life as a commercial fisherman, Jerry had a thing for hair. He was a natural stylist. If a man had a more unusual combination of temperaments and abilities, he would not be found among the hunting fraternity.

Bob met Jerry at a hunting camp in Colorado the year before they flew to Africa. Jerry was a tough, quick man, about five and a half feet tall. He had brown hair and eyes that took in everything. In Colorado he talked enthusiastically about an upcoming polar bear hunt. For instance, he planned to paint the back of his bow white and wear a layer of white over his insulated suit. (The back of the bow was the side that faced the polar bear; the face was toward the archer.)

Unhappily, not long after the Colorado outing, a horse threw Jerry, and he broke his leg. He canceled the polar bear hunt and began physical therapy. When Bob, seeking to cheer the bedridden bow hunter, described a hunt he was planning in Mozambique the following May, Jerry realized his leg was already feeling better, and he signed on.

Neither Bob nor Jerry had ever been to Africa. In the '60s it was still the Dark Continent, and maps bore names like the Belgian Congo and Tanganyika and Rhodesia. Apartheid was law in South Africa. Nevertheless, the nations were beginning to shed white colonial control. They eventually achieved this at a horrible price in blood and corruption, which unfortunately continue to this day.

Few archers had hunted in Africa then, so Bob and Jerry didn't have much of a plan, but they knew about Saxton Pope and Art Young, Howard Hill and Fred Bear. These hunters were the pioneers of bowhunting in Africa. Bear had publicized his 1964 adventures in Mozambique by connecting with '50s national radio and television personality Arthur Godfrey and the popular television shows *American Sportsman* and *The Late Show.* The 1967 group of archers, which included Bob Eastman, his bride, Ann, and his bowhunting mentor, Roy Colter, was still in the first wave of archers in Africa.

Competing Personalities

Bob and Jerry didn't realize that by throwing themselves into the midst of a hunting expedition with Safarilandia Mozambique, the storied concession camp owned by Baron Werner von Alvensleben, they were harnessing the competitive energies of their professional guides. Fast friends, Rui Quadros and Amadeu Peixe were Africans of Portuguese descent. Quadros was thirty; Peixe was thirty-two. Both were national trap and skeet champions, as good with a shotgun as they were with a rifle. Neither had a clue about the bow and arrow, however.

The Americans were surprised when, on occasion, Rui Quadros would take over the driving and watch for big game and game birds. Seeing the flush of a francolin or a dove, he might grab his shotgun

In the sixties, Bob Eastman (right) took his first leopard with guide Amadeu Peixe. Called Fish by his American clients that included Fred Bear, Peixe was a Mozambican of Portuguese descent.

from its place beside the steering wheel, load a shell, shove the barrel out the window, and drop the bird without veering from the rutted savanna path. Then, the guide would turn and grin, as if to say, "Did you see that?"

These young men were cocky and utterly self-assured, but they were as different as a gnu and a gerenuk.

Rui Quadros was a moody, intense man. He rarely smiled and could become unexpectedly morose. He was a passionate hunter, but he was also a man who openly expressed his sympathy for the animals. A poorly placed shot or a client's failure to follow his directions precisely might set Rui off, cursing and on the edge of apoplexy. His fists clenched and his face contorted, he would redden as if he were going to hold his breath until his eyes popped out. At such times guests could be certain that Rui was considering using his fists to enforce his authority.

This difficult, angry man had a genuinely soft side. The songbirds and the butterflies, even the bats of Mozambique, were his private passion. He could identify them flitting through the brush and on the wing, and he would volunteer their names and information relating to their lives and habitat.

"African fire finch," he might mutter to no one in particular, his eyes straining to peer through the tree canopy, as if his clients had come to Africa on a bird-watching expedition. "Seed eaters. Big nests."

Before dawn each morning, Rui insisted his clients stand by the Toyota while he and his tracker and the driver packed for the day's adventures. When a client was late or had jogged back to one of the picturesque thatched huts to retrieve his hat, Rui brooded as if the sun might burst above the tree line while he was killing precious time. Impatient to be away from camp, he would curse, at first quietly and, if the delay were more than a few minutes, not so quietly. He paced and drummed his fingers on the roof of the white truck. And if a client eventually noticed that Rui and his men had forgotten to pack water for the day, the guide refused to return to camp, muttering, in a mixture of Portuguese and Shangaan, something that sounded like, "You came here to hunt, not to hang around the campfire. Suck it up (you soft Yankee bastard)."

Jerry drew Rui for a PH, and Bob drew Peixe, whom everyone called Fish (in English his name meant "lance fish"). Which of the American hunters had the long and which had the short straw may never be fully understood. Unlike the easygoing yet professional Peixe, Rui never quite seemed to care whether his clients were having a great safari, the time of their lives, or getting their money's worth. Rui was all about the work, the effort, the animals. If, at the end of the day, his clients were too exhausted to eat, he was happy. If they were bitten by flies, if their clothing was shredded by thorns and their throats parched with thirst, Rui perhaps believed they were experiencing the real Africa. And if a client succeeded in downing a record-book kudu, despite Rui's unspoken belief that clients were stumbling dolts, well, that was their business. Rui might smile and pose for a picture, but he made little effort to celebrate. By the end of a hunt, most clients probably hated Rui, but, in spite of their personal feelings, they took home trophies.

Although either guide could walk all day without water, rest, or food, Amadeu Peixe was Rui's alter ego. Rui had the husky physique and bold good looks of a movie star. A few photos survive, frayed and fading, glued permanently into Rui's dilapidated album. (Rui and Peixe lost everything, including most of their photos and souvenirs, when they, along with hundreds of thousands of others, fled Mozambique in the aftermath of the 1974 Communist takeover.) In these photos it is not some shy, unheralded black tracker or driver who stands near the smiling client, but Rui himself. In most cases he has stripped off his shirt to kneel close beside some proud rifleman and his trophy. The guide is an exotic, black-haired presence, like Tarzan. He stares straight and unsmiling into the camera with a glare that heightens the sense of safari. He knows he is a handsome brute.

Amadeu Peixe, on the other hand, was tall and thin, with a dark mustache and a curling goatee. The respected PH had guided Fred Bear, a prince of Spain, movie actors, and industrialists. While Rui was the gruff disciplinarian, Peixe was the cheerful, patient coach, the guide who meticulously prepared for each day. Peixe never lost his temper and never left camp without spare water cans. His was the perfect attitude for a nervous bow hunter excited about his first African safari.

Peixe laughed at Rui for hauling clients out of bed at 4:00 AM.

"You'll just sit out there in the dark and wait for the sun to come up. You can't see anything. Who wants to walk around in the bush before you can see? There are lions and hyenas and snakes!"

His teasing and heavily accented English sounded almost comical, even effeminate, while Rui's face reddened and his brows furrowed in anger.

Neither of the American archers recalls precisely how the competition began between Rui and Jerry, Peixe and Bob, but it seemed to arise naturally from the loneliness of the veld. After all, here were two novice American bow hunters—both had hunted extensively in America, but they were novices in Africa—and two intensely competitive professional guides. In the early days of the hunt, every effort at humor, any small joke to scrub away the wildness of the bush, led to a challenge and then to a wager, although both Jerry and Bob swear money never changed hands.

In those days—forty-four years ago at this writing—there was game everywhere. This was before the revolutions and the resulting horrors of civil war and ecological collapse that decimated entire countries. Back then, it was natural enough to place a friendly wager on which team of hunters would take the greater number of game animals. Although the archers understood that their goal was not to score a great quantity of

Roy Colter was one of Bob Eastman's childhood mentors. Roy taught him bowhunting skills in Westchester County, New York, and eventually accompanied Bob to Tanzania where, thirty years ago, he took this magnificent kudu.

big game but to experience an African safari and perhaps to take several high-quality animals, the competitiveness did sharpen the day's work.

Jerry recalls, "Our bets were similar to those of fishermen who heighten their group's enthusiasm by boasting that they will be the first to catch their limit or will catch the largest or the greatest number of fish."

Today, such a wager may seem disrespectful to the animals hunted and maybe to the experience itself, but it was not thought to be so a half-century ago. A similar wager today would be judged by different standards and by the spirit of the gesture.

"I told Jerry to shoot, shoot!"

Elephants belong to the order Proboscidea, of which there are only three members: elephants of the African savanna, elephants of the African forest, and the Asian elephant. It is the order of nose and ears. Elephants and the ludicrous proboscis monkey are the Jimmy Durantes of the animal world.

An elephant's most important appendage is its trunk. It could get along without a tail, lost to the bite of a lion. It might live with a leg crippled by a snare. But cut off its trunk or stick an arrow through it, and that pachyderm is dead.

The African bush elephant, *Loxodonta africana,* uses its precious trunk to multi-task. With the trunk it grasps food and hauls to its mouth everything from small trees to a single blade of grass. It drinks by sucking water into its trunk and spraying the water into its mouth. The elephant breathes and smells through its trunk and fondles its mate with that same trunk. And occasionally there is a report that an elephant has seized some hapless person; with its trunk it squeezes him without mercy before crushing him beneath its ponderous feet or with its forehead.

Thirty-two-year-old Jerry had switched his sights from the Arctic to Africa, from polar bears to elephants. In those days, not many elephants—perhaps three or four—had been taken with a modern bow, but Jerry was convinced that, using a heavy arrow and a sharp broadhead, his 89-pound recurve could achieve sufficient penetration to kill a mature pachyderm, bypassing the ribs and slicing through an inch and a half of hide.

Before guiding Jerry to an elephant, though, Rui made him shoot several baboons. Easy to tip over with a gun, the sharp-eyed primates were a challenge with relatively slow and high-arcing arrows. A troop of baboons will not sit still with humans present; they will run. Jerry took shots at these small targets, moving in their peculiar limping arm-and-leg gait. It amazed and delighted the Portuguese-Mozambican guide and his black accomplices when Jerry's arrow stuck one at sixty yards. (Perhaps, at that distance, it amazed Jerry as well.) Rui's tracker and driver immediately charged the dying primate and gleefully hacked it to death with their machetes. It was a violent and primal foreshadowing of conflict in the Congo and, years later, in Zambia and Rwanda.

"My men say these nasty little buggers sneak into villages and steal whatever they can lay their hands on," Rui said. "And believe me, brother, if you have ever been in one of these bush villages, you would hardly believe baboons would waste their time. But they raid the vegetable gardens, and that pushes the women over the edge. In this part of Africa only women are gardeners, and whatever they can grow themselves becomes the majority of their food.

"Baboons have been known to snatch babies. Once the babies get a little large, too large for the baboon females to carry, they abandon them. Then the leopards get them. So the Shangaan hate baboons."

Having successfully graduated from the baboon-culling phase of his elephant hunt, Jerry had had a long day before he and Rui located a herd. They began to follow it, at first by vehicle and then on foot. There were many more elephants in Mozambique in those days, before AK-47s became commonplace in the bush and before a surging tide of humanity threatened to sweep all but a handful of Babar's kinfolk from the wilderness.

Recurves in Mozambique. Bob Eastman's party of archers—California's Jerry Gentellalli (right) and Roy Colter (left) who was manufacturer of the Cat Quiver—hunted with Werner von Alvensleben's Safarilandia Mozambique along the Save River in the '60s. They were often guided by Rui Quadros (center), a terrific guide, but a man with little sense of humor and an obstinate—some might say ornery—passion for Africa's big game.

After a ten-mile hike, Rui and Jerry finally discovered a bull elephant slightly separated from a herd. The setup seemed perfect, as if it were designed by the gods of the hunt themselves. The lone bull, apparently asleep and leaning against a thick termite mound, appeared in front of the hunters. The sun, the wind, and maybe even their astrological signs were aligned in their favor.

Like most professional hunters in the '60s, Rui was accustomed to riflemen, who could take shots at elephants from much farther away. Riflemen only had to be concerned that the bullet was carefully placed and that, when it reached the beast, the round would still carry sufficient kinetic energy for a mortal wound. A bow hunter's concerns were identical, though his range was insanely close.

At seventy-five yards, Rui, not the most patient of guides and admittedly inexperienced with bow hunters, began to hint that Jerry should loose an arrow. Jerry, however, knew he was outside his effective range. And, though a rifleman might aim for the ear canal or make a frontal brain shot, there was only one place that would allow an archer to take the animal cleanly, Jerry believed. He must slip the arrow between the elephant's ribs and into its lungs. The elephant would run away, the hunter hoped, leaking blood in such quantity that even an inexperienced tracker could follow, and the beast would expire within the hour.

African PHs are not especially keen on blood trailing, and therein lies their customary argument with bow hunters. Who knows what is lurking in the bush while one is down on his hands and knees, searching for droplets of blood? To this day, leopards, lions, and hyenas kill and eat people in East Africa, prompting us to reconsider which species truly occupies the top of the food chain. Only the rare casualty involving a hunting client, unfortunate tourist, or other nonresident is widely publicized.

Typically, it is not the PH who does the serious tracking, however. Safari companies employ local individuals to work in support roles, and one is the role of tracker. Such men are always black Africans. They are usually more skilled in bushcraft than the PH, whose primary job is to look after the client. It is the trackers, bent over as they scan for tracks and droplets of red blood in the sand, who are vulnerable on a hot and thirsty track. And tracking a wounded elephant has been known to last for days. Armed as he is with a .375 or some heavier-caliber rifle (or perhaps a shotgun loaded with buckshot to shoot a wounded leopard at short range), a decent PH knows this and is protective of the unarmed and defenseless men in his charge.

So when Rui began urging Jerry to shoot, even though he was still out of range, it was not with complete lack of consideration for the archer.

That day was hot—practically all days are hot in central Mozambique. Jerry and Rui and their tracker slipped closer to the elephant, using the termite mound as cover. Halfway there, Jerry's throat began to cry out for water. It was a natural reaction to thirst compounded by excitement.

Eventually, the men were only ten yards from the sleeping giant. For Jerry, the opportunity disguised a problem. Not only was the elephant leaning against the termite mound, effectively covering its vitals—the exact area an arrow would have to be placed to make the quickest killing shot—but it was also on the opposite side of the mound. So, despite Rui's urgently whispered warnings, Jerry crept closer and closer, edging to his left, and calculated the angle that would permit his arrow to slide between the ribs and into the elephant's great lungs. Finally, he was not five yards away. Then four and even three. Three yards . . . less than a heartbeat.

"I whispered to shoot," Rui continued the story, after forty years still astonished at the bow hunter's temerity. "That elephant was just on the other side of an anthill, sleeping, and Jerry kept getting closer until he was only three meters from it. I said, 'Jerry, watch out for the wind changing.'

"So Jerry goes to his left, and the feathers on his arrows—they're fluttering a little bit in the wind, you see—get the attention of the elephant. It wakes up, and it opens its eye to look at those feathers. We freeze, but we are so close that if the elephant suddenly charged around the anthill, it would be on us instantly.

"Then its trunk snakes around toward the arrows in Jerry's quiver. Trying to smell them, feel them, because it didn't know what they were, and I think, *Sh@#. We're all going to get killed here, and Jerry's going to be the first one to die.* And that elephant begins to shift its weight off the anthill, and Jerry notices this. How could he not notice? He could have leaned forward and touched it with the tip of his bow. The instant that elephant moved, Jerry reaches down and does this incredible disappearing blackflip, and I think, *Oh, no. He's hurt!*

"So I get up and I hit him, the elephant—*boom!*—and knock him down.

"Jerry could easily have been killed by that elephant that day. He was never interested in elephants after that . . . and I have never understood how a grown man with a bow and arrows in his hand on uneven ground can suddenly perform this perfect backflip. Incredible."

Jerry remembers the day, too. He recalls the elephant growling like a dog.

"I never heard anything like that," he says.

What is unsaid is that he never wants to hear it again, either.

* * *

Jerry Gentellalli never returned to Africa. He never made his trip to Alaska for polar bear, either. He recalls the elephant episode vividly, though, and he remembers how, a few days later, an unruly wildebeest charged, breaking the tip of his recurve. Jerry was the only hunter ever known to have been threatened with bodily harm by a gnu.

In the end, the count of big game compiled by Rui and Jerry was one more than that claimed by Peixe and Bob. And even though Jerry's elephant was credited to his professional hunter, Mr. Back Flip took a magnificent Cape buffalo, plus bushpig, waterbuck, eland, warthog, nyala, greater kudu, oribi, bushbuck, and sable . . . not to mention baboon, which is really what put him and Rui over the top.

Inside the Magic Kingdom

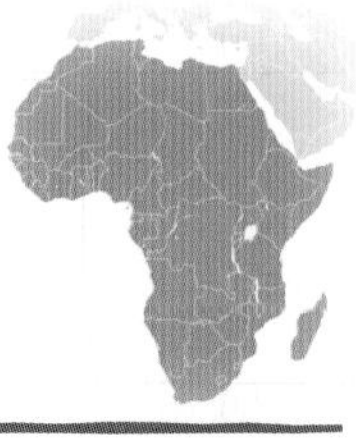

1969

Chapter 2

A peculiar virtue in wildlife ethics is that the hunter ordinarily has no gallery to applaud or disapprove of his conduct. Whatever his acts, they are dictated by his own conscience, rather than a mob of onlookers. It is difficult to exaggerate the importance of this fact.

A Sand County Almanac[1]
Aldo Leopold

It was the adventure of a lifetime.

Scott Young was only seventeen, and he was not large for his age. Nevertheless, his parents let him go to Africa with someone they didn't even know. Perhaps the clincher was the money. Isn't it always?

Scott needed a couple of thousand dollars to make the trip, and his folks told him, "If you can come up with the money, you can go." They probably figured it wasn't going to happen. Scott worked as a "box boy" in the supermarket for minimum wage, which was $1.25 an hour in 1969, and raising the money for an African safari must have seemed to him like raising a million dollars.

But Scott caught fire. If someone had told him he had to raise a hundred thousand dollars before he could stow his bow and board a plane to Africa, he would have counted the nickels and dimes in his pocket and confidently announced, "I've got thirty-five cents. That means I

[1]Page 178.

have only ninety-nine thousand, nine hundred and ninety-nine dollars and sixty-five cents to go."

In hindsight, those seem like innocent times. This was before Scott spent thirty years in law enforcement, most of it with the Los Angeles County Sheriff's Department. Tough neighborhoods. Many languages. Lots of bodies. Enough blood and broken bones, broken lives, to satisfy a sadist. And needles. Almost as tough a neighborhood as Mozambique when the killing started there in the '60s, except that in Africa they meant to kill—randomly, in abundance, and, often—and to inflict intense pain and suffering in the process. The killing practitioners on the Dark Continent appeared to enjoy their work, and they were very good at it.

But Scott was still an innocent kid, and for bow hunters Africa was still the Magic Kingdom.

But First, Santa Catalina

The modern hunter knows very little about Catalina Island, originally named Santa Catalina and before that San Salvador. Who knows what it was called in the language of the Pimuvit (or Pimungan) people the Spanish sailors encountered there five hundred years ago.

Catalina is as much the birthplace of modern bowhunting as Michigan or Wisconsin, though the island was never so intended. But most things turn out differently from the way they begin or from the designer's original idea. God surely looks down at the world and scratches his head: "What was I thinking?"

At sixteen, Scott Young bowhunted the pigs and goats on that dry Pacific island. "Seeded" there by early American whaling ships, the animals were a ready source of fresh meat on a difficult two-year voyage around Cape Horn. The realization of a canal across the Isthmus of Panama was then a century or more away. So Scott was shooting goats

Scott Young, later to pursue a career in law enforcement in Los Angeles, was just seventeen years old when he first accompanied Bob Eastman to Africa. Bowhunting in Mozambique in 1969, his first big-game trophy was this black wildebeest.

at sixteen, and barely a year later he was running for his life from a trio of charging bull elephants in southeast Africa.

Catalina gave Scott—and thousands of others—a bowhunting opportunity. Owned by the Wrigley family, America's chewing-gum impresarios, the island was overrun by hardy critters who, though not necessarily native, had reached a rough equilibrium on the arid, cactus-covered land. What harm could they possibly do? Even the Wrigleys would occasionally mount up, grab their .22 rifles, and chase goats from horseback.

Only twenty miles southwest of Los Angeles, Catalina was not a tourist attraction in the '50s and '60s, or even in the '70s. Bow hunters looking for a weekend camping and hunting trip flew over on seaplanes. Movie stars like Charlie Chaplin, Howard Hill, Errol Flynn, Johnny Weissmuller, and John Wayne—their yachts packed with "fine food, better booze, and broads with big boobs"—motored over to anchor at Avalon, the island's rustic but hospitable port. In those days Catalina was a seldom-visited gem awaiting the curse of being discovered, a picturesque backwater fishing village not far from one of the fastest-growing cities in America.

"Seaplane fare from Los Angeles to Catalina was only fifteen dollars," Scott recalls. "Even then, that wasn't a great deal of money, although I was a kid and had to scrimp and save for the cash, so we hunted there as much as possible. The fee for a three-day hunt through the Camp & Cove Company, which had the concession for quail and goats and fishing from the Wrigley family, was eighteen dollars."

It was through archery and trips to Catalina that Scott met Bob Eastman. Both men were archers, and although Bob was ten years older, he was gripped by the same hunting fever as the teenager. Bob, who had his pilot's license, even talked Scott into taking up flying, although spending six hundred dollars for ground school and sufficient air time to qualify for a license seemed outrageously expensive in those days.

"When I had a lesson, Bob always wanted to come along for the ride," Scott said. "That meant I had to rent a larger airplane, step up from a Cessna 150 to a 172. It got to be expensive."

Long before Bob and Scott flew to Africa, the piloting experience provided its own death-defying moments. With the youngster at the controls, they flew over the Pacific to Catalina and "buzzed goats, chased them down ridges," Scott recalls. "In those days that was just good, clean fun. Today, we would never let our kids do some of the things that we did."

It all set the stage for their first African adventure.

The Times They Are a-Changin'

"Then you better start swimming or you'll sink like a stone, for the times they are a-changin'." So goes the Bob Dylan song "The Times They Are a-Changin'." For Bob Dylan, the times were 1964.

That year, FRELIMO (Front for the Liberation of Mozambique) began a series of bloody cross-border raids deep into the Portuguese colony. A decade later, this political and military movement would bring the impoverished country its independence, though at a terrible cost in lives and suffering.

Five years after Bob Dylan penned these ominous yet promising lyrics, two years after the Summer of Love, and despite an armed counterinsurgency movement named RENAMO—sponsored by apartheid South Africa and Rhodesia with U.S. backing—Mozambique was on the verge of a-changin'.

To this day, Mozambique's national flag features a symbol of resistance and war that is recognized around the world: a Soviet-era Kalashnikov AK-47 rifle. The only state banner in the world with such a symbol, the flag also depicts a primitive hoe, although a fleet of modern tractors would be insufficient to change a poverty-stricken national mentality that remains obsessed with colonial-era repression.

It was onto this volatile background of international intrigue and rebellion that three green bow hunters—Bob Eastman, Scott Young, and Dale Gray—ventured in 1969. Bob wanted to hunt an elephant; Scott intended to operate Bob's Super 8mm movie camera but took his bow "just in case"; and Dale went simply for the experience.

"I was a kid from the white suburbs of L.A.," Scott says, reflecting on his naïveté about Africa and big game and the international power struggle that swirled around their cocooned camp on the Save River. "I had no means, no right, to be in Africa hunting with the bow and arrow."

Obviously, the kid was smitten.

"Means," in the sense of wealth, knowledge, or power, is not something a seventeen-year-old usually possesses. Scott spoke no Portuguese or Shangaan, Shona or Swahili; he had no education past high school; and he had no survival skills beyond sheer spunk. So perhaps what he meant was that he was young, scared, and a long way from home. One lion, three elephants, and Africa itself helped Scott grow up fast. His professional hunters, Rui Quadros and Amadeu Peixe, and his friend Bob Eastman supervised the process. Bob had once again booked with Werner von Alvensleben's Safarilandia Mozambique.

Still, something more subtle than the charge of a trio of ten-thousand-pound elephants may have contributed to Scott's immediate sense of helplessness.

Like Catalina, the camp on the Save was a hangout for European princes and Hollywood celebrities. Don Juan Carlos, the future king of Spain, hunted there, as did American writer Robert Ruark, who elaborated on the camp's story in best-selling novels. Bowhunting pioneer Fred Bear, accompanied by Arthur Godfrey, had made von Alvensleben's camp legendary in bowhunting circles, though such circles were narrow in those days before the compound bow.

These famous men and not a few women, all people of "means," signed their names to the whitewashed wall in the camp's dining hall. Scott eventually wrote his name near that of Fred Bear, but it never occurred to him to take a picture of the wall.

The California kid—who has now hunted in Africa six times—is still in awe of his good fortune. "I'm in Africa," he reminisces. "I'm seventeen years old, signing my name next to Fred Bear, and only a handful of people with a bow had hunted there!"

It would have been odd not to feel overwhelmed.

The Missed Shot

An airplane flight halfway around the world and one's first overnight stay in a five-star hotel in the capital of a foreign country make memories for a seventeen-year-old. And they were only the beginning.

In those days, the bow and arrow were not condoned in Mozambique, but the Portuguese colonial officials quietly turned their heads for reputable and free-spending safari outfitters. After all, the officials were born in and spoke the languages of the country, and they understood the writing on the wall. Through a haze of denial, they realized better than anyone else that their time as masters of southeast Africa was drawing to a close.

The officials certainly had bigger fish to fry, and if they ignored archers, then the professional hunters, though puzzled that people would bring such inadequate gear to Africa, would not fuss a great deal either. They soon learned that American bow hunters worked hard, rarely complained, and did not judge their hunt in the same manner as riflemen. Ultimately, bow hunters would become as obsessed with record-book minutiae as were gun hunters, but that moment was still a generation away.

* * *

Bob had hunted with von Alvensleben two years before, taking blue wildebeest, nyala, sable, kudu, impala, warthog, and even that shyest of all big cats, the leopard.

Right away, Scott realized that the fabled camp was not going to be a five-star hotel in the bush. Perhaps he had pictured Hemingway's campsite in *The Snows of Kilimanjaro*: "This was a pleasant camp under big trees against a hill, with good water, and close by, a nearly dry water hole where sand grouse flighted in the mornings."[2]

Though neat and comfortable, von Alvensleben's concession camp, located in a swamp near the Save River in southern Mozambique, was beset with tsetse. Flies made any trek through the shadeless scrub exhausting, miserable.

To this day the Save is an important national landmark. The river separates the subtropical Shangaan people to its south, in Gaza and Inhambane provinces, from the tropical Shona people to the north, in Manica and Sofala. The Shangaan are adherents of FRELIMO politics, and the Shona profess more reactionary RENAMO politics.

Safarilandia and its experienced second-in-command, Wally Johnson Jr., forbade hunting or shooting within a mile of camp, so the days began, and often ended, with time-consuming hikes away from the river through the mopane scrub, a three-dimensional wall of almost leafless brown, interspersed with dry clearings and camelthorn acacia.

At first, the landscape reminded Scott of California, for it was hot and dry. Yet Save River country seemed inhospitable to an astonishing degree, as if no big-game animals could possibly survive there. It was an arid environment where the carpet of dull and lifeless brown was dotted by tiny water holes and roofed with an equally dull and lifeless dome of pale blue.

A five-minute walk from camp into the mopane confounded the bow hunters' sense of distance and direction. It was a thirsty land, a hungry land that looked on Scott and Bob not so much as visitors or predators but as prey.

[2] Page 4.

Despite the evidence of their eyes, the guides swore game was abundant. The trick to finding it was to look for outlines, watch for tracks, and be alert for spoor. Perpetual hunger hung over the land, so even droppings soon disappeared. Carrying the 8mm camera gear and

In the '60s Bob Eastman (left) and Scott Young honed bowhunting skills on California's Catalina Island before their first great adventure in Mozambique where they took this waterbuck. The Catalina Island Conservancy has since closed most hunting.

his own archery equipment, walking rapidly while swatting flies and continually wiping sweat from his eyes, Scott found that watching for lions and even for elephants was more difficult than he had imagined while dreaming of Africa amidst the tidy green lawns of suburban Los Angeles or in the hills of Catalina.

Every now and then, the bow hunters' guides patched up one of the camp's battered Toyota Land Cruisers so the group could set off in style. It was on one of those days that Scott faced off with a warthog.

Scott had missed a shot at the four-legged snuffler, but it did not run far. Scott jumped out of the truck, followed by Peixe. When they found the warthog's den—which was little more than a hole in the ground large enough to contain its chunky, inelegant body—the animal turned and backed down into it, presenting wide-set black eyes and a grimacing mouth filled with tusks like daggers.

Here was a wild African hog, only a few feet away, and all that was visible was an ugly, bony face. The perplexed teenager drew the string of his 65-pound recurve to anchor at the corner of his mouth and, from a distance of less than ten yards, attempted to brain the pig. Its head, which is almost as impenetrable as the forehead of an elephant or a rhinoceros, deflected the sharp broadhead. The impact of the 40-foot-pound tap on its frontal lobe brought the pig out of its den at full throttle.

Scrambling backward, Scott lost his balance and fell heavily. He was relieved to hear the roar of his professional hunter's rifle, for even a teenager from L.A. knows he will be safe as long as he sticks by his pro and follows his directions.

Dusting himself off, Scott picked up his bow, checked it for damage, and looked around, expecting to see a dead pig.

"Where's the warthog?" he asked.

Peixe shrugged.

"I missed," he replied in heavily accented English, and stood there grinning.

Scott had never imagined a professional hunter might miss, and it came as a shock to the boy that he could actually get hurt in Africa. It was a lesson he would not forget.

The Gang That Couldn't Shoot Straight

Everyone has an off day now and then. A day when the boss grumbles no matter how hard you work and the machine won't release a cup before it pours the coffee. A day when traffic slows to a crawl and the pending appointment is especially important.

Even skilled bow hunters have bad days, although they work hard to avoid them by practicing distance judging and tuning their equipment. But when the inevitable day comes, it is the rare bow hunter who will talk about it. Unlike a gun, the bow and arrow makes everything personal.

A hunter with any type of weapon deals with the lives of big-game animals, many of them magnificent creatures that are masterful in their domains. Since the earliest days of man the hunter, the omnivore, wounding an animal has been an unavoidable, if occasional, consequence of the hunt. One sees rare video footage of lions and tigers that attack, wounding a Cape buffalo or even an indigenous farmer, only to be fought off and driven away, leaving an aftermath of deep scars and crippling infection.

* * *

Bob wanted a lion, and Scott's mission was to be the boon companion and film that event and any other exciting portion of the African experience. But lion hunting is no casual pastime, no sure or safe thing, whether one grips a high-powered rifle or a Maasai spear and shield. It does promise a great deal of excitement—pulse-pounding excitement that hardly diminishes later on a television screen. Prior to the hunt,

Scott had never handled a movie camera, and he had never been close to a lion except at the zoo.

* * *

Amadeu Peixe and his men are building a double-layer machan, a spacious platform, in a sturdy camelthorn acacia. The lower layer will hold the hunters; the higher layer, the trackers and driver. They are a hundred yards from a water hole that is the same diameter as the distance. Peixe drags a stained and tattered mattress out of the back of the Toyota for the hunters' comfort.

"The lion will know we are here," Peixe says, "and I guarantee the smell will not offend it."

Next, Peixe shoots a Cape buffalo, cuts it open, and drags it around the water hole behind the Toyota. He places the carcass fifteen yards from the machan, positioning the belly toward the archers. In theory, a lion would walk around the buffalo to the soft underbelly, avoiding the rib cage and the backbone. This practical decision is meant to give the archer an easy reverse-quartering shot, but when hunting the king of beasts, things are never quite so easy.

That evening Scott, Bob, and Peixe climb into the shaky machan and settle onto the mattress. The two black trackers and the driver climb past them into the top of the tree and onto the even shakier upper level. Baboons bark in the distance, and a troop scrambles to the water, drinks, and hastily retreats, the baboons constantly looking over their shoulders. The ever-present call of Africa's doves ceases; nightjars flit in the twilight; darkness falls. Stars twinkle; the Southern Cross whirls overhead. Beyond that, there is nothing except the sharp, distant chuckle of a hyena.

Nothing. And more nothing. Soon the waiting bores the seventeen-year-old. Hunting without lions is like fishing without fish. The night

Hunting with Safarilandia in Mozambique, Scott Young killed a superb kudu in 1969 and poses with his trophy beside hunting buddy Bob Eastman (left) and their Portuguese-Mozambican guide, Amadeu Peixe (center). Like his friend Bob Eastman, who lived in California at the time, Scott hunted only with a recurve bow.

is cool, and Scott curls up on the mattress, his feet hanging over the edge of the platform. Despite the soft chatter of the men on the upper level, the exotic nature of the experience, the relaxed concentration of the professional hunter, and Bob's relentless effort to divine movement in the darkness, there is nothing. Scott falls asleep.

He wakes to a hand on his shoulder. Peixe is leaning close, his stale breath warm in Scott's face: *"Shh."*

Because finally there is noise in the bush, not close, but it becomes a roaring groan just as Scott sits up. Peixe holds his shoulder, urging him to be slow and to make no metallic sound.

"It is maybe a mile away," the guide whispers, his accent strong but soothing.

The stars cast a false light, and Scott peers over the edge of the machan. Even if something were standing out there, moving toward him for the kill, preparing to spring upward into the thorn tree, he could not see it.

Another roar, much closer this time.

"It's coming," Peixe whispers to Bob, who, in the dimmest perceptible light, nocks an arrow, more by feel than by sight.

The archer checks the rest on his recurve bow and pulls forward into a kneeling position, his feet beneath his buttocks. All seems in order until another roar rips the stillness.

To call it a roar would be to misunderstand, although it is a roar of sorts. It is more an announcement, a declaration, followed by the lion's throaty *chugga, chugga, chugga,* which is all blood and bone, dirt and hunger and panting power. It is the scream of every man or woman killed and eaten, every child orphaned by a cat since the beginning of time. And the hair on the boy's arms, the hair on his neck, rises in anticipation—and fear.

It is fear, to say it like it is, because the night is suddenly silent as a stone lying in still, cold water, and this is the worst part. Bob is tense; Peixe grips his rifle. Scott struggles to hear past the blood pounding in his ears, and he understands. Even though a creeping anxiety has not swept through him, and he does not yet feel the terror from within, he knows something is out there in the dark, and he knows it can see him, and it is hungry and patient. To such a killing beast Scott is little more than a rodent. His humanity, his dreams, his truth and his lies amount to a small meal. Nothing special. Nothing more.

Scott's radium-dial watch reports it is past midnight when a lion shape appears, wraithlike, over the buffalo carcass. For all Scott knows, it has been there for some time, watching, listening to the men breathe, hearing their hearts pound, a sound that now seems almost as loud as the beast's own *chugga, chugga* open-mouthed panting.

Instead of walking around the buffalo to begin eating, thus giving Bob the bow shot he needs, the lion rolls the buffalo over. Now it can dine while keeping an eye on the noisy tree and its nest of humans. This is unanticipated.

Scott scrunches forward on the mattress and peers into the dark. All he can see is blackness with some hint of movement.

For hours, the lion eats and grunts and scuffles in the dirt as it fusses with the carcass. Bones crack. Lips smack. It burps and passes gas. The sound is casual and therefore unnerving, yet not as frightening as the quiet that eventually descends. A few hours before dawn, the lion ceases to feed. Its belly full of buffalo guts, it simply lies down next to the carcass, perhaps resting its gore-spattered head on its paws.

Eventually the hunters hear something behind them, something moving through the brush, and they cautiously turn to face it. It can only be the lion, which has moved silently around the tree, perhaps curious about the human odors drifting down from the machan. Surely it is no longer hungry, although it might kill them anyway, as a cat sometimes kills for sport. Of course, a different lion might come, for lions rarely live or hunt alone. The veld is dangerous, even for lions. Whole handfuls of minutes pass, possibly an hour, but the lion makes no move to climb into the tree. The thorns, which a tracker has trimmed with his machete so that the humans can climb safely, surely give it pause.

The lion is directly beneath them now. It could leap into the tree and easily kill them all. In the confusion of such an event, the machan—a construction of sticks and twine—would shatter. The hunters would panic and fall on their broadheads and scrabble helplessly between the

Scott Young was only seventeen, but he was determined to save enough money to go to Africa with Bob Eastman in 1969. His personal guide was Amadeu Peixe (right), a professional hunter who guided princes and millionaires for Safarilandia Mozambique owner Werner von Alvensleben. On that hunt, Scott shot this fine bush duiker.

excited lion's paws. Peixe would fire and hit it . . . or he might not. But, with day approaching and its immense hunger satiated, the lion ambles away in the direction of the buffalo.

The men's eyes have grown accustomed to the dark. Peixe whispers to Bob to be ready and flicks on a hand-held light, shielding it from Bob's eyes. Bob edges forward to the quivering edge of the mattress. Half balanced and half falling, he draws and releases his arrow.

Scott recalls, "All hell broke loose."

In the dim beam of the flashlight and the merest hint of sunrise, the men's muscles ache from the long night of balancing on the hard, tilting platform. The thin mattress had hardly cushioned the rigid sticks beneath, and, Scott recognizes years later, the older men had given him as much room as possible to lie down and stretch and turn over. It was generous, for with three men the machan was cramped. And any stray movement would have brought them into contact with thorny branches.

Bob's arrow hits the lion, and it roars and screams at the same time. Whirling, it bites at the arrow.

"It was a horrendous sound," Scott recalls, "but then it disappeared, and everything got quiet."

The Pis#@ng Contest

Bob is excited. It is understandable. Everyone is excited. Above them the trackers and the driver chatter and peer down at the hunters.

"It was a good shot," Bob says to the men, mentioning, by the way, that the lower limb of his long recurve bow hit the bottom of the machan as it sprang forward, an impact that would diminish the energy delivered to the arrow and could steer it off course.

"But it was a good shot," he insists.

And so the men talk in muted tones, although the action is over, the lion is gone. So many things to consider now. A big cat with an arrow. Other members of its pride. An arrow does not kill on impact, but it kills just as surely as one of the giant slugs of lead from Peixe's .458.

At daylight, they climb down and out of the tree. They stretch. Drink water. Pee in the bushes. Peixe converses with the trackers. They load the Toyota. One man stands on the bumper, one runs in front.

The grass is waist high, patches of it as high as the tracker's shoulders. Scott and Bob stare, but rarely notice so much as a smudge or a droplet of blood. It is practically impossible to follow a lion in this sea of grass. Yet the tracker forges ahead, bent over at a steady lope.

Then the grass ends; a broad zone of rock and sand stretches out ahead. Peixe stops. They climb down. He confers with the trackers, then picks up his .458 and hands Scott a double-barrel shotgun loaded with double-aught buck.

The act is symbolic of the times—either trusting or thoughtless. Scott lays his bow in the truck and takes the gun. It is three or four times as heavy as his bow and quiver. Forty years later, Scott will say no professional hunter would ever do such a thing today because the chance of error is great. The edge of the grass is close, and it is thick and tall. A lion could burst out and be on top of them in a second. In panic, Scott might shoot the lion, but the chance of shooting Peixe or Bob or one of the trackers is just as great.

Scott is excited holding the heavy shotgun, but the feeling does not last. On the dry, rocky ground they quickly lose the sign. With daylight, a breeze rustles the grass. Peixe sets it on fire. The dry brush bursts into flame instantly, and they watch as the occasional game animal bolts from the sour smoke and slow-moving flame.

All day they move and fire the grass and wait. Peixe watches through binoculars, passes them to Bob and Scott.

"It was a good shot," Bob insists, attempting to draw the others into agreement.

But there is nothing. Nothing by day's end except exhausted, disappointed, thirsty men who reek of smoke and sweat, men who want a quick bath, a quick dinner, perhaps a shot of whiskey and a peaceful cot. It is a story the teenager decides his parents will not appreciate.

They load the Toyota and drive away; they have done a day's work and more. No one speaks until the truck grinds to a halt. They open the hood, and steam gushes from the engine compartment. The men sit in the shade of the truck, waiting for the metal to cool. Eventually, Peixe discovers the radiator is dry.

At least it is not a blown tire. Tires burst every day in the bush, when the trucks are flying twenty or thirty miles per hour across uneven terrain, the drivers dodging holes and swerving around trees and cactus, watching for game instead of stumps and rocks. But when a truck is almost on its side after sliding down a bush-covered embankment, or in one of the most inhospitable spots, like the deep sand of a wash, von Alvensleben's men are expert at righting the vehicle and patching the tube.

And some of the tubes have fifty patches, Scott thinks, marveling both at the men's self-taught mechanical skills and the truck's amazing toughness.

Peixe fishes under the seat for a wrench and a screwdriver, then wiggles under the truck. It is tight, and a shift in the sand could kill him, but in a few minutes he emerges, sweating and dirty. There is this thing between the radiator and the hose, he says, flapping his hand back and forth.

"A valve," Bob suggests. "Yes, I think that is right, and sometimes it gets stuck."

"Everyone take a sip from your canteen," Peixe instructs, "then pour what's left into the radiator."

"We need more," the PH announces, and before anyone can ask what to do, he climbs onto the bumper, unzips his trousers, and pees into the radiator—or mostly into the radiator.

"Now you." He points at Bob.

One by one, Bob and Scott, the trackers, and the driver take turns pis@#ng into the radiator. It is barely enough, but it is enough.

* * *

A year later. Scott is eighteen. The phone rings. It is Bob. Peixe has called from Mozambique.

"Another hunter, an American rifleman, has shot our lion," he says.

Bob describes its size and the length of the black mane.

"But how do they know for sure? How do they know it was our lion?" Scott asks.

Bob says when they skinned it, they found a lump near the spine, a cyst, and inside that was a Bear Razorhead. It almost looked new, right out of the box. Protecting the lion, the cyst had inadvertently protected the broadhead as well.

Three Elephants in the Bush

Scott was at that age of rebellion and back talk and indifference to parental experience that moms and dads and teachers believe will never end, or they fear it will end suddenly in some secretly anticipated, violent event. Scott couldn't quite get over how amazed he was at being in Africa and hunting at the camp that Bear and Godfrey, Ruark, and the prince of Spain had made famous.

I'm in Africa and I'm seventeen years old, he thought, *and only a handful of people have ever hunted there with a bow!*

It was a dream for a young hunter, but it was also hard work, and it could be frightening, as Scott had realized from his night in the lion machan.

His elephant encounter started unexpectedly when the lumbering Toyota unexpectedly came upon three bush women dipping drinking water from a dark pond surrounded by tall yellow fever trees.

The bush women are kneeling, Scott recalls. They will not look the men in the face. They speak in an unusual wavering, high-to-low pitch. To his American ears and eyes, the women are very black, and small and dusty. They are shoeless, dressed in rags. Their hair is cropped short against their skulls. They are barely animated lumps in the drab landscape of mopane scrub.

Yes, they have seen elephants recently. Yes, today. In fact, they waited while the elephants drank. The elephants will not be far. Perhaps at a different water hole in "that direction," and they point with thin, fragile arms. Peixe thanks them, and the men drive on, turning slightly to the left.

"Shouldn't we give them something?" Scott asks.

Peixe looks at him almost sadly, Scott thinks, years later, when each of them has endured his own stormy life.

"What do you want to give them?"

Scott considers for a moment.

"Well, maybe some money? They looked really poor."

"They weren't poor. They were bush people," Peixe answers quietly, his voice only slightly louder than the groan and bump of the truck. "You don't have anything they want or need, least of all money. Bush people can live in places where you and I would starve. Everything they own they carry with them. Whatever you gave them would only slow them down. Anyway, it wouldn't last long, and they would just throw it away."

Moments later, the driver hits the brakes. The trackers jump out and slip forward into the scrub. Soon, one of them returns and points, holds up three fingers. Everyone looks, but Scott cannot see anything through the dusty brown depth of mopane.

"Elephants," Peixe whispers. "Get out."

Going forward, they hear a high-pitched whistle. It is a sound elephants make breathing through their trunks, similar to a whistle through a hose or an elk bugle, from low to high, as if the animal suffers allergies or has a cold.

The tracker stops again and points: "There!"

Still the young man cannot see them.

"You'd think an elephant would stick out," Scott says later, "but unless you see movement or a silhouette, they're mottled gray and massive and blend into any background."

The men move forward in single file, following the trackers, moving quietly and deliberately in the behemoths' wake. In anticipation, Scott begins filming. Then a light breeze brushes against their necks. Ahead, they hear elephants running away.

"That's it," Peixe says, halting and wiping his forehead with a red bandana. "You can turn the camera off. We'll never catch up with them. They may not stop for hours."

But he is wrong. As the hunters rest in the shade, one of the trackers appears and motions to them.

"Come on," he tells Peixe, in whatever language they share. "The elephants have stopped not far ahead, maybe a mile. There is this clearing . . ."

They take up the track again and at last emerge from the thicket onto a plain broken by gullies and dotted with termite mounds. There are three elephants and plenty of tusks on at least one of them, but the beasts are nervous, no longer moving in a straight line. They are milling, undecided. Keeping a termite mound between themselves and the elephants, the men move forward onto the prairie.

Scott begins to film again, but as the camera runs, whirling strips of film across old-fashioned internal sprockets, it makes a clicking noise.

"Turn it off," Peixe whispers, but it is too late; the wind has shifted.

The elephants turn and, in a line, advance deliberately toward the men, their long, heavy strides kicking up dust as they come. They cross a hundred yards practically in an instant.

Now the wind is weird, swirling. Behind him, Scott hears footfalls. The unarmed trackers have fled. Now the elephants are running straight at the men huddled near the termite mound.

"Get behind the mound," Peixe says, and the three men make themselves as small as possible, which is silly because elephants have stereoscopic vision and eyes the size of dinner plates. There are three elephants and only one gun, and it is too late to run.

Peixe pushes the safety off his .458 Winchester Model 70. He has three rounds in the gun. This is all he has brought from the truck. Bob nocks an arrow, although the better course might be to throw the bow at the pachyderms and bolt.

At forty yards, Peixe fires. Bob sees a puff of dust on the forehead of the lead elephant. The two trailing bulls swing left. Peixe shoots again, and that's enough for the teenager. The memory of his PH missing a warthog at close range is still fresh. Suddenly he is following the black trackers at his most motivated speed.

Bob begins flinging arrows at the charging bull, which stumbles to its knees upon Peixe's second shot. It gets up and rushes forward again. Bob shoots quickly until his quiver is empty. Finally, Peixe shoots a third time, and the elephant collapses.

With one of their number down, the other elephants turn away and, enormous as they are, disappear across the plain. Scott returns with the trackers. There is small talk, and the men walk around the bull, admiring it, thinking what a shame it is. Bush people appear out of thin air—men and women with machetes, homemade knives. They hang back at first, apparently waiting for a sign. Then Peixe acknowledges them.

Two, three, a half-dozen, then a dozen or more naked people swarm around the elephant and begin hacking at the carcass. It is reminiscent of the lion attacking the buffalo carcass a few days before. When one person tires, another takes his place—cutting, sawing, slicing into the belly, and the great mass of guts that is an elephant pours out, steaming. This incites the people to a frenzy. Soon they are climbing onto the animal's side and hacking down through the thick hide; knife blades jut upward unexpectedly from the inside. Occasionally there is a yelp of pain, but no one stops. Men and women are covered with gore, but they are hilariously happy, sweating and chattering as if the day were a giant party in their honor, with gifts for everyone.

Scott is horrified and feels vaguely ill. The day is warm and the stench is powerful. Someone wraps the liver in leaves. Others trample in the guts and chew small pieces as they go. Flies and hornets by the thousands swarm the carcass and the people. It is disgusting, a vision of ancient days, a vision of hell, but it is also the most powerful thing Scott has ever seen in his life, and, while he wants to turn away, he cannot take his eyes off it.

Please, he thinks, *don't tell my mom.*

First Elephant: Showdown in Angola

1975

Chapter 3

. . . he felt death come again. This time there was no rush. It was a puff, as of a wind that makes a candle flicker and the flame go tall.

The Snows of Kilimanjaro[1]
Ernest Hemingway

It should be among the most famous photographs in hunting, alongside that of a blustering Theodore Roosevelt on safari or the rare photo of Jim Corbett, that steady hunter of man-eating tigers and leopards. It belongs with photos of Ishi, the "last wild Indian in America," or with a photo of Fred Bear, posing with his amazing Alaskan brown bear.

Still, this photograph is virtually unknown. Although the subject is well framed, the photo is teasingly out of focus. The man and his trophy are easy to identify. What is not easy to identify is what it all means.

* * *

Bob Eastman is a young man. In the field photograph he looks tired—tired but happy, perhaps proud as well. Clothes disheveled, jeans dirty. Hair prematurely thinning, eyes sunken, two days' growth of beard.

In his left hand Bob holds a recurve bow from Bear Archery. On his left forearm he has tied a leather armguard. It protects him from string

[1]Page 18.

slap and keeps his long-sleeved tan shirt away from the oscillating path of the bowstring as it thunders through the arrow's launch point.

In his right hand, dangling almost casually from its nock end, is the arrow—an arrow tipped with a Bear Razorhead broadhead.

The bull elephant is dead. It has fallen in the dry bush of Angola. Its massive ivories are visible, and Bob is leaning against one of them. He is not disrespectful, just tired, and at the same time happy, with that mixture of elation and exhaustion that hunters who have endured hardship in the bush understand. It is the look of a man who has passed through fire and, emerging singed, is nevertheless alive and thankful.

It is January 1975. Eastman is making his fourth African safari. With one terribly unconventional and controversial shot, he has killed the largest elephant in the world. He has a right to be happy. And proud.

A Meeting with the Master

In 1975 Bob Eastman killed the largest elephant ever taken with a bow in modern times or maybe in all time, for elephants are not easy to kill, especially with a bow.

Prior to his first safari, Bob drove to Grayling, Michigan, to consult with Fred Bear. The president of Bear Archery, Bear was one of only a few living hunters—among them Howard Hill, Bob Swinehart, and Bill Negley—who had killed elephants with a bow and arrow.

In June 1964 the sixty-two-year-old Bear had hunted Mozambique. His professional hunter was the redoubtable Walter Johnson Jr. of Safarilandia Mozambique. About this hunting adventure Bear had mused simply, without poetry and curiously without passion, "I want to kill an elephant with a bow and arrow."[2]

[2]Bear, *Fred Bear's Field Notes,* page 183.

In the '60s and '70s, before revolution tore the country apart, the men of Werner von Alvensleben's Safarilandia Mozambique were expert at balancing loads to cross the Save River in Mozambique.

Guided principally by Amadeu Peixe, Bear collected his trophy and displayed it for many years inside the Fred Bear Museum, first in Grayling, then in Gainesville, Florida. It is now on display at Bass Pro Shops in Missouri. His bull elephant's tusks weighed 81½ pounds. It was a fine elephant, certainly by today's diminished standards for ivory, but not a great elephant.

Stories about Bear's elephant hunt subsequently appeared in several national magazines. The lanky master of the stick and string believed in self-promotion. The American public looked on Bear's exploits with interest, even favor, perhaps because he had partnered on that African adventure with the most dynamic radio and television personality of the era, Arthur Godfrey.

Bob read Bear's stories. Then he wanted to talk elephant hunting, tactics, and safari companies with Bear. Perhaps he wanted the blessing of the old master as well, for all bow hunters eventually seek to measure themselves against the great Bear.

The two men eventually spent a quiet Saturday afternoon in Bear's sunroom overlooking the Au Sable River. They talked bowhunting, elephant, and Africa. They discussed professional hunters who would take archers, and they spoke of the endless possibilities for big-game hunting on a continent blessed with abundant and diverse game but doomed to continuous social, economic, and political upheaval.

When the conversation turned to elephant, Bear cautioned Bob that he could kill one with a bow but would have to be obsessively careful about wind direction and noise. Bob had to be an exceedingly patient stalker. He had to position himself for a clear shot within twenty yards of the largest and most temperamental animal on earth. And finally, if he wanted to live a long and happy life after releasing the bowstring, it helped if the bull was alone and not surrounded by other elephants.

But all of this was not the hardest part, said the dean of American bow hunters. The hardest part began the moment the hunter drew the bowstring.

In those days, virtually every bow hunter shot recurves and used no sights. Lightweight and graceful, the recurve's drawback, in a fluid on-the-ground situation, is effective shot placement and the effective delivery of kinetic energy. Few men can hold an 85-pound recurve at full draw longer than a split second; most cannot even pull one to full draw. And even these heavy stick bows do not deliver an arrow with sufficient power to bust through an elephant's rib cage and penetrate its vitals.

"That's bowhunting," the older man said, somewhat needlessly.

It was not like shooting a .458 Winchester. At the moment of decision, the heavy bow would "stack": It would pull straight up the force-draw curve that described the bow's energy storage potential. In practice, Bob would feel as if he were trying to snap a tall pine tree with his bare hands. In the field, however, when an elephant stood just twenty yards away, adrenaline would drip into Bob's bloodstream, and drawing an 85- or 90-pound bow would either seem like child's play or become impossible. The response was unpredictable.

In the evening Bob went home. He drove south through gloomy Michigan forests and east into open farmland and toward the growing suburban sprawl. And in subsequent years, although he knew he had Fred's best wishes on the 1975 hunt, he rarely spoke of that afternoon.

The Angola Hunt

Safaris came and went. Bob shot various thin-skinned plains game, but an elephant eluded him. Nevertheless, he had the three essential qualities for elephant hunting. He had the time, he had the money, and he was absolutely determined.

By his fourth safari in 1975, Bob began to feel he could fill his trophy room with lion and black rhino, with Cape buffalo and eland, and perhaps, one day, even a secretive forest bongo. A wild elephant, however, one that would die on his arrow like a defeated Roman general falling on his sword, was proving elusive and expensive.

Then he took a chance and moved his base from Mozambique to southeastern Angola, near Mucusso.

Now, as Ishmael observed about Captain Ahab in Herman Melville's *Moby Dick,* reality can exceed expectation. After all, more than one hundred years ago, bulls with stunning "teeth" were already quite rare.

"The ivory proved better than I had expected," wrote professional ivory hunter Arthur H. Neumann in *Elephant Hunting in East Equatorial*

Bob Eastman's trophy elephant, taken in southern Angola with Antonio Guerrero of Angola Safaris in January 1975, carried 133- and 137-pound tusks. It is the largest ever taken with a modern bow. Bob was shooting a recurve in the 90-pound weight class.

Africa[3] in 1898. "Three of the bulls had tusks of about fifty pounds apiece, which is about the limit of a full-size 'herd-bull's' teeth."

As with Ahab, so, eventually, with Eastman's elephant. When he finally caught up with one, reality surpassed every possible expectation.

* * *

Three decades after that hunt in Angola, Bob remembers his shot well because he defied conventional wisdom and the great Bear's advice. And he remembers the tracking—seemingly endless tracking through a brown and parched Angolan outback—and being wary because of the civil war raging to the north. Bob had worked very hard to teach his guide about the limitations of the bow and arrow, saying, "It is deadly, but I must be very close, and you will be uncomfortable."

Bob, professional hunter Carlos Fortunato, and their tracking and skinning crew followed elephant spoor continuously for two days, from before sunrise until darkness swept across the bush. Then they would chew biltong, wrap in blankets, and lie down exhausted in the dirt, with a small fire to keep the hyenas and wild dogs at bay.

"Following spoor" sounds easy, as if anyone with common sense could do it. But an elephant can defecate up to two hundred and forty pounds of partially digested vegetation and urinate as much as thirteen gallons every day. To compound the problem, Bob's bull was only one of many elephants living in the neighborhood of the Cuvango River.

So time became a weary process of gauging the heat in piles of elephant dung nearly as high as Bob's knee. Thrust a fist into the pile and feel around. Cold and firm meant distant and old. Warm and fragrant meant check the wind and watch out.

[3]Pages 197–98.

Bob Eastman and professional hunter Antonio Guerrero pose with Bob's world-record tusks. Given the uncertain dynamics of the wildlife populations on the politically unstable continent of Africa, his Angola trophy will almost certainly never be eclipsed, by a bow hunter or a rifleman. It is a trophy for the ages.

Suddenly, Antonio Guerrero of Angola Safaris told him to hurry. "Come forward," he said, in heavily accented Portuguese-English.

Now, Bob told himself, *It's like shooting a trophy whitetail. Don't look at the antlers. Wait until it moves, then draw and take the shot.*

Incredibly, the giant bull had not seen or smelled them, and when it finally moved, Bob drew and released from a distance of little more than twenty yards. Instead of taking the side-on shot, he wanted the whitetail angle, reverse quartering. There would be no giant ribs to stop the arrow, and his heavy bow could punch the arrow forward, through the tough skin and into the bull's vitals.

Bob released, and the elephant lunged ahead, as if it had been hit with an electric prod. For a few seconds, Bob and Antonio and their party of skinners and trackers heard the elephant crashing through the brush. After that, Bob heard only silence and the beat of his heart roaring in his ears. He recalls holding his breath and, when the elephant rushed away, gasping for air.

As they chased after the bull, they spotted occasional sprays of blood, watched for vultures, and listened cautiously for hyenas and lions. None too soon to suit Bob, the trackers located his elephant. It lay gigantic and quite alone in the scrub—a colossal hump of flesh with two immense ivories. Stunningly immense ivories. Combined, they weighed two hundred and seventy pounds. Such size was almost inconceivable.

Bob's elephant dwarfed any other taken with a bow and most elephants taken by gun in recorded history. Beside it, Bear's 81½-pound bull seemed diminutive.

He had endured heat, bushels of crawling ticks and swarms of biting flies, trickles of warm water from rank canteens and the ebbing of his own adrenaline tide, which can leave one momentarily exhausted. And so, as the trackers whetted their knives and chanted the "meat song," the flame of Bob's desire for a trophy elephant flickered and was satisfied. He leaned against the belly of the beast and smiled for one fuzzy photo.

Heavy Bows, Long Tracks, Danger Close

A good hunting story should end with handshakes, some backslapping, and the taking of pictures. Perhaps a congratulatory long-distance call to Bear, who was, after all, Bob's mentor in the matter of elephants. This one does not.

Of course, there is no single elephant experience, any more than there is one whitetail experience. No hunting story unfolds exactly like another.

Motives cannot be duplicated. Reactions one has not practiced, instincts one is unprepared for, sometimes appear without warning, uncomfortably and uncontrollably. And there is the animal, which presumably is not interested in expiring and will run or fight or both to save its life.

It remains true, however, that an elephant—bull or cow—is a dangerous foe.

"I've hunted elephants five times," says Bob Eastman, "and each time but one, the wounded bull has spun around and charged. Elephants are tough, tough and dangerous. A man can get killed. It is very, very difficult and very dangerous.

"You are standing twenty to thirty yards from a very large, very wild animal. Your professional hunter is beside and slightly behind you with his loaded rifle, and there are native porters and skinners nearby. Your hunter only has one gun, and at that distance, with a bolt-action rifle, he is only going to get one shot.

"If the elephant charges, you are going to run around trees. A wounded bull will run over them to get at you. Alone, you don't have a chance.

"The African elephant is the most dangerous big-game animal in the world. It's smart and it's mean. I know hunters who have survived lion mauling and leopard attacks, even the charge of a Cape buffalo. I don't know anyone who has survived being stomped by an elephant. An elephant's favorite trick is to knock you down and crush you with its forehead. That's got to be an awful way to die."

The instant an elephant hears your shot or feels your broadhead penetrate, it whirls and searches for the cause of its calamity.

There is universal agreement among hunters. Elephants are a very dangerous business.

"[H]e suddenly rushed at me," Arthur Neumann wrote[4] a century ago, after he had shot the bull twice, pulling both barrels of his .577 double

[4] Ibid., page 112.

Portuguese-Angolan professional Carlos Fortunato guided Bob Eastman for big game on several occasions in the '70s, originally in Angola and later in Sudan. "Carlos was one of the quiet adventurers," Bob recalls, "one of the big-game guides who relied on his work in the field and his personal integrity to build a loyal client base. He was a specialist in the easy smile, the shrug of the shoulders, and one-word answers to the most complex questions." The eland horns in the center are still the largest ones on record taken with a bow.

rifle. "As there were not more than ten yards between us and he came straight for me at a quick run, there was no time for hesitation. There was luckily a little opening to my right; into this I slipped, crouching to be less readily noticed."

California bow hunter Jerry Gentellalli says if he had not been athletic, the elephant he stalked “back in the ’60s” (see chapter 1) would surely have trampled him. At twenty to twenty-five feet, the wind changed. The bull whirled and came for him, trumpeting and growling like a dog.

With a 48-inch, 89-pound draw-weight recurve in his left hand, Jerry performed an acrobatic backflip, landing behind a termite mound. His professional hunter aimed for the base of the bull’s nose. At that distance the .450 slug would have hit with as much as 5,000 foot-pounds of energy, enough to blow a strong man twenty yards and reduce him to the consistency of bloody Kleenex. The bullet apparently glanced off the skull, slid beneath the skin, and emerged from the animal’s forehead. The shot turned the bull, which, except for one hell of a headache, was apparently none the worse for wear.

If even an elephant gun cannot always stop a charging elephant, what chance is there for a bow?

Eastman no longer recalls the particulars of his gear setup. After all, the kill took place long ago, during the brief presidency of Gerald Ford. Eastman does recall that he took an extremely controversial shot angle.

An elephant’s lungs are larger than microwave ovens, and its heart can weigh sixty pounds. Bob believed then (and he believes now) that the best way to accomplish a killing shot is to stick an arrow in the liver. This requires a reverse-quartering shot, virtually in the same manner one would arrow a big whitetail.

“An elephant’s ribs can stop an arrow from a one-hundred-pound bow,” Bob says, “but if it can be shot quartering away, behind the rib cage so your arrow slices forward, a broadhead to the liver is absolutely deadly. The liver is the size of a whitetail deer. It weighs at least one hundred pounds.”

Actually, elephant livers can weigh more than one hundred and fifty pounds.

Arguing About Elephants

No other big-game species causes as much divisiveness as elephants, unless it is dolphins or mountain gorillas—certainly not tigers, polar bears, or pandas. Every aspect of the elephant—including the disposition of ivory, sharing authority for issuing hunting permits, and shot placement—elicits hysterical and uncompromising opinions from wildlife organizations, government offices, and private citizens, hunters included, around the world. The elephant has fulfilled the ultimate promise of the Hindu story about six blind men attempting to describe it. Each feels a separate anatomical part and hypothesizes, incorrectly, about the whole animal.

Toward the end of his life, Fred Bear adopted a curious position on bowhunting elephants. From personal experience with elephants (and, it must be noted, with polar bears, although Bear never mentioned this part of his story in public), he knew that more elephants and rhinos were dispatched by professional hunters than through the quick and painless hemorrhage caused by a well-placed broadhead.

A longtime secret smoker, Bear was afflicted with emphysema and, during his last decade, needed a canister of oxygen to breathe. In a private note to Bob, typed with two fingers on an Olympia manual typewriter, the dying dean of American bowhunting wrote, "[L]et's not shoot any more elephants. I think that one should be enough for anyone. As a matter of fact I wish that I had not shot any. I have destroyed my elephant pictures and wish I had not done a chapter on it in my book. I have taken the stand that elephants and rhino are too tough for the bow."[5]

[5]Fred may have thought about destroying personal photographs of his elephant hunts, but that was apparently as far as it went. Photos still hung on the wall of his home in Gainesville, Florida, as long as his widow, Henrietta Bear, lived there. The childless Bear sold his company in 1969, and after his death nineteen years later, his company was bought and sold numerous times. In June 2003, when Escalade Sports of Evansville, Indiana, purchased the assets from Bear Archery's bankruptcy, plenty of those photos were still available. Indeed, enlarged copies still hung in the entrance hall at company headquarters in Gainesville, as well as inside the Fred Bear Museum, until the museum's contents were sold to Bass Pro Shops and Fred's museum was closed.

Was Fred searching for some type of broad public redemption at death's door; was the master jealously attempting to project his glow into the future; or is there a secret truth in what he wrote? We will never know because a year later, at eighty-six, he was dead.

Perhaps Bear's condemnation was simply nostalgia in the face of change, the case of an elder statesman falling behind the technological development of the sport he helped establish. After all, in the decade prior to his death, the ability of even a modestly weighted bow to deliver a killing force of kinetic energy through a stiff carbon shaft and surgically sharp modular broadhead had increased dramatically.

Bear also condemned Bill Negley's classic *Archer in Africa,*[6] in which Negley wrote that he "had hunted with a rifle since childhood, and at age thirty-eight, I had given up the rifle because it had grown too easy." Negley should have been a natural ally for Bear's promotion of bowhunting around the world.

Initially, Bear had hoped Negley would film his African adventures and contribute the film to Bear's anticipated television show. In a private communication with Negley, Bear reasoned that with just a couple more films, Bear Archery would have enough adventure footage to offer a complete quarter of television programming. Besides, he argued, Negley used Bear equipment on his safaris.

Alas! When Negley finally set his bowhunting experiences in ink, he refused to sugarcoat them. He journaled the good and the bad, the quick kills and the missed opportunities. He told the truth as he saw it and lived it, then published it, warts and all. His frank approach to archery in Africa opened a chasm between the two men. Some would argue that Bear was more concerned with the promotion and image of bowhunting than with unvarnished truth.

"The whole book is not good," Bear wrote in a supreme fit of ego.

The great Bear was wrong.

[6]Page 4.

Companions in the Survival Ark

Acknowledging all opinions, we must choose those who will travel beside us day by day in this fragile survival ark. The regrettably maligned Bill Negley said it very well in the final chapter of *Archer in Africa:* "Regardless of what violent, intemperate or even sophisticated arguments the contras might propose, I feel in good company on the side of the hunters."[7]

This means that, in spite of our differences, we are sailing with the likes of Bob Eastman and Art Neumann, Bill Negley and Fred Bear. Elephant hunters all, and good company.

Statistically Speaking

According to Doug Luger, Safari Club International's Trophy Records and World Hunting Awards manager, Bob Eastman's 1975 Angola bull is the only bow-killed African elephant in SCI's top one hundred. Eastman's 270-pounder ranks number five and is only 32 pounds lighter than the greatest elephant ever recorded by SCI, Marc Pechenart's 302-pound tusks shot in 1970.

In the twenty-first century, only three African elephants have scored among the SCI (Safari Club International) top one hundred. Michael Wilmet's 177-pound bull, which fell to a rifle bullet in June 2002, is the largest of them.

Publisher Ludo Wurfbain of Safari Press says the world-record African elephant was shot in the foothills of Mount Kilimanjaro in 1898. The hunter was an African named Shunti, the slave of an Arab trader who lived in Zanzibar, off the coast of what is now Tanzania. The ten-foot tusks, on display in the Natural History Museum, London, weigh an astonishing 440 pounds. Listed in Rowland Ward's record book as the largest in the world, they are sixty-six pounds larger than the number two entry.

7. Ibid., 234.

Freedom

1975

Chapter 4

I always have the feeling that there is something new just over the next hill or in the next village, and the habit patterns of this enormous cruel child which is Africa are positively sinister in their fascination.

The Honey Badger[1]
Robert Ruark

The famous guides and professional hunters of Africa were, at least on the surface, an extraordinarily undisciplined lot. Not at all like today's certificate-bearing cherubs, who gain experience through "internships" with various game commissions, who absorb knowledge by reading books and taking examinations, and who could no more repair a broken motor mount in the Range Rover or track a bleeding buff in high grass than they could negotiate with one of the minor princes of Italy about a greater kudu.

In the old days the professional hunters smoked and drank and spit and whored and, when they thought it necessary for their client, ignored the law. They were mischievous and could be hugely entertaining or downright mean. Many of them were great hunters in their own right, men who knew every bush sign and every signal of day or night, and what it might mean for the game their clients were paying them to locate. They spoke numerous obscure local dialects of Kikuyu or Shangaan, as well as English and German, Portuguese and Italian. Having fallen deeply in love with Africa and its big game, they preferred that their clients hunt

[1] Page 428.

hard and have fun but kill rarely. The PHs reluctantly agreed to shoot "their" precious animals only when nothing else was to be done.

Other guides were quiet professionals, dedicated to the chase, the animals, and their clients. This group resisted the Hollywood stereotype of brave and lonely white men on a dangerous Dark Continent, the image that sold the fiction of Hemingway, Ruark, and Capstick. These PHs were reliable and resilient and altogether serious about their work.

In the old guild of hunting professionals, one and all shared a passion for the outdoor life. They preferred to be deep in the bush with only two or three companions: a guest hunter, a gunbearer, and the inevitable and invaluable tracker. They preferred this lonely wilderness existence to everything else in life: art galleries and operas, newspapers and nightclubs, electricity in wires and water in pipes. And in the end they paid for this choice, for snubbing their noses at convention. Escaping the misdirected Communist revolution in Mozambique with little more than the shirt on his back, Amadeu Peixe fled to Brazil. Toward the end, Rui Quadros, Peixe's great friend and rival at Safarilandia Mozambique, lived on scraps of fish and begged from his former hunting clients, eventually dying in Maputo broke, dispirited, and in ill health.

It has always been like this with the men of the bush, and perhaps it always will be. Robert W. Service (1874–1958) wrote about them in his poem:

The Men That Don't Fit In

There's a race of men that don't fit in,
A race that can't stay still;
So they break the hearts of kith and kin,
And they roam the world at will.
They range the field and they rove the flood,
And they climb the mountain's crest;
Theirs is the curse of the gypsy blood,
And they don't know how to rest.

The English-Canadian poet may have been writing about the Yukon, but he instinctively understood the life and death of old African hunters. Failing at love, professional ivory hunter Arthur Neumann put a bullet in his head in 1907. William Charles Judd was horribly speared and then crushed by a bull elephant in 1927. Denys Finch Hatton was killed when his biplane crashed near Nairobi, Kenya, in 1931. Bror Blixen, the former husband of writer Isak Dinesen, died in an automobile accident in Sweden in 1946. Such men did not go quietly or easily. Few of them died in their sleep, surrounded by grieving children and grandchildren.

To go quietly, easily, painlessly, get a desk job. Work for an insurance company or the government or sell real estate. Accumulate for retirement. Own a small business, pay taxes, and count the nickels and dimes until the day death appears at your back. On the deathbed, having traded risk and adventure for security for three score and ten years, wonder if "safe" was a life well lived.

A man has the choice of these two tracks in life, and the older professional hunters were among the handful of risk-takers who existed for the day, the hour, because they truly never knew when the mamba would bite; when the bullet placed a few inches too high on a charging elephant would slide up and over the bull's massive skull; when the tracker might suddenly appear in the tent with a panga, having secretly "gone over" to a rebellion during the night.

It is the risk-takers, however, who have enriched our literature, our civilization, and our imagination with tales of screaming lions, with terrific bow and rifle shots taken when only perfection would save them, with an Africa—indeed, a world—that is fast disappearing.

In Sudan with Carlos

Portuguese-Angolan professional Carlos Fortunato was one of the quiet adventurers, one of the big-game guides who relied on his work in the field and his personal integrity to build a supportive client base. He guided Bob

Eastman for big game on several occasions, originally in Angola and later in Sudan, before that desperate country was ruined by war and dismembered by the politics of oil. Carlos was a specialist in the easy smile, the shrug of the shoulders, and one-word answers to the most complex questions.

Carlos hunted for Angola Safaris in the southwest corner of Angola, the exotic Mucusso zone, in the '70s and '80s. This area is north of Namibia (formerly German South-West Africa) and, crucially, north of the east-flung neck of the Namibian guitar, the curiously and artificially constructed Caprivi Strip. At any minute you expect the map to collapse and the peoples of Namibia's narrow corridor along Highway B8, from Divundu to Katima Mulilo, to join one of the bordering nations: Botswana to the south, Angola and Zambia to the north, or even Zimbabwe to the east. In some directions this zone along the Zambezi and its tributaries is moderate, and in others it is either too wet or too dry, but, curiously, all are rich in big game, and here Carlos was home.

And so it was puzzling that Carlos left Angola for Sudan and a company called Safaria Aviation. He subsequently guided in South Sudan for five years. Upon returning to Angola, he explained tersely, in typical Carlos fashion, "It wasn't working out."

Thirty-five years ago, Bob Eastman hunted with Carlos in South Sudan, long before that region became the Republic of South Sudan, balancing the Muslim north with a Christian and an animist tradition. South Sudan is a landlocked region bordered by poor relations, and its borders are choked with the vicious ethnic militias of Ethiopia, Kenya, Uganda, the Congo, the Central African Republic, and, of course, Sudan itself. To this day Bob remembers the capital city of Juba as a wretched hellhole. He recalls butchered goats in the marketplaces, crawling with flies and maggots. But he also remembers one special eland, a lion, and, several years later, a sitatunga in the great swamp bordering the White Nile, the Bahr al Jabal. This is the story of that East African (Patterson) eland.

* * *

Carlos Fortunato was one surprisingly tough guy back then, says Bob Eastman, the American bow hunter's mind wandering back thirty-five years.

"He wasn't tall, and I don't imagine he weighed one hundred and forty pounds soaking wet. But he was wiry. Durable. Brown as a coconut husk, with black hair and a thin black mustache."

Except for the mustache, Bob might have been describing himself before the endless nights of building a business and paying taxes, the endless worries of raising children and studying the competition for an advantage. Bob was about Carlos's size, but the bush-hungry guide possessed an endurance that astonished the Yankee archer.

"He drove through the bush like a racecar driver," Bob says, describing Carlos's one raw edge, "and I don't mean on roads or even on dirt tracks. Right across the country through grass and brush, bumping and pounding around anthills and across warthog holes. I can't imagine how a truck could take that kind of abuse day in and day out. It was all we could do to hold on. If he saw something we were going after, he drove like a madman, and to hell with the truck.

"But every day I hunted with him he knew exactly where he wanted to go and usually took the shortest possible route to get there. It didn't matter if there were rivers or ditches or buffalo lying in the grass or a pride of lions skulking across the plains ahead. He took off, and, of course, as his client, I knew enough to shut my mouth and go along for the ride because, as reckless as he could be behind the wheel, when it came to getting close to trophy game, he was the best."

Bob recalled that the Safaria Aviation hunting concession appeared to be the same in all directions—empty, with sand trails running endlessly through the bush with no apparent beginning, direction, or destination. Apparently Carlos Fortunato knew the way, though. After one headlong race through the countryside, in which they saw not one other human being or beast for hours, Carlos stopped suddenly and pulled out a compass and a set of beat-up field glasses. The guide blew on the eyepiece and the objective lens and wiped them with a dusty handkerchief.

"Where are we?" said Bob.

Carlos explained that they had come forty-five miles from camp. This, he said, was where he wanted to hunt. To the American, every square inch of territory in the flat to gently rolling countryside looked exactly the same. Bob admits that if Carlos and the native had gone off for a walkabout and left him behind, he could never have found his way out of the wilderness. Perhaps he could have followed the sun toward the east, in the general direction of the Nile River, or he could have followed the path of the vehicle on the stony, hard-baked ground over which they had driven helter-skelter. For anyone except an experienced native tracker, though, the tire tracks would quickly have disappeared.

Carlos and the Record-Book Eland

Bob was excited to be bowhunting in Africa, even though this was by no means his first safari. He was an experienced big-game bow hunter on the North American continent and, after five trips to the Dark Continent, considered himself an old hand there as well. He expected to work hard in unfamiliar circumstances, but this particular day puzzled him.

His professional hunter, Carlos, was apparently comfortable—he had no maps in the truck, and he paid no attention to the radio in these days before satellite communications or GPS (global positioning systems). But the countryside was featureless and had no landmarks that Bob could identify. There was no point of reference, mountain peak, giant tree, or creek that he could follow. It was all a bewildering maze of thorn and acacia trees, interspersed with sharp gullies and barren meadows. Without grass, the land lay prostrate to the burning sun, and at the height of the African summer in January and February, only a few degrees north of the equator, it would become mind-numbingly hot.

Carlos drove the truck onto the occasional hillocks and scanned the landscape with the native tracker. To Bob, just looking out on the jumble of brownish-green was disconcerting. It was the dry season, but he felt as if he were in a small boat in the middle of a vast ocean, and it would have taken no less than an elephant, an explosion, or some brilliant burst of color to get his attention.

Glassing from the roof of the truck, Carlos unexpectedly pointed into the distance, and Bob heard an *"Ohhhh."* Even in Carlos's broken English, the American bow hunter understood. Bob immediately scrambled up beside him and, shading his eyes, tried to discover what Carlos found so interesting. Even standing atop the cab of the truck, Bob saw nothing that stood out, nothing except thornbush, and he had no idea in what direction the guide was pointing, except "over there." Neither did he know for sure whether they were in Sudan. Although the border was occasionally marked, the posts were often missing. It was not obvious what had happened to them.

"Are we in the Sudan or Uganda?" Bob asked.

Carlos did not answer. Instead, he handed Bob the field glasses and oriented him to a distant speck. It was an eland, now subcategorized by Safari Club International as an East African or Patterson eland, and it was standing very still. If one could anthropomorphize it, it seemed to be lost in thought.

Bob realized Carlos was talking to him rapidly, urgently, but Bob could not understand what the guide was saying because, in his excitement, Carlos had lapsed into Portuguese. The guide took back the binoculars, thrusting them again to his own eyes. Bob finally got the message that this was a magnificent animal, a giant, perhaps a world record. Here, less than half a mile away, was an animal worthy of stirring the hunter's blood.

Carlos jumped down and conferred with the native tracker. He motioned to Bob to take his bow and arrows and to follow them. A veteran of long, thirsty days in the bush with other Portuguese-African guides, Bob knew enough to take a canteen of water also.

Bob could never understand how they got within bow range of the eland, which had moved very little, in the monotonous Sudanese countryside. Now, as Carlos peeked over a slight rise and saw the animal to their right, he turned and began speaking to Bob again in an animated manner. This time Bob quickly made it clear that he could not understand a single word.

"He has a broken horn," Carlos said. "Do you understand what that means? This is not just a record-book animal. I believe it is much bigger than that. I believe it to be maybe the biggest in the world. The biggest, even with the horn broken!"

At that moment the eland began to wander away, and the hunters crept from cover to cover until Bob could take an open shot.

He realized the shot was longer than he wanted when the animal paused around forty-five yards away, the limit of his recurve bow's abilities. Carlos, who had guided only three bow hunters in his long career and had little exposure to archery, wanted him to "Shoot—shoot!" When Bob finally released, the eland turned its head and practically watched the arcing arrow until it sliced into its chest. The sharp Bear Razorhead from Bob's 65-pound bow did the rest.

Bob was thrilled when the Dinka tracker located the dead eland, but Carlos was even more ecstatic. There was no mark on the male to suggest why it had lingered in relatively open positions and allowed the hunters to get close for the killing shot. The eland did not appear to be injured or sick. It was, Carlos explained, just its time to die.

Even with its left horn broken, Bob's East African eland scored a remarkable 95 inches in the SCI bowhunting record book (adding the length of the horns to the circumference of each at its base). Thirty-five years ago, bowhunting trophies were few and were not considered serious claimants to entry in the African record book. Today, the score would have made it a bowhunting world record for all species of eland, and that record would have stood, even with a broken horn, for eleven years.

If the eland's horns had been roughly the same—as they typically are on eland and most spiral-horned antelopes—the eland would have scored about 108 inches. This would have stood as a world bowhunting record for an amazing twenty-four years.

Carlos by Phone: La Vida Boa-Libra

When Bob Eastman and his sister, Stephanie, who speaks fluent Portuguese, finally caught up with Carlos Fortunato, the old guide was working in a hotel somewhere on the Atlantic coast of Portugal, north of Lisbon. True to form, the quiet man spoke with a minimum of energy and volunteered few facts or details about his life in the bush or his current circumstances. It could be surmised that he was working a shift, perhaps in the kitchen or as a part-time desk clerk, although he would not clarify his responsibilities.

Carlos was born in Portugal in 1940, on the eve of war in Europe, and his family "fled to Angola" when he was small, he said. Indeed, under the rule of António de Oliveira Salazar, dictator for life, thousands of Portuguese citizens were encouraged, though not exactly forced, to relocate to Portugal's African colonies, principally to Angola and Mozambique. Salazar believed that a strong presence of Europeans would render the colonies impervious to movements for independence. It was in Angola that Carlos and his two sisters attended grade school.

Carlos loved Angola. But in the '50s an incipient independence movement, the MPLA, or People's Movement for the Liberation of Angola, began organizing in the countryside. International pressures, principally from a Soviet-led coalition of nations, began mounting against the Western European colonial powers. It became increasingly dangerous for Europeans to live in Angola, and histories talk about one million destitute

Portuguese, both white and black, *los retornados,* eventually returning to Europe from the colonies. Carlos's family fled from Angola in 1955 "for political reasons" and also because remaining in that southern African nation was dangerous.

As soon as he could, Carlos returned to Angola and began his new career—as a poacher. He loved hunting and "had a wonderful life." He eventually became legitimate as a professional guide, and, most important, he was free. That was what he preferred—indeed, it was all he cared about. Now he says simply, "I had a good life."

Because the natives had no work or working capital, the government had no strength, Carlos said. The police were ineffective, and the towns were, in his words, "riddled with crime." Competing political gangs fought openly, and in 1975 Portugal gave the country its independence.

Carlos offered these facts in his own manner, almost reluctantly, as if he were hesitant to revisit a time of his life when he was young and free.

Carlos married but never had children. He volunteered that if he had had any, he would have wanted them to be hunters.

In his day he only guided three archers, among them Bob Eastman. The rest were all gun hunters. Carlos was never bitten by a snake or attacked by a lion or leopard, never gored by a buffalo or chased by a hippo. He hunted in Kenya and other East African countries, but the political situation made a stable base difficult.

Carlos guided hunters with Angola Safaris, and he also guided in Sudan for five years, working for Safaria Aviation.

In 2011 Carlos Fortunato was still working at a hotel in Portugal.

"One has to work in order to live," he said.

He didn't sound happy.

The Persistence of Memory

1980

Chapter 5

The hunt led inflexibly to death. The real hunters knew no fear.

Watchers at the Pond[1]

Franklin Russell

"All those things that happened are part of me now," says George Gardner.

It took the Michigan archer, a friend of Bob Eastman, seven years to give up his guns. When he did, though, he never looked back. That determination to move forward is characteristic of this friendly and soft-spoken man, a gentleman with a sense of humor.

George Gardner started bowhunting the moment they let him out of the navy in 1946. Until 1953, he hunted with both a gun and a bow. After all, the bow season was short in those days, and hunting from tree stands was against the law in some states. (Even homemade tree stands—boards nailed to trees—are simply tools that help archers "level the playing field.") Archers killed deer by slow, silent stalking and deer drives; at least, that was how a lucky and determined 5 percent killed their deer. The other 95 percent used a gun or went without.

Deer camp in the fall was a release from the daily grind, an opportunity for a special kind of camaraderie that men prefer. Most men of that era had been permanently scarred by the Great Depression and the two world wars. And 1953, the end of the Korean War, was

[1]Page 108.

Bob Eastman has hunted in Africa more than thirty times since his first trip to Mozambique in 1967. "Back then it was like waking up in a movie by National Geographic," he says. "Everything was exotic and exciting. In Africa in those days, it was common to see bare-breasted women carrying suckling babies."

the first year they could hunt does in Michigan. As Gardner recalls, during the last three days of that season, one could take any deer, as long as hunters in camp still held unfilled licenses.

George walked into the woods that cold November morning, gloved hands clutching his rifle. It was the final day of the season, and he expected to shoot something. Hours later, George indeed dragged his deer out, but he needed help dragging the others, for he had shot six deer in all. He had filled everyone's tag with a doe.

"We always had fun running around the woods with guns," he says, "but I thought, 'I love to hunt, but shooting all those deer wasn't so much fun.' I never shot anything with a rifle again."

Bob Eastman understands that, for he has been a bow hunter all his life.

A Man's "Better Half"

After a half-century in archery and perhaps a dozen hunting trips around the world, more than half of them to Africa, George's trophy room is festooned with forty or so big-game trophies. From his easy chair, it is a painless flight of memory to the 1946 Osage orange self-bow, and to his old recurves and wooden arrows. Now, as he weaves his way past eighty years of age, he carries a crossbow into the field. He's still a killer.

He says visitors to his home inevitably ask if his wife, Betty, his bride of fifty-seven years, hunts, and when he replies that indeed she does, they ask if he has "taken her to Africa."

Betty hunted South Africa with him eight years ago, he says, recalling the trip as the first time he took a crossbow to the Dark Continent. His wife, as it turns out, took four shots with that bow and took four "pretty nice animals," all of which are mounted now in the family trophy room.

According to Betty, "People see our trophies and ask, 'Betty, do you hunt?' I tell them, 'Yeah, I went to Africa with George.' They ask, 'Well, did you get anything?'"

And right there the trouble starts, for Betty is not a lady who is content to sit quietly in the back when the front is available.

Betty continues, "Do you see those two impala on the wall? The big one is mine. The small one is George's. Do you see the two impala beside the fireplace? The big one is mine and the little one is George's.

The warthog with the great big tusks, by the way, is the one I shot; the little one beside it . . ."

People eventually get the picture.

Before the couple booked their hunt, Betty decided she wanted a duiker, a diminutive African antelope. George wanted a more robust gemsbok. As events unfolded, George shot a superb duiker with unscarred six-inch horns, and Betty took the big gemsbok.

To get even, George mounted her smallish, 2007 white-tailed doe beneath his big buck of that year. So much for this husband's sense of humor.

Where Are Your Guns?

These days George Gardner does not recall every trip, every date, every shot in his long hunting career, but he vividly relives a few of them, and he has advice for "anybody who is a bow hunter and hasn't been to Africa. Go as soon as you can."

His leopard hunt was special, although not because anyone was killed and eaten or because the cat scored high in the Safari Club record book. The hunt was special because it took several trips to harvest a cat. That would have been in the late '70s or early '80s, he thinks, those days before AK-47s and the intervention of nongovernmental organizations decimated the game in so many areas. He says he hunted one of those countries north of South Africa that has changed its name—maybe Rhodesia; it wasn't the Congo. It could have been any number of places, but Bob Eastman, who was his friend on the hunt, says it was Tanzania.

* * *

"Where are your guns?"

That was how the outfitter welcomed the American bow hunters to Africa.

"We're bow hunters," the men replied, pulling recurve bows out of their travel cases, "and we can only shoot effectively out to about thirty yards."

"My gun hunters usually shoot a hundred yards," the outfitter huffed. "There ain't no damn way you're going to be successful here at twenty-five yards. Leopards, especially, will never let you get that close. Oh, they'll talk to you and tell you they know where you are, which will raise the hair on the back of your neck, but you'll never see one. Forget it. You'll never get a shot."

The outfitter was right, at least on that first hunt. George did not kill a leopard. For ten days he hunted and never saw a cat. George only shrugged and booked a ten-day hunt for the following year. The outfitter pushed his hat back and scratched his head.

The next year, George hunted diligently for nine days without letup or discouragement, arriving at his blind in the morning darkness and creeping away quietly after sundown. In the middle of the day, he left, ate lunch, napped, and hunted plains game for trophies and to replenish the leopard bait.

"I'm surprised you booked to try again," the outfitter said, happy to take George's money but not so happy to have failed to deliver a leopard for his client. "You didn't even get a shot last year. At this distance, you're never going to get a shot, you know."

Now, George believes bow hunters occasionally need a little break, a little luck, but by the last day of his second hunt, he had still not gotten a leopard. And the bush plane was scheduled to land on the camp's grass runway at 2 PM.

"Well, you're here," his professional hunter said on the final day. "You ought to give it one last try and hunt this morning. At least check the baits to see where we should have set up last night. After all, you have come a long way. Might as well make the most of it."

George had had his fill of leopard hunting. Enough is enough, he thought. Sometimes it is a matter of knowing when to ask for seconds

Scott Young (left with professional hunter Amadeu Peixe) took a gross of arrows fletched with feathers and tipped with Bear Razorheads. The game was plentiful, and he often saw more than five hundred animals a day.

or when to fold your cards and push away from the table. Despite the outfitter's encouragement, with the ride home a scant seven hours away, George decided he would rather take a leisurely shower, pack his gear, and eat lunch beside the river. The option was to sit for several hours in a cramped, increasingly hot blind, then rush through the packing and mount the creaking steps into the bush plane breathless and sweating. After nine straight "oh-dark-thirty" wake-up calls, he thought a morning dithering about the camp and enjoying a final shower in the African sun and shade, without the tension of waiting for a mythical leopard, would feel just fine.

At the last moment, George had second thoughts; he grabbed his bow and ran out of the thatched hut.

"Wait!"

Meanwhile, his guide, a driver, two trackers, and two dogs—the outfitter's black Labrador retriever and a mongrel—had mounted up and were turning around to drive out of camp to check the baits.

When the guide asked about his change of heart, George just shrugged in his best *"Aw,* shucks" sort of way, grinned, and settled down among the trackers and dogs for the jarring morning ride through the bush. After all, he was paying a great deal of money, and, regardless how frustrating, it was Africa. He ought to wring every possible moment from this final day.

"What are the dogs for?" he asked.

"I used them when I hunted for the army during the war," his guide said, leaving which war unspecified. There is usually sufficient organized bloodshed taking place in Africa to please the most trigger-happy homo-hater.

The mongrel dog, it turned out, had a reputation. The dog knew when a game animal was going to lie down and die from its wounds, and they would not give up a chase until it was found. On the other hand, if the animal had been hit but was not going to die, the dog

would soon quit the track! Whether that was a convenient explanation or an explanation of convenience was never clarified.

It was too bad George was leaving, the guide said, without shooting anything of significance that might allow the dog to demonstrate its talents.

"I Said, Shoot Again!"

An impala carcass hanging near blind number one has not been touched; neither has the dead baboon at blind two. For leopard bait the guide prefers fresh baboon or impala, both of which are plentiful: "Leopards love baboons. A leopard will fight a pack of hyenas for a chance to eat fresh baboon. It's like birthday cake."

The path to a third blind requires the driver to downshift and to negotiate the Toyota Land Cruiser's trail uphill on a rocky dirt track that has eroded severely during the annual rainy seasons. In the outback there is no road maintenance. The trackers are expressionless. The dogs are panting and uncomfortable from the jarring ride. They give off an odor of sour woolens. To George Gardner, the jolting of the truck bed in the nearly horizontal morning light is painful.

I left camp for this, he thinks.

At the military crest of the hill, the guide stands up and studies the bait with binoculars. It is nearly 10:00 AM, and heat waves have begun to dance across the open veld. George checks his watch: four hours until the plane arrives. If the truck blows a tire or a hose bursts, he could miss his ride, and that would mean paying a

Standing beside his professional guide in 1972, Bob Eastman takes a practice shot while on a lion hunt. It took many years for the modern bow and arrow to become legally accepted for big-game hunting in Africa—and many more for the professional hunting community to recognize that a well-placed arrow kills as surely as a well-placed bullet.

thousand unnecessary dollars for an unscheduled flight. Time to get back to camp.

But the guide stands very still, concentrating. He says something in Swahili. Both trackers stand up next to him and, shielding their eyes, stare in the direction of the bait.

"There's a cat on your bait, George."

Mentally packing his gear, unscrewing broadheads from aluminum arrows, rolling his socks, and shielding his face from prop blast while boarding the airplane, George is slow to stand up, and, as he does, he thinks, He's just giving me a little thrill before I leave.

"No, no," the guide insists.

The plump baboon carcass has been pulled off the limb and is dangling partially on the ground. With his knuckles the guide thumps twice on the roof of the pickup, then leans out from his perch in the back to speak to the driver. The white truck edges forward over the low hilltop, bounces ahead a couple of hundred yards, and eases to a halt.

"Let the dogs out. Come on, George. Bring your bow and we'll follow the dogs. It's rocky here, and the dogs might push something up a tree. You could get a shot."

Sure, George thinks. A long shot.

Silently, the dogs streak toward the bait, all happiness at their escape from the rocking truck, ears flopping, tongues lolling. They race toward a leopard that could turn and kill them with a single swipe, a leopard George still has not seen and only half believes is possible.

They have not gone a hundred yards when the guide spots a leopard in the low branches of a tree, just as he had predicted. Finally, George

Freelance professional hunter Peter Dafner was born in Africa. He began his apprenticeship with an old Zambian professional named Jeff Wainwright, who is now in Tanzania. "Cat hunting can be really tedious," he says. "It isn't uncommon to spend ten days just waiting, and then a hunt can be over in a couple of seconds."

sees it, and the dogs, all nervous energy now, prance back and forth, ignoring the stinking baboon carcass.

"Shoot!" the guide growls, but it is seventy to eighty yards, and George is well out of range, especially with a screen of branches and brush between his arrow and the leopard. Focused on the excited dogs, the big cat has not yet spotted the greater danger.

"If that leopard sees you, he's gone," the guide says. "You'll never see him again. I guarantee it."

"I have to get closer," George insists.

With the impatient guide at his back, he begins a careful stalk through the dry brush toward the treed cat, keeping as much cover in front of him as possible. At around twenty-five yards, his vision narrows; he focuses only on leopard spots.

Snarling, showing its yellow, killing teeth, the cat is balanced delicately on a low branch that curves upward from the bole of the tree. It watches the dogs jumping and yelping harmlessly below.

What a leopard thinks is unknowable. It is quicker than the dogs. One-on-one, it would kill them both, even if the dogs were game. Its experience suggests that, individually, they are only noisemakers. One swipe of its claws and a dog will yelp and flee. But a leopard's instinct is to climb above the hyenas and the wild dogs. Instinct now forces it into the wrong decision. Tense, aware that this is not a game, it waits. These are strange dogs, but they are just dogs. There are other dogs on the veld more powerful, more cunning.

The leopard understands these pack runners, though, and is programmed not to fear them, for they are only a gang of children in a world ruled by cats, cats like itself. Yet dogs have a pack mentality, they hunt together as a herd, and that makes them dangerous, like jackals or hyenas. Dogs survive by confusing their prey, running in teams, in contrast to the stealthy stalk and sudden charge of a great cat. Dogs prosper because they have ingratiated themselves to the hairless ape who walks on two legs. Individually, dogs are nothing, and the leopard is prince of the plains. This, also, George's feline understands in its deepest marrow because it has dealt with dogs longer than humans have walked the earth.

George nocks an arrow, draws the recurve, and releases. The broadhead slices cleanly through the spotted cat, center of mass, just behind its front shoulder. The shot is perfect, and the leopard slumps forward and down on the branch without losing its balance, perhaps stunned at this sudden and unexpected pain.

"Shoot him again!"

The instant George shoots, the guide runs forward.

"He's dead," George says, in his self-possessed manner. "He just doesn't know it yet."

"God damn you," the guide swears, fingering his double-barrel rifle, "I said shoot it again."

At this point in the tale, George's memory is taut as a bowstring. It is as if he has, mentally, sat up and leaned forward in his chair. One can almost hear him chuckling.

He steps into the open and slowly, casually, takes the classic archery stance, shuffling his left foot slightly away from a direct line to the wounded leopard.

The cat lifts its head and, as George begins his draw, springs out of the tree, straight at him. Whether it intentionally charges or simply springs away from the dogs and happens to leap in his direction, George cannot guess, even after twenty-five years. And he has thought about it a lot. The archer completes his draw and lowers his point of aim, and his second arrow hits the bounding leopard dead center in the chest. It is an exceptional shot with a recurve on a charging leopard.

"It started doing twirlies," George recalls, "chasing its tail."

He shoots again, his third arrow in less than thirty seconds, and the cat tumbles. The dogs catch up with it now, whirling around it, worrying it, nipping its tail and hindquarters, staying away from its still lethal teeth and claws.

"God damn it. I don't believe it!" George's guide says, pushing his hat back from his forehead and uncocking both rifle triggers. "I can't believe I didn't shoot when it charged."

Ten minutes later, the guide is still mumbling: "I can't believe it."

What he himself could not believe, George says, is that he did not shoot immediately, as soon as the cat sprang out of the tree.

"But I was very confident of my shot. And maybe I stepped into his shooting lane—accidentally, of course—and besides, Bob Eastman and I had talked with him many times about only shooting if it was absolutely necessary. So, as far as I'm concerned, my guide did the right thing."

* * *

Embarking on his fifth generation now, if a generation is considered a twenty-year span, George sips a scotch ice and remembers the good times with the bow and arrow.

"My leopard is over the fireplace now, glaring at me from a tree branch, just like I remember out there in the bush. It could have happened yesterday. . . . And we didn't miss the plane, either."

The Unlikely Combination

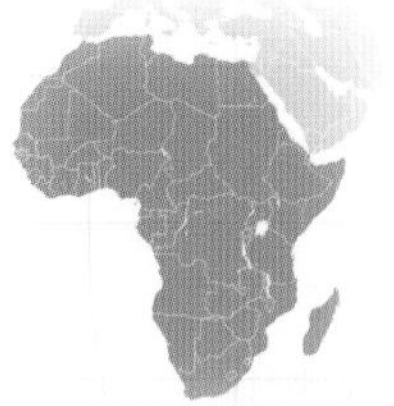

1980

Chapter 6

Rashness in my clients was always a source of concern to me for no one knows what a wild animal may do. A professional hunter learns to expect a certain type of animal to behave in a certain way and nine times out of ten he will be right. But there is always the tenth animal and he is the danger.

Hunter[1]
J. A. Hunter

Every traveler venturing into the African bush leaves with lifetime memories. Whatever the reasons for the visit, though, everyone is bloodied—especially the nonhunters. Christian missionaries stir up intractable tribal conflicts. Muslims appear willing to force their world view upon the entire population, regardless of the cost. Businessmen find irreconcilable opposition between their government's laws about business ethics and the continent's insatiable demands for *suborno* and *takrima*, bribes and gifts. Tourists in Cairo are startled to discover that the disintegrating pyramids have become joyless suburban parks, ringed by police with automatic weapons and hucksters selling holy relics made in China. At the opposite end of the continent, in Johannesburg, guests are warned not to wander away from the hotel and not to sightsee without an armed escort certified by the hotel. In any of the capital cities, white visitors are lectured that the whores, no matter how beautiful, how young, how affordable, are already dying from AIDS.

[1]Page 59.

George Gardner's brush with mortality came on a trip to the Republic of South Africa a generation ago. He wanted to hunt zebra, while his friend and hunting partner, Bob Eastman, was after a hippopotamus.

Hunting in South Africa today bears little resemblance to the exciting free-for-all action available a generation ago. Except for rhinoceros, which have been poached almost to extinction, the animals, for the most part, are as wild as they were a thousand years ago. The hunts, however, are as tame as those for food-plot whitetails. Riflemen drive a ranch while comfortably seated in the back of a truck; bow hunters wait inside enclosed or dark blinds near water holes. With rising populations, the expansion of poverty-stricken cities, and pressure on natural resources, it won't get better.

A zebra-and-hippo combination hunt is a most unusual pairing. It is a combination of cheap and expensive ventures that would normally take archers in separate directions with different guides and possibly even with different outfitters.

Zebras are skittish, thin-skinned herd animals. The color of a new soccer ball, a zebra is readily observed on the plains but must be carefully stalked, for wind direction is important, and any unusual noise or movement panics the entire herd. This is a prey animal, nowhere near the top of the food chain, and somewhere deep in its DNA the zebra seems to understand its role of converting grass energy to blood energy.

Many bow hunters believe their whitetail setup is suitable for such plains game. This may be true if one hunts from a blind beside a water hole where a shot is a known distance and the animal is not moving. Inside the blind, one may sketch, even casually range the distance, read a book, drink a beer, text one's spouse, all without being detected through the narrow shooting slit. On old-fashioned safaris, however, where the closest fence may be five hundred miles away, shots are rarely within an archer's thirty-yard comfort zone. When buying one

A woman of the Ndebele tribe of Zimbabwe wearing neck rings. Their color and variety testify to her social position, family wealth, and perhaps even her or her family's power. Women of this tribe once wore heavy brass and copper rings around their necks. These rings gave the appearance of lengthening the neck.

of these hunts, the rule is to expect longer shots and to crank up the bow's draw weight accordingly.

The hippopotamus, not one of the planet's daintier mammals, is as easy to spot as a zebra and is especially visible when it is lounging, grunting, and fighting in a pack in an African river. (However, we shall see that even an alert hunter can walk past without noticing!)

To kill a thick-skinned hippo, most archers hunt from a brush blind along a hippo path. The blubbery behemoths usually come out of the water in the evening to graze in nearby fields and vegetable gardens, returning at dawn—a habit that understandably annoys a river valley's human inhabitants. To take a hippo from only a few yards, one must deliver a heavy arrow and sharp broadhead just below the crease where the foreleg folds into the body. Shots from a short distance deliver maximum kinetic energy and penetration.

Despite Disney's charming hippos, dancing to Amilcare Ponchielli's "Dance of the Hours" in the movie *Fantasia,* one must remember that nothing would please a hippo more than to stomp a hunter to death, for, deep within its psyche, a hippo is a mendacious and calculating beast.

After humans and perhaps disease-carrying mosquitoes, the hippo is Africa's most earnest killer. Inscrutable as a crocodile. Quick as a mamba. Deadly as a lion. In the water, hippos are as delicate and graceful as synchronized swimmers; on land, as formidable as battle tanks. A hippo is an endearing brute without a brain, a killer without a conscience.

The trophy fee for a Burchell zebra, hunted on a South African ranch in 2011, is about sixteen hundred dollars; a mountain zebra, about twenty-eight hundred dollars; and a hippopotamus, about nine thousand dollars.

White on Black or Black on White?

Zoologists suspect that zebras are black animals with white stripes, the stripes being a survival mechanism in a land of high grass and color-blind predators. George Gardner admired zebras, for they are sturdy and wild and apparently untamable. He wanted one. Whether it was white-on-black or black-on-white was immaterial.

Like the zebra, Africa was then—and remains—black with white stripes. There were few newspapers in South Africa in those days, and there are fewer today. Few news outlets in the land of apartheid were free to report events or arguments that were unpopular with the government. For those who do not recall apartheid, it was a political, social, and economic system that separated black men and women from white men and women. Apartheid was unfair and unjust, although the current "post-apartheid" democratic system has proven little better.

Although it suffered international sanctions because of its white-supremacist apartheid policy, a generation ago South Africa was a land of apparent opportunity with magnificent natural and wildlife resources.

George and Bob chose John Brooker as the outfitter for their trip. Brooker was not only a respected professional hunter, but he was also widely recognized as a specialist in wildlife capture who supplied zoos, game farms, and animal research facilities around the world. The man indeed had a foot in camps with widely divergent philosophies.

The game capture business is altogether different from guiding clients. Originally, game capture involved lassoing and then darting animals from the back of a racing Land Rover, dodging stumps and crashing out of ditches. It was hard, dirty, hands-on work, and it was terribly dangerous, especially if the chase was conducted from a low-flying helicopter.

Brian Herne writes of game capture pioneer Carr Hartley: "Carr usually caught his game by lassoing from a speeding vehicle. Over the years he paid a high price for his daily handling of dangerous game. He was severely mauled several times by lion, twice tossed by rhino, trampled by a buffalo, and an oryx put a horn through his knee. In Carr's view, elephant were the most dangerous of the Big Five, followed by buffalo,

In 1975 Bob Eastman took one of the largest elephants of all time, but before that, he shot an elephant by bow that subsequently turned and charged. The guide was forced to shoot the bull with his rifle, and it dropped to the shot immediately.

leopard, lion, and rhino, despite the fact that his most serious injuries were caused by lion and rhino."[2]

In his camp beside the Limpopo River in the northern Transvaal province, Brooker told the American bow hunters that zebra should not be a problem, even for an archer, because they were plentiful. This pleased George Gardner. The professional hunter also had obtained a rogue (or marauding) hippo permit, and this pleased Bob, who was skilled at hunting and capturing hippo.

The Game Tracker

Brooker understood the limited range of a bow and arrow, and he set George in a clump of brush beside a wide ravine. Natural shooting lanes afforded an unobscured view of any animal moving through the eroded cut.

Zebras used the ravine, Brooker explained, to avoid the high, sandy bluffs along the river. It gave the single-toed ungulates access to water during the dry season and limited cover from lions. There were often zebras and other game animals coming and going along the ravine's sandy bottom, so Brooker's plan was to drive the cut slowly on foot from the river. This would push any zebras present in George's direction.

The outfitter's plan worked to perfection. As a harem of perhaps a dozen zebras trotted by, George drew the bowstring and released. He sensed he had shot a little low, but he remembered to follow through and to continue the slow tracking with his bow after the shot.

In those days, George hunted with a game tracker unit screwed into the accessory insert on the back of his bow. A strong but lightweight synthetic thread, like dental floss, was spooled inside the unit's plastic

[2]Herne, *White Hunters: The Golden Age of African Safaris,* page 310.

housing. It was attached to the arrow behind the broadhead. Normally, it uncoiled smoothly, providing an invaluable tracking aid that, at distances up to thirty yards, did not interfere with the flight of an arrow. This was especially helpful in the African bush, where danger from wild

Today the hippopotamus kills more people in Africa than lions, leopards, and crocodiles, even when those numbers are totaled. "People are under the false assumption that these are just big teddy bears," says Bob Eastman (holding bow), who has taken several hippos by bow. "They are not. They are very tough and very aggressive. If you are the least bit careless, they will kill you."

predators and human opportunists was as omnipresent as it was in the overcrowded, underemployed cities of Johannesburg and Cape Town.

Indeed, it was via the game tracker that George Gardner and Bob Eastman became acquainted. George, who had assisted its inventor, brought the device to Bob's attention. The two avid bow hunters immediately developed a passion for its game-finding possibilities. Bob saw a business opportunity, and the Game Tracker became the foundation for his success in developing a broad-based archery and outdoor products corporation. In the process, the men became friends.

In the case of George's zebra, the string, tracking the fleeing stallion, zinged out nearly fifty yards after his shot before snapping. The tracking system was in its first of several mechanical versions, and the businessmen were still perfecting it. Every part and fitting had to work together seamlessly—bow poundage, string weight and tension, wrap tension around the spool—for the game-tracking unit to operate as designed.

The recurve bow, with which George and Bob hunted, was ideal for use with such an arrow-tracking device. A recurve stacks weight progressively but smoothly, building to a peak of tension, at which moment the archer pulls through his draw, releases, and follows through with the shot.

A compound or cam bow, on the other hand, builds draw weight suddenly and releases even more suddenly. This dynamic is expressed by the bow's force-draw curve, and it is not consistently efficient with the smooth flow of tracking string.

Classic shot mechanics emphasize a relaxed hand grip on the bow handle (also called the riser) because gripping the bow tightly causes it to twist and results in imprecise left-right arrow placement. This was an unexpected problem for early Game Tracker models. When an archer shoots with a relaxed grip, the bow takes on a life of its own once the arrow leaves the string. Typically, when simply sitting "at rest" in one's hand, the top limb of both recurves and compounds rocks backward

Inspecting his trophy rhinoceros with guide John Brooker near the Limpopo River, Bob Eastman (right) reflects that the skin is so thick that arrow placement is critical; this is true on all big game, but especially on elephant, rhino, and hippo. "If you hit a rib, an arrow from a hundred-pound bow can bend and bounce right back at you," he says.

quite sharply toward the archer's face. Following a shot, however, the momentum drives a bow forward and down. This changes the angle of the string running out of the enclosed spool after a shot, causing it to rub against the housing. The friction increases the already high tension that results when the arrow sticks in a moving target.

Since the turn of the twenty-first century, sophisticated shock-absorbing stabilizers have been developed. Stabilizers balance the bow in the shooter's hand, allowing it to remain relatively vertical after the shock of a shot, and they dampen the vibration that causes noise.

Now Would Be a Good Time to Panic

These were only a few of the engineering puzzles Bob was studying when George discovered that his tracking string had broken. Still, there was a blood trail and a bloody arrow that apparently had zipped completely through the zebra. This meant the wild horse would leak from both the entrance and the exit wound, leaving a well-defined blood trail in the sand of the gully.

* * *

Absolutely forbidden to follow a blood trail without Brooker and his trackers, George relaxes and sits down to wait for them. Brooker is not only afraid that a client alone in the bush might encounter some unexpected predator—a lion or a wild dog, for instance—but also that he might become lost. A lonely death in the bush would certainly be worse for the client. And losing a client would ruin an outfitter's reputation and perhaps cost him his license.

Brooker appears, and they set off on the track. George first returns to the blind for his bow and quiver of arrows. It is at this very moment when, "out of the blue," George recalls, the hippo rams its way up the ravine from the direction of the river. Mature hippos, *kibokos* in Swahili, laugh at crocodiles and, other than small but deadly parasites, have no enemy but man. Now, plowing over brush, insensitive to the noise or disturbance, the hippo charges the American hunter. Brooker and his trackers have apparently walked right by the gray, dust- and mud-covered animal, although even the experienced trackers are at a loss to explain how this was possible.

Spying George, who is momentarily rooted to the floor of the ravine in astonishment, the hippo swerves toward him. George does the only sensible thing. He runs for his life. He scrambles up the side of the ravine, either because that is the direction in which he has been walking or because he instinctively understands that the steep, sandy banks will slow the ton of blubbery vegetarian. George scrambles, and screams for Brooker. The archer expects to reach the top of the ravine and catch his breath while the guide runs the hippo back to the river with a shot or two in the air. The hippo, however, tiptoes up the wall of the ravine with an ease that belies its magnificent girth.

Adding to George's consternation is the fact that he cannot send the universal distress signal by firing three times in the air. He can, but he will then need to dodge falling arrows. And the hippo is making a great deal of noise. It snorts and slobbers and gnashes its immense ivories, all the while gaining steadily on the scrambling archer.

At the top of the ravine, George turns to see how far from the beast he has come, but, to his surprise, the hippo is closer than before. Screaming again for Brooker, he backs away from the edge just as the hippo's head appears. The sight, seared like a brand into George's memory, is that of bulbous, bloodshot eyes, framed by knots of thornbush. It is demonic in composition.

The hippo scrambles over the top, and George retreats from the edge. Unfortunately, he is wearing a popular brand of head-to-foot camouflage from Winona (Minnesota) Knitting Mills—a lightweight, two-piece knitted wool suit—and he immediately backs into a large thornbush. With its millions of tough, two-inch thorns, the bush pins him as securely as a choke hold pins a wrestler. (This would be an excellent time to panic.)

One moment George realizes he is inextricably trapped in the thorns, and the next, just as the hippo tops the ravine, he realizes he is in grave trouble. Pawing the ground and snorting, the hippo—whose eyesight may not be spectacular, but who makes up for it with uncomplicated malevolence—is barely ten yards away.

The tape that runs through George's mind calls for the PH to appear and shoot the hippo, thereby saving George's life. While George believes in miracles in general, he nevertheless feels that possibility is remote, since it happens too often in novels to be true to life. So George quits struggling and stands quite still. He barely breathes. Except for the sweat dripping down his face, the camouflaged man might, for a hippo's intents and purposes, be part of the bush. Later, George will realize that this surrender may have saved his life. The hippo now pauses, searching for movement from its panicked victim.

Just then a voice, deep and reassuring, says, "George, I'm here. Don't worry. I have a gun on the hippo. Just move out of there slow and easy."

Hearing George's cries for help, Brooker has raced back down the ravine. The problem is that George cannot move. When he is motionless, the thorns do not prick him, but they are inextricably enmeshed in his woolens.

"I can't move! I'm pinned by the thorns," George whispers.

We can surmise that his reply was almost certainly more vivid.

Oh, no, Brooker recalls thinking. *I've got a client stuck between me and a hippo. That's not a helluva nice situation.*

He does not say this to George.

Brooker asks George if he can unzip his jacket and slide out of it. He barely manages to do it, and abandons the jacket in the bush.

"The hippo just stood there and looked at us," Brooker says. "It was really a mean-looking animal, a big old bull, a huge thing. When it closed its mouth, the tusks were so long that they went through the top of its lips. So I threw a rock at it, and, quite amazingly, it pushed off."

The hippo spins, executes a perfect *pirouette en dedans,* like in the Disney movie, and races toward the river. No one shoots; no one dies. The entire episode has taken only a minute or two at the most, but it is during minutes such as these that a man's existence can spin off in any direction. This particular minute spun George Gardner in the direction of life, and he admits that, as John Brooker and the trackers extricated him from the thornbush, his hands trembled in silent gratitude and in fear.

"Well, George," Brooker said, "we'd better go find Bob and see if we can get an arrow into that hippo, eh. Want to come along?"

"No, you guys are crazy. I want to find my zebra."

George has had enough of hippo.

* * *

Brooker works the hippo like a pro golfer on a fairway surrounded by sand traps, Bob recalls. Cautiously but steadily, the guide stalks within a stunning five yards.

The professional hunter motions two assistants to circle around the hippo bull, to make noise and leave their scent on the wind. But as the hunters close in, Bob feels a breeze tickle the back of his neck. In a single fluid movement, the hippo's head springs up, and it spins in their direction and charges, but not before Bob, at that age slender and quick, releases an arrow. (He was slender and quick in those days.)

For some reason the bull swerves to the side and lumbers toward a shallow pool in the drought-plagued river. It may be the arrow's impact and subsequent deep penetration that has spared them, but probably it is the fortuitous log in front of them.

Bob Eastman's Michigan friend and hunting partner George Gardner with an old and yellow-fanged lion taken in South Africa. Gardner advises any hunter who has not yet been to Africa to go as soon as possible. "Old Africa is fast disappearing," he says.

Later, sitting on the bank, Bob and Brooker wonder how to lure the mortally wounded animal out of the water without being caught on the wide-open muddy flats between the hippo pool and the dry riverbank. The difficulties seem insurmountable. Eventually, George joins them.

Brooker decides to return to camp for the Land Cruiser and a set of strong ropes, leaving the bow hunters to keep track of their quarry. These two are not men to sit idly by when a problem needs solving, however. Soon, without a specific plan, they scramble down from the bank and begin walking in the direction of the hippo. This, of course, motivates the wounded river horse, and once again it charges. ("We ran like hell," George says.) Snorting blood, it races across the flat ground, and, as it begins to scramble up the bank, Bob shoots again. The arrow sinks to its feathers.

Halfway up the steep bank the hippo pauses, perhaps feeling the red bite of the razor-honed steel head. Then, the massive animal seems to fold in on itself, Bob remembers. It stumbles, then slides backward, and the ponderous land-whale begins to slip and fall and roll. The bow hunters watch, relieved, as it comes to rest, twitching momentarily, at the bottom of the low ridge.

An hour later, Brooker's white Toyota, with Brooker himself at the wheel, crashes through the forest behind them. At first Brooker does not see the hippo beneath the lip of the bank.

"Well, I think we have enough rope to winch it out onto solid ground. I better put it out of its misery," he says, lifting his rifle from its cradle behind the cab.

"Ah, don't worry yourself, John," Bob says. "George and I have already taken care of that."

* * *

As he talks, George remembers more of those days. As he recalls the heat and the animals, the bright black-and-white adventures of Africa become immediate once again. The ice in his glass melts, diluting the untouched scotch.

"I've had some fun, all right. Hunting for a Cape buffalo, we lay out in tall grass and had a thousand buffalo feed around us one day. They were close, only ten yards. I could have reached out and touched one or two. . . ."

The memory locker is undone. Images, wisps of conversation, flights of fancy, trophies, failures—they come fast now. George is ready to talk.

How Brooker Remembers It

John Brooker, South African lodge owner, game capture professional, and hunting guide, remembers the hunt with Bob and George, but he recalls it unfolding differently. George was hunting impala, not zebra, he thinks . . . but it has been a quarter-century, and who really knows any longer.

"I'm one of those people who—well, don't tell me something can't be done," Brooker says, "because I'll work as hard as I can to prove you wrong."

And so, when the American bow hunters challenged him with a combination zebra (or impala) and hippo hunt, Brooker took it as a personal challenge.

According to Brooker, the most demanding of the Big Six is hippo, especially when hunting with a bow and arrow.

"They're the most dangerous animal in Africa. There is no such thing as a 'mock charge.' A hippo isn't going to stop until it bites you. An elephant or a lion, sometimes you can stand your ground, shout them down, unless they have been wounded at some time. With hippo, there's no second chance, even though it may not charge you out of aggression. It may charge, actually, out of fear.

"Hippos kill more people in Africa than any other dangerous animal, and they are especially dangerous when people get between the animal and the river when they are returning from grazing in the morning. Deaths usually happen—not always, but usually—when they're trying to get back into the water.

"I have hippos out my door at the lodge north of Johannesburg. They're totally wild, and I have a huge amount of respect for them. They are closely related to whales and dolphins, and they communicate quite well. They're highly intelligent animals.

"The year before Bob's hunt with George, Bob and I tried to get a hippo down in Lesotho. We sat up all night in a blind in the freezing cold. I nearly got pneumonia.

"So this year hippos were raiding the crops, and Nature Conservation told us about them. We were going to move them out, but they said, 'No, no. Shoot the stuff.' So I said, well, let me bring out a client, and that's how we got the permit to hunt hippo."

The PH recalls, "They couldn't get into the thicket where the hippos had run, so I got a couple of my Africans to go down fifty meters around by the river, and I told them, 'For once in your life don't keep quiet. Talk to each other.' The hippo concentrated on them, and we went in on a path, a hippo trail that led behind this thing. And I told Bob that if you step on so much as a leaf, I'm going to shoot you first because if the hippo charges, we're never going to get out of here alive.

"There was a broken tree stump, and we kind of climbed in behind that, and the hippo was—Bob could have touched its backside with the tip of his bow, that's how close we were, so if you want to know what the backside of a hippo looks like, we can tell you.

"I told Bob to take his time and pull back and make a good shot. Bob at that stage began to shake quite a bit. He was getting a little nervous, and I whispered in his ear, 'You'll be fine,' and he settled down.

"Then the wind changed, and this thing spun around, and Bob let go an arrow, but it just bounced off."

Bob later said it ricocheted off the thick, tough hide because the angle was too great.

"The hippo came straight for us," Brooker continued, "and I raised the rifle and thought, I'm going to shoot this thing, but the log was what saved us. We were so close that a bullet wouldn't have stopped it. But when it ran into the log, it went down, knocked off its feet. It spun around and went out of the thicket toward my Africans, who scrambled up a tree to get out of its way.

"Bob eventually got a twenty-yard broadside shot and stuck it perfectly. The trackers found it lying on its side in a clearing.

"I thought, Bloody hell. This thing looks dead, or else it's mortally wounded. And so I went in and got behind a huge wild fig tree and watched it for a while. I saw blood spouting out of its side and realized Bob had a lung shot, but when I moved away, it stood up and ran around, and I decided if it charged me again, well, hell, I was going to blow it away. I let off a shot in the air and backed behind the tree, and that turned it down toward the river, but not in the water, funny enough.

"We saw it standing about three hundred yards away, across the sand. When I walked down the bank, it went into a pool in the river, where it would submerge and come up. Finally, it charged out at me, and I ran back toward the bank where Bob was.

"I told Bob we were going to lure it out of the water, but he should run behind a fallen tree and from there take his second shot. It worked. Bob's second arrow went right up to the feathers. This hippo was huge, larger than most taken with a rifle.

"Then we got very, very drunk that night with a bottle of Scotch or two."

A Most Unusual Talent: An Interview with John Brooker 1980

Chapter 7

The aloneness of the hunter, and his thoughts of his hunting past, are the very genesis of primitive energy. He is always a young man, then, and making his most daring journeys. He will not think of middle age, and even the responsibility of his family will be dim as he pauses, every sense alert for the sound of what he plans to kill. This is really the only time that he is fully alive. All the rest is the dreaming time.

The Hunting Animal[1]
Franklin Russell

Bob Eastman built a hunting lodge in Michigan's north woods. More properly, he rebuilt a hunting lodge. The former establishment, a hodgepodge of creaky trailers and cabins, wooden sheds, outbuildings, leaky pipes, and blind alleyways, burned to the ground. Good riddance.

Built on a square mile of forest and bog, the new place has polished hardwood floors, a wraparound porch with rocking chairs, and enough hot water to shampoo a herd of buffalo.

Bob calls his property "Tens or Better." The name suggests that a hunting guest must find a whitetail buck with five antler points to a side before shooting. There are plenty of deer on Bob's place, but not many 10-pointers; indeed, there are not plenty of 10-pointers anywhere. No guns are permitted, so that minimum requires a lot—especially of archers.

[1]Pages 2–3.

Bob Eastman's spacious new lodge at his "Tens or Better" hunting camp in northern Michigan replaced an old system of sheds and trailers that burned in 2008. The lodge is surrounded by rolling hills, thousands of acres of hardwood forest and swamp, and a superb population of white-tailed deer.

Robert Eastman is a brilliant man. Quintessentially American, he never stops making contacts, searching for commercial advantage, that extra point or two. Even on safari, he is obsessed with work and family. On safari, during lunch in the *miombo* tree's high, thin shade, he reads a business book. In the evening by the campfire, he pulls it out again. He sleeps lightly, if at all.

But this chapter does not concern Bob Eastman specifically. It is about a professional hunter who has guided him throughout southern Africa, a man named John Brooker. Brooker is much more than a PH, as if that weren't enough. He is also Bob's friend.

I interviewed Brooker by telephone from Bob's new hunting lodge in the fall of 2008, and again in the spring of 2009 from my office in Florida.

Bob and "The Brook"

Bob Eastman knew of John Brooker by reputation, and on Bob's 1984 safari, when his Mozambican PH, Rui Quadros, "was elsewhere," Brooker took over. The two men hit it off right away.

"He was just great," Bob says. "It surprised him when we didn't show up with guns. Rui didn't bother to tell him that, but because of Brooker's expertise in capturing big game, he knew the importance of getting close to animals. That was perfect for bow hunters."

Brooker recalls that when he met Bob Eastman's party in a hotel in Johannesburg, he asked, "Where are your rifles?" and they said they weren't shooting rifles; they were shooting bows and arrows.

"Well, that was something different," he says.

It was January or February. Hot as hell, Brooker recalls.

"Bob wanted to shoot a giraffe, so I made arrangements with a friend who owns a ranch called Thornybush.[2] It is situated next to Kruger Park. Thornybush has the largest giraffe population in the whole of Africa. A positively tremendous amount of giraffe down there.

"Bob shot at a giraffe and missed, but a little while later he got a better one, and we started tracking around eight-thirty or nine o'clock

[2]www.thornybush.co.za

in the morning. Just the two of us. He said, 'Aren't you going to take your rifle?'

And I said, 'No. You want to kill a giraffe with a bow and arrow? You're going to kill it with the bow and arrow. I'm not going to take a rifle.'

Bob looked at me skeptically, as it's lion country, and he said, 'What happens if we come across something?'

I said, 'I hope you can shoot straight.'

"We tracked until one o'clock in the afternoon, and Bob said he was thirsty: *'Nina kiu.'* He asked if I carried water, and I said no. When it got to two o'clock, he offered me a hundred dollars for a Coke.

"We didn't find the giraffe until the next morning. It was dead and not far from where we left off the day before. That was my first experience with a bow hunter. After that we hunted in various places for plains game, hippo, giraffe, nyala, lion, and so on."

The Making of a PH

John Brooker was born in Norwich, England, in 1945. His father, an officer with the British Tank Corps in North Africa, fought with colonial troops from South Africa and the former Bechuanaland, now Botswana.[3] When World War II ended, Brooker Sr. deactivated his African troops and threw his lot in with them.

John Brooker says his father had "fallen in love with Africa." Compared to the British Isles, Africa seemed vast and empty and ripe with potential. Game ran everywhere; regulations were, for the time being, lax; land cost little or nothing; workers were readily available.

[3]The United Kingdom established Bechuanaland as a "protectorate" in 1885. When it gained independence on 30 September 1966, it became the Republic of Botswana.

From South Africa he sent a telegram to his wife: "Pack and move down here as soon as possible."

The young Brooker thus grew up in two hemispheres, but his lifelong enthusiasm was Africa's wildlife. At just seventeen, he started his own business, capturing animals for export to zoos. Bilingual in English and Afrikaans,[4] he also spoke a smattering of several native dialects, including Swahili, and could make himself understood anywhere in southern Africa.

With no family fortune or powerful political allies, with only a young man's passion for big game, it was natural for Brooker to become a professional guide. By the '60s, the world had begun to recover from the direct effects of the Second World War and had settled into its Cold War posture. Western economies boomed, but African independence and freedom movements were gaining popular support. They were supported, it must be said, by the Communist Eastern Bloc and resisted by the free, Western colonial democracies, sometimes including the United States.

Guides like Brooker are essential for hunting in a foreign land, but also for any quality adventure abroad. Someone must translate, and only natives or those with total immersion in a language truly understand a dialect's nuance. Nuance is often the difference between yes and no, right and wrong, humor and anger, courtesy and defiance. Someone must understand the currency and local customs, or trouble will most certainly result. Thus, being a guide is an honorable profession, and the services of a thoughtful, knowledgeable, positive guide are invaluable for a traveler.

[4]Afrikaans is a linguistic variation of the Dutch language that was taken to southern Africa by white settlers in the late 1600s. Afrikaans is a principal language of South Africa and Namibia, together with English and a number of Bantu tongues, nine of which have official status in South Africa.

The tradition of guide as professional hunter surely began thousands of years ago. Poor people hunted because they were hungry; the rich hunted for sport, eating the boars and stags, but also for excitement. Whether it was hunting hares with falcons or lions with spears or even French Protestants (Huguenots) with matchlocks in the very Catholic Louis XIII's shooting parks, someone had to organize and be responsible for the event. Someone had to clean the game for the pot, cure the skin for the rug, and drag offal to the boneyard.

John Brooker also became a specialist in the terribly difficult and dangerous art of game capture. Zoological gardens (zoos), game parks, and even wealthy private collectors the world over require species of unusual game for exhibit: elephant, lion, zebra. Wildlife management agencies required game populations to be in balance with their ecosystem, needed samples for scientific study, and occasionally wanted captured game to restock areas that had become barren as a result of war, disease, or poaching. Brooker traveled around the world and made a good living capturing animals. Guiding hunters was a sideline for him.

The Kamikaze Way

"Ted Riley, who owned this tiny little reserve out east in Swaziland, and I started the first private, professional game capture business in South Africa," John Brooker says, "although it was interrupted when I went off for my two years of compulsory service in the infantry as a military parachutist.

"At first we would go screaming through the bush at forty or fifty miles per hour in a Land Rover with a souped-up engine. We would try to lasso running animals with a catchpole (an eight- to twelve-foot pole with a rope noose on the end). If that didn't work, we just grabbed them by their tails or horns and threw a net over them or wrestled them to the ground by hand. It was incredibly scary and exciting, the kamikaze way of capturing animals."

In fact, Brooker says, his first wife "told me there was no future in it and that I was going to kill myself in the bush." Then she walked out.

"In 1962, when I was seventeen, we imported the first tranquilizer gun, called a Palmer Gun.[5] Darting animals to immobilize them probably saved our lives, but it also had a very big downside: a small margin of error. At first we lost more than eighty percent of the game because, using nicotine-based drugs, dosages were hard to regulate, and the equipment we used was really out of the Dark Ages.

"Since the '70s, though, we have used M99, etorphine hydrochloride. It is a morphine derivative, and, with some other drug supplements, we have solved most of the really distressing losses we had experienced earlier.

"We also learned how to minimize the stress on animals. For one thing, by planning better, we don't chase them for very long, and not during the heat of the day. We learned how to build good holding pens and to separate the males from the females and how quickly we could introduce nonnative foods, but mostly we learned about proper drug dosages for the larger and more expensive animals. Just because an animal like a rhino is three or four times as big as an eland, for example—and an eland is a big animal—doesn't mean the M99 dosage should be three to four times as great. For instance, you need more M99 for a zebra than for a rhino. Using drugs really is an art, and we had to learn that.

"At one time, before I stopped capturing in this country [South Africa], I was moving between seven thousand and nine thousand

[5]Game capture is practiced around the world. Members of the industry not only supply zoos with animals, but they also assist with projects such as relocating endangered species. The 1962 movie *Hatari!,* starring John Wayne, featured animal capture and opened with a rhino. The Palmer Cap-Chur company, of Powder Springs, Georgia (www.palmercap-chur.com), still markets hardware for animal capture. The company prefers to use the term "projectors" for their CO^2 and powder-blank-firing .22 "guns."

animals a year, either on specific assignment or to auctions. I supplied animals to safari parks and registered zoological gardens worldwide, as well as some of the local ranches, game farms, and reserves.

"Game capture has gotten to be a bit of a dogfight these days. People want to haggle over your price, and they tell you they have to go with the cheapest. But you contact them after a few months and ask them how many of the shipment they've got left, how many survived, and they tell you maybe eight or nine out of twenty. So then I ask them how much the surviving animals really cost. We cost more in the beginning, but we have got capture down to a one-percent mortality rate.

"Most people don't know that I also brought a lot of animals back from zoos, especially African buffalo, because all of our native buffalo here in South Africa have endemic diseases.[6] So when we couldn't move them internationally, I brought back and relocated at least two hundred, and now there are more than two thousand from that group that are disease-free."

Brooker explains that he got into the hunting side of the business "by default."

"For me it was more a pastime than a profession," he says, "although I have an international professional hunter's license. My main business is still game capture. We have been around the world locating and catching rare species and placing them in breeding programs: Spain, Mexico . . . We also got into the movie industry, sort of by default, and have done more than four hundred movie productions at our farm north of Johannesburg."

[6]Hoof-and-mouth disease is an acute and highly infectious viral disease of cattle, domestic buffalo, and some wildlife species, including elephant. Although morbidity is high, mortality is relatively low. Once an animal is infected, however, there is no known treatment. Hoof-and-mouth is endemic in South Africa. Corridor disease is a highly infectious disease in Cape buffalo. It is spread via a protozoan passed through tick bites.

A roaring fire in the bush can turn an uneventful evening into an unforgettable memory. The evening is also the time to check equipment for the morning and to reflect on the day's events.

Glen Afric

Today, John Brooker and his wife—he eventually found another girl, Jenny, who would stick by him—own a ranch north of Johannesburg and west of Pretoria in the North West Province. They named it Glen Afric, after the National Nature Reserve near Strathglass in northern Scotland.

"We bought the ranch in 1986," says Brooker. "Now we have a game lodge and do van drives and photographic safaris and elephant walks. We have the Big Five here—although we're temporarily out of rhino—and we do movies, also."

A travel site on the Internet describes the Brookers' ranch as follows:

Set in the splendor of the Magaliesberg Mountains, Glen Afric Country Lodge utilizes the Brookers' original hilltop homestead, built in the classic East African style by John Brooker in the mid-1980s and turned into a luxury lodge in the mid-1990s. The lodge offers spectacular views and sunsets from our deck.

Enjoy the sociable ambience of the Main Lodge, with its five luxurious en-suite rooms. Other facilities include swimming pool, guest lounge with satellite TV, and the "Big Five" Bar. Tantalize your senses in our elegant restaurant or experience the ultimate taste of Africa in our boma. Glen Afric is the home of 32 species of African wildlife, including

Bob Eastman is one of few hunters in the world ever to take a giraffe with a bow. He says, "A giraffe is as difficult to penetrate as a Cape buffalo. It is deceptively fast and its long legs can easily disembowel and crush a man."

lion, cheetah, hippo, elephant, and buffalo, plus over 340 identified bird species and a vulture restaurant, feeding over 120 birds[7].

Although it is sometimes difficult to understand that a professional hunter, world-traveling game capture specialist, and internationally acknowledged lodge owner must occasionally "get away from it all," Brooker says he must do just that.

Brooker, who describes himself as six feet tall with hazel eyes and brown hair, says his favorite get-away hobby is flying.

"I'm a qualified fixed-wing and helicopter pilot, also," he says. "I used to fly a lot and have logged more than three thousand fixed-wing hours and twice that many in a chopper."

Even in the bush, with so many exotic foods available, Brooker says he "loves to eat out, especially sushi."

Brooker's Future in Africa

John Brooker has traveled to every continent, and he understands that Africa is changing; that conflict seems unavoidable; that the future is, at best, uncertain.

"Well, take Zimbabwe for instance," he says, referring to the former Rhodesia, which suffers at present under the repressive dictatorship of Robert Mugabe. "With the turmoil up there, the first thing to go is the wildlife because the people kill it for food. The wildlife is under terrific strain. In Zambia the tourist trade has saved it.

"The only way wildlife will survive in Africa is if it's got a commercial value, from hunting and photographic safaris to everything else. If it doesn't have a commercial value, it's gone. That's the bottom

[7]The mailing address of Glen Afric is Box 54, Broederstroom, RSA 0240 NW Province. The Web address is www.glenafric.co.za.

Are they white on black or black on white? Zoologists suspect that zebras are black animals with white stripes, the stripes being a survival mechanism in a land of high grass and color-blind predators. Although there is no record-book category, a zebra stallion is a striking trophy for a bow hunter. "Zebras are fast, very sensitive to their environment, and can be aggressive," says Bob Eastman.

line. Sustainable utilization. It's the only way wildlife anywhere in the world will survive. People come first, unfortunately.

"In South Africa today, we have thriving game ranches catering to tourists and hunters where cattle ranches cannot survive. In places where you could run one cow, you can run five wild animals because they are indigenous. They don't have to be fed artificial supplements, and they don't have disease problems because they are born and bred in those areas.

"But even here we've got a few of these animal rights types who don't understand that their philosophy doesn't work. I think the world is waking up to these organizations like PETA [People for the Ethical Treatment of Animals[8]], which have such high administrative costs that they won't put any money into the real work of doing what's right for wild animals in a world where humans come first. They think animals are people. . . . That's a pet subject of mine, and when you get me started, I can go for a week."

Brooker feels that Americans have "figured it out." Organizations like Ducks Unlimited raise millions of dollars to preserve waterfowl habitat. After all, he says, the natural order of things is habitat first and healthy wildlife populations second.

"The only reason that ducks have survived there is hunting," he says. "DU even pays farmers not to drain and plant, and the farmers get more money than from actually farming."

The government-financed biofuel movement and gasoline at four dollars per gallon may change that, however.

"In places in Africa [such as Kenya], where they stopped all hunting and all extractive wildlife use, the safari and tourist business collapsed," he says. "Poachers went in and people exploring for minerals. When

[8]In 2010 the Florida Department of Agriculture and Consumer Services' Gift Givers Guide reports the following statistics for PETA: $33.203 million annual income with $1.402 million administrative expenses (four percent) and $4.060 million (12 percent) spent on fund-raising.

they found a little something to mine, they built highways, and the poachers used the highways.

"It was only when hunting came back that anti-poaching patrols organized by hunters drove the poachers out and the wildlife recovered. The parks got money again, and some of the meat went to the villagers. The Selous in Tanzania, for instance, is a highly successful wildlife project—a huge area with plentiful wildlife, and it's generating lots of money due to hunting. Even here in South Africa there are more animals now than in generations, and it's due to hunting and game capture and restocking."

Despite the stresses, Brooker says, game populations in Africa are overall "very, very good right now."

"So good, in fact," he continues, "that they have to be thinned out. They shoot thirty thousand buffalo a year in Kruger National Park because having an abundance of buff allows hoof-and-mouth disease and corridor disease to spread. And Kruger is 'redlined,' meaning that animals from the park area cannot be traded or shipped out without first being quarantined and vaccinated because of the endemic presence of these contagious diseases."

The abundance of game opens a potential market for enterprising Africans, according to Brooker.

"It's different than in America or Europe, where venison is on the menu every now and again. The general African housewife doesn't have a clue how to prepare game, although there is a tremendous potential market because it is low-fat meat and quite good and healthy."

John and Jenny Brooker believe they have a good future in South Africa. The economic and social problems facing the country and the sub-Saharan zone of the continent are in some ways endemic to all nations, he says.

"Speaking of Zimbabwe, it has nothing to offer the West. A few gold mines, maybe. It is a beautiful and wonderful country with fine people, but there's nothing else there, and the West won't invest unless it gets something back.

"The big corporations that control America and Europe want a return, and there is too much wealth in South Africa for it to turn into a Zimbabwe, with the white people being driven out of the country and their businesses and property confiscated by the government. The Indians and Asians would be next, and the nation would descend into chaos. I don't think the world is interested in that happening in South Africa. Plus there are the sea lanes around the Cape of Good Hope. Nobody wants a bunch of pirates working there.

"Zimbabwe only has two ethnic groups—like Rwanda, with Tutsi and Hutu—though in Zimbabwe they are Shona and Matabele. The ethnic mix here in South Africa is much more complex."

Still, Brooker is a realist.

"Africa stands with its hands open. All the countries want is aid from the West, and the system is absolutely corrupt. Material aid goes immediately to 'the boss,' the president or prime minister, or some tribal chief, and a few weeks later it's for sale on the black market in Russia. Cash goes directly into their Swiss bank accounts.

"If you live in Africa, you must have a sense of humor. The blacks now make the rules, and you have to learn them and learn how to play the game. Here, if you want something done, you have to start at the top and work down; don't start at the bottom, or you'll bleed out buying gifts before you get anywhere, before you reach anyone who has any influence.

"Play the game, though, and you can achieve a lot. In Botswana, playing the game means you must become a member of the golf club, even if you don't play golf. In Zambia, it is the flying club, even if you don't fly, because everybody who is in *Who's Who* drinks at these clubs. It's like an old boys' network. This is the way it works. It's networking. It's what you do. It's what you have to do."

The Mentor

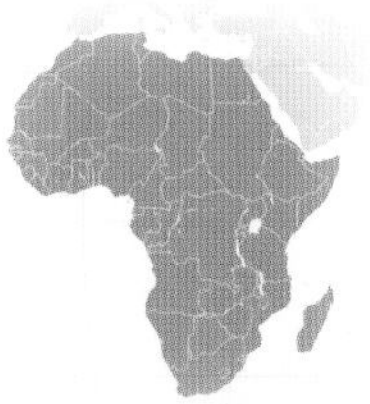

1982

Chapter 8

The thing I like best about the Old Man is that he's willing to talk about what he knows, and he never talks down to a kid, which is me, who wants to know things. When you are as old as the Old Man, you know a lot of things that you forgot you ever knew, because they've been a part of you so long.

The Old Man and the Boy[1]
Robert Ruark

According to legend, the Greek goddess Athena sprang fully formed from the head of Zeus. Armored with shield, breastplate, and greaves, she is usually pictured at the moment of birth, carrying a spear and a sword—halfway out of her father's brain. It is curious that this magnificent warrior woman was the patroness both of intellectual wisdom and of crafts and technology. This was the legacy of her father, who was also her mentor.

Not everyone is fortunate enough to have an all-powerful, all-knowing mentor, although "fortunate" may not be the right word, for Zeus had a mercurial and complicated personality. For us mortals, learning from the old man may be practical and economical, but it has always been fraught with difficulty.

Bob Eastman's bowhunting mentors were a couple of his neighbors in New York's Westchester County, Roy Colter and John Borg. They recognized something in the young man, whatever mentors look for when they take a kid under their wing—an intelligent eagerness, perhaps. Bob had that.

[1]Pages 21–22.

Guided by Hunters International in the Moyowosi region of Tanzania, Bob Eastman (left) took this record-book waterbuck (SCI 47⁴⁄₈) in 1975. Beside him to help celebrate a fine shot with a recurve bow is Bob's friend and bowhunting mentor Roy Colter.

These days Westchester County barely eludes New York City, which sprawls just minutes to the south. Westchester County has the image of being overrun with people and highways, in the peculiar style of shabby Yankeedom depicted in the opening of *The Sopranos,* although that technically was New Jersey. In the '50s, however, there was a surprising number of deer, and there were very few bow hunters in the county. It was then that Colter and Borg bought the kid a recurve bow and a handful of arrows.

In the half-century separating us from those days, Colter has died, but Borg has accompanied Bob to Africa several times.

"Bob was twelve or thirteen years old," Borg recalls. "His dad owned ten acres in Westchester County, and we had lots of deer back then. One day we were walking along the fence line with our bows and arrows, and Bob saw us. Well, he came running over, wondering what we were doing. 'Bowhunting deer,' we told him.

"When we came out of the woods that evening, he was waiting. 'Did you see any deer?' he asked.

We told him that yes, we saw deer. Well, by the next weekend, I had made him up some arrows, and Roy had a bow, and we got him started. Every weekend after that, he wanted to go with us. Once he got the hook in his mouth, he was off and running."

* * *

Having mentors who can help avoid the pitfalls of business or politics is an obvious asset, especially when one is young and restless, eager to make a name or build a company. It can also be a trap. This is especially true when one crosses the boundaries and invites a mentor in one field to comment on a plan or an innovation in another.

One could argue that the Eastman Companies, especially those divisions that revolve around outdoor products, were built on a small device called the game tracker. The theory was straightforward and brilliant and, like so many inventions through time, simply another iteration of an old idea. Attach one end of a spool of thread to an arrow and the other to the bow. When the archer subsequently shoots at a deer or a bear, the line spools out, and one can readily find the arrow—always a time-consuming task, especially if one has missed—or track the wounded animal. To construct such a device proved difficult but not impossible. One difficulty was that archery equipment, relatively static for thousands of years, was suddenly changing. By the late '70s, the switch over from longbows and recurves to higher-energy compound bows had already begun in earnest. From an energy point of view, that changeover had a great impact on the game tracker.

When Ted Lawson showed Dale Gray's early model of the game tracker to Bob Eastman, a young man whom John Borg described as "a driven, creative person," Bob was not only interested but enthusiastic.

"He's a compulsive worker, twenty-four/seven," Borg says. "Bob Eastman plays a lot, but all the while he's playing, he's thinking, thinking about products and marketing. If he's off on a ten-day hunt and something occurs to him, he'll pack up and go home early."

So it was natural that Bob would share the idea of the game tracker with his bowhunting mentors, who were very different from each other. Roy Colter worked with his hands and had "a big heart," Bob recalls. John Borg had an especially varied life and a broad point of view. Bob thought Borg would be enthusiastic because he was a schoolteacher and administrator, a private pilot, and a former paratrooper.

In fact, John had the opposite reaction.

"I said it was a harebrained idea and would never work," Borg recalls nearly thirty years later, and chuckles at his presumption. "Fortunately, Bob went ahead and developed it."

So Bob's life was blessed with mentors. At home, his father, Robert Eastman Sr., introduced him to the world of business; outside, in the woods, Colter and Borg taught him about hunting with the bow and arrow. It was an effective, one might almost say lethal, combination, and in less than a generation, the mentors were tagging along behind Bob to Africa.

The Ancient Ones

In a paper titled "History of the Bosjesmans or Bush People; The Aborigines of South Africa," which was compiled and published in England in 1847, Bushmen were depicted with the scientific understanding and humanity of the day—not impressive insight by today's standards. A number of the Bushmen were presumably seized and taken captive to London and were put on display, exhibited in museums and theatres as "specimens of rude nature." The paper describes them, in part, as follows:

> . . . having no settled habitation, sleeping in bushes and wandering from place to place to supply their daily wants; their weapon of offence or defence is the bow and arrow, with which their aim is unerring; they evince great expertness and cunning in securing their prey, "and when in search of the ostrich they disguise themselves with the skin, having stuffed the head and neck, which they hold in one hand, mimicking very accurately the actions of the bird pecking on the ground, etc., and are thus able to approach the unsuspicious bird. When within the required distance, they strike down the bird with their poisoned arrows."

All of which, if you are fond of ostrich, sounds both sane and effective.

And although the author of the paper refers to Bushmen as "stunted both in intellect and stature," he nevertheless affords them a nineteenth-century compliment: "Hunted down through a long succession of generations, by races corporeally more powerful, but mentally less cunning than themselves, they have still contrived to propagate and perpetuate their breed."[2]

For millennia, the Bushmen of Africa were the world's quintessential hunter-gatherers. Their lives swung like a pendulum between hunting and being hunted, hunted first by that continent's great cats and wild dogs and later hunted by human enemies. It was a terrible position for a people whom, genetic evidence suggests, may be one of the oldest surviving races in the world.

American geneticist and anthropologist Spencer Wells calls the African Bushmen a "genetic Adam" from which all humans ultimately trace their biological heritage. Although that heritage is inconceivably deep when imagined by an individual member of the species, it is not so deep compared to species of sparrows or lions or ants. The human heritage extends backward in time—if time can properly be said to "extend" in any lineal direction—barely five or six million years. The celebrated Olduvai Gorge region of northern Tanzania contains the most ancient findings of humans in the world, footprints of proto-Bushmen, technically named *Homo habilis.*

The black men with whom we hunt in Africa—in Tanzania, in particular—are primarily Bantu, although their tribe or social group may be Iramba or Chagga. They speak a common Swahili language across tribal and linguistic lines and are very different from the original Bushmen, who today are collectively referred to as the San or Khoisan.

When Bantu tribes expanded from East Africa into Central and Southern Africa, beginning perhaps as early as 1,000 BCE and reaching the most extreme portions of Southern and East Africa by around 400 CE, they found the land occupied by the San and nomadic Nilotic

[2]Anonymous, *History of the Bosjesmans, or Bush People.*

groups, such as the fierce Maasai, who were obsessed with cattle. The numerous Bantu—agriculturalists who possessed iron tools and weapons and had a complex social hierarchy—rapidly drove the wandering San bands of hunters and fishermen to the margins, the deep forests and the hot deserts. They made peace only where necessary with the Maasai and the Arab traders along the coast.

The policy of exclusion continued after the invasion by whites, and, when the invaders could not force the San to change their cultural practices, they were eradicated. They virtually disappeared. Curiously, the C. G. Jung Institute of Los Angeles[3] notes that there may still be one hundred thousand Bushmen left in Africa. They are the people a visiting hunter almost never sees, or, if he sees them, he does not notice. Small in stature, they are the working hands, or, in Joshua's words from the Old Testament, "the hewers of wood and drawers of water."

Thus, it was little short of miraculous that nearly thirty years ago, Bob Eastman and a hunting party encountered a group of the San people while on safari west of the Olduvai Gorge in Tanzania. The hunters included Bob's former mentor John Borg, who played a prominent, if unfortunate, role in the event. What happened illustrates the difficulties when one group of aliens encounters another.

In the Bush

"We were scheduled to hunt the Moyowosi district in the west near Lake Tanganyika," John Borg said, "but our outfitter, Tanzanian professional hunter Paulo Shanalingigwa, was not awarded that concession. So we hunted with him in the Selous."

[3]http://junginla.org/pubprograms/040511_ZF_Presseheft_engl.pdf. "Spirit of the Rocks" dates from 2007.

Africa allows hunters to experience not only diverse big-game opportunities, but also gives them a chance to interact with people not normally met "back home." In some regions of East Africa, governments have developed decision-making structures that give local peoples responsibility to manage big game. This preserves populations by giving animals an economic value and ensures income for the community from a local resource.

Almost right away, Borg recalls, Bob Eastman shot an ostrich. "He made a terrific shot on a running bird from the back of a moving truck."

It was better than terrific; it was phenomenal. Placing an arrow into the vitals of the largest flightless bird in the world, a bird that sprints forty miles per hour, while drawing and aiming a heavy recurve bow from the back of a speeding safari vehicle that is bouncing along the veld—hell, it was the shot of a lifetime!

But when Bob tried to duplicate that amazing shot when stalking a wildebeest, things went wrong. Larger and slower than an ostrich, a

The early bow hunters—Saxton Pope, Arthur Young, Howard Hill, Bob Swinehart, Fred Bear, and Bill Negley—carried recurves or even longbows to Africa. Beginning his safaris in the '60s, Bob Eastman began hunting with a powerful recurve and never changed, except for twenty-first-century experiments with one of the crossbows his company manufactures. With a recurve, he has taken virtually every big-game animal available on the continent.

wildebeest would seem to be an easier target, but in archery a puff of wind at the wrong moment, or the sudden shift of the game animal's body, can mean the difference between a solid hit and an arrow that is slightly off target. Thus, when the horned bovid ran off, carrying Bob's arrow—placed a little too far back, a little too low—the professional hunter followed it with his field glasses. His young trackers did not need binoculars. It was gut-shot.

The group piled onto the Toyota. Bob, John, and Paulo occupied the high seat immediately behind the cab, while a tracker rode on the front bumper—a dangerous perch on a prairie strewn with warthog holes and termite mounds. Easing the truck forward, they began a patient track, three, four, five miles per hour, and soon the wildebeest lay down to die. The sharp broadhead had cut it and bled it and strangled it quickly and efficiently as the blue gnu ran.

As they lurched across the veld, the cooler with the men's field lunch took a terrific beating, sliding back and forth in the unoccupied truck bed. When the wildebeest expired, one of the trackers opened the cooler and beheld the mess that had been their midday meal. Hardboiled eggs, smashed. Containers of salt and pepper, open and spilled. Bottles of beer, water, and soft drinks, broken, their contents soaking and soiling everything. Even the smoked meat was ruined, covered with fragments of eggshell and glass.

It was not a disaster, exactly. No fortunes were lost, no lives sacrificed, no reputations stained beyond redemption. But the food in the cooler was inedible, and the drinking water was insufficient for five men.

Bob posed for a quick photo, and then Paulo and a tracker set to work field-dressing the wildebeest, intending to use the meat for lion

Bowhunting partner and mentor Roy Colter tests the weight of Bob Eastman's first leopard. In the '60s and '70s it was still the custom for hunters to leave an arrow in a downed game animal, or even replace it for photos, if it fell out.

or leopard bait. Paulo's second tracker, the Toyota driver, emptied the cooler by slinging its contents into the scrubby brush, instead of walking ten yards into the bush and pouring its contents onto the ground.

The day was already hot, John thought, and the darting tsetse flies made it worse. The long ride back to camp would be hot and thirsty.

"Where they came from, I don't know and couldn't imagine," Borg says, referring to the half-dozen people who sprang out of the ground like Athena, fully formed from the head of Zeus.

"We were out in the middle of nowhere, miles from the camp field, dressing a wildebeest, and no one, not even our trackers, had noticed them. They just emerged from Hades, I don't know, like dandelions springing up in your yard the day after a rain, just from nowhere. They came over to us, and Paulo began to converse with them.

"I can't say these people stepped out of a tourist brochure. They wore tattered garments, mostly old shirts and shorts, but no one wore shoes, and that plain was covered with sharp rocks and thorns that would have torn my feet apart in ten minutes. A couple of them were women, and even they were wearing old clothes—rags, really—held at the waist by pieces of string and rope. The women did not look directly at us, did not speak, but did not seem afraid, either.

"One of the women carried a bowl, a gourd, on her head, that was half the size of a big watermelon. She seemed curious about the spilled contents of the cooler—maybe she was looking for something to eat—and walked over to look. She set the bowl down near the mess of broken glass and spoiled eggs on the ground.

"Because she was close to all the broken bottles, I used my foot to push the bowl out of the way so her people would not cut their feet, but, instead of sliding, the bowl tipped over, spilling what I later found out was cornmeal onto the ground. Whatever was in there was pretty much ruined."

The woman screamed. It was as if she gave the group an electric shock, and at this critical point accounts diverge. John recalls that the woman was upset but rather quiet. Bob remembers her being terribly distressed, voluble, and demonstrative.

Even Paulo, who normally chooses his words carefully, recalls the incident, though it happened nearly three decades and hundreds of clients, thousands of safari incidents, ago. The woman, he says, nearly went "over the edge."

"Apparently, it was an insult to these people that I had pushed over her bowl with my foot," John Borg recalls, "but I didn't do it on purpose. I was just trying to be a 'Mister Clean' guy, I guess, keep them from stepping in the broken glass. It wasn't malicious or anything, just an accident while trying to do the right thing."

The woman and her group of ragged and virtually penniless San had walked barefoot across the open plains for many miles and many hours to buy the kilo of cornmeal. Where the money came from, or what they had to exchange for this bit of edible treasure, no one could know—perhaps cured meat from a dead impala or even a few rock lizards. Paulo offered to drive them to the nearest village to buy fresh meal for them and then return them to the spot of the accident, or take them even farther toward their destination. This was not sufficient. Their larger band was still "out there" in the bush. They waved to the west, in the direction of the great lake called Tanganyika. The lake forms the border between the United Republic of Tanzania (which is only united in its imagination) and the Democratic Republic of the Congo (which gives the term "democratic" a bad name). They said their band was already moving on, could not wait, and would soon be lost. The woman said her group might not find them "for many suns," Paulo translated, and that would be very difficult for the separated families.

Paulo ignored the hysterical woman and negotiated with the San men in his most soothing voice—a reasonable but persistent tone, achieved through years of training in "polishing the mouth" as a member of the Tanzanian government. For a time, nothing worked; everyone was unhappy. Eventually, Borg says, Paulo gave the group part of the wildebeest, a fistful of Tanzanian shillings, and some chewing gum. It was the chewing gum, the professional hunter believes, that clinched the deal. (Tanzanian chewing gum is imported from Saudi Arabia.)

The San lifted the meat; the offended woman silently picked up her gourd, after salvaging as much of the cornmeal as possible, though Borg recalls it was thoroughly mixed with dirt and bits of grass; and the Bushmen disappeared. The vast plain simply swallowed them, as if they had been no more than the shadow of a passing cloud.

It was as if Athena, from the high brow of Zeus's forehead, surveyed her arid world and chose to sink back into oblivion.

Why You Want a Lithuanian Backup

1982

Chapter 9

The experiences of other wandering hunters have always had so much interest for me, that I have ventured, perhaps presumptuously, to conclude that my own may possibly be thought worthy of perusal by those with similar savage tastes.

Elephant Hunting in East Equatorial Africa[1]

Arthur H. Neumann

Michigan's Mat Dunaskiss, an internationally known state senator and businessman, says, "I'm 100 percent Lithuanian." The story he tells—which his hunting buddy, Bob Eastman, confirms—has a lesson. When the chips are down, choose a Lithuanian to watch your back.

When Mat and Bob went to northern Tanzania twenty years ago to hunt with Paulo Shanalingigwa's Pori Trackers, they experienced a string of mishaps that would have dismayed anyone, or almost anyone. Remember that Mat is a Lithuanian-American, and Bob is one of the most dedicated bow hunters and businessmen on the planet. These two men are not easily dissuaded from their goals.

The backstory is that Mat had hunted with a gun until Bob turned him on to bowhunting. So Mat's plan was, "Why not do both." He took his new archery setup—bow, arrows, broadheads, and accessories—and a Remington 7mm Magnum to Africa. Bob, of course, never hunted with anything other than a recurve bow.

Paulo met the travelers and their photographer, Jeriot Dowland, at the Mount Kilimanjaro International Airport, about forty miles east

[1]Preface.

of Arusha. Arusha is a city of one million people sandwiched between immense outdoor tourist attractions: the Serengeti Plains, Ngorongoro Crater, Lake Manyara, Olduvai Gorge, Tarangire National Park, Arusha National Park, and snowcapped Mount Kilimanjaro itself.

From Kilimanjaro the group drove to the smaller municipal airport west of Arusha. There they planned to hop a bush plane into the Moyowosi region of Tanzania, nearly four hundred miles farther west. The objective was to hunt the abundant buffaloes, lions, and plains game that could be found there.

On the truck to Arusha, Bob and Paulo hatched a plan to hunt sitatunga, Africa's "amphibious antelope." No modern bow hunter had ever taken one, and few had even seen one. Paulo suggested the animals might be attracted to a bait pile of cabbage. What the hell, the men thought; it's worth a try. They bought several croaker sacks full of the leafy green vegetable, and it was at that point their troubles began, hours before they got off the ground.

The Flight

The commercial flights from Detroit through Amsterdam to Tanzania were uneventful. At Arusha airport, workers crammed five people, with their luggage and hunting and camera gear, into a Cessna 340 that theoretically would take five passengers but was ideal for four. Paulo sat beside the pilot, with Bob, Mat, and the photographer, Jeriot, behind them. Then the workers topped the load with sacks of cabbage, and even a blind man could see something at the end of this rainbow that didn't look like a pot of gold.

Bob asked if they were overloading the airplane, but the pilot smiled, shrugged, and, speaking to Paulo, said the plane was powerful and there was plenty of room for everyone.

"Not to worry. I am the pilot. It is for me to worry."

Those words, Bob later realized, should have served as a warning.

No one recalls who volunteered his lap for a sack of cabbage. ("Not me. Not me!") The plane lumbered down the runway without gaining speed or altitude until the final few moments, when its wheels miraculously lifted off. The authorities were lengthening the runway, but, Africa being Africa, the workers had piled a great mound of dirt and rock at the end of the tarmac instead of on the side. Perhaps positioning it on a hard surface made it easier for them to remove it later, or perhaps they thought it would be a great practical joke.

Except for the poorest manual laborers, all the white-collar architects and site supervisors—the foremen, contractors, and suppliers—were relatives of local "big men." So whether the project was accomplished to specifications or accomplished at all was unimportant. The men who dug the foundations and swung the axes and hauled the cement would never get to fly.

The overloaded twin-engine airplane bounced across the top of the mound of rubble and, with a terrible screech like fingernails on chalkboard, left behind its rear landing gear and a significant portion of its horizontal stabilizer. Mat says it was the only time he ever saw Bob—who is also a private pilot—become excited and curse. His emotional outburst was almost certainly attributable to the gaping hole that opened almost beneath his feet, for he was not excitable by nature. As the men stared down through the hole, additional parts of the tail and wheel assembly fell away.

Mat believed there was a good chance he was going to die. Bob insisted they circle and land immediately, but the pilot looped east toward Mount Kilimanjaro International Airport, where there were fire and rescue capabilities in case they crashed on or near the runway. At first the pilot acted as if nothing had happened, but he soon began having difficulty with the rudder, which eventually fell off the airplane entirely. At Kilimanjaro he made a skillful, though ruinous, landing on the plane's belly. The airplane was completely demolished, and some of the cabbage was lost, but no one on board received so much as a scratch. (Bob says the lost cabbage was the reason he failed to connect with a sitatunga on this trip.)

Mat recalls this as the most harrowing twenty-three and one-half minutes of his life.

The Usual Charges

Bob remembers the charge of a buffalo in the bush. "It ran alongside, butting the Jeep with its horns," he says. "If we had turned over or blown a tire, that buff would not have rested until it killed us."

He remembers Mat's solo excursion into the bush and his parting words, "*Aw,* I'll be fine."

Bob also recalls the hours spent finding him.

"You can't imagine how dangerous that was!" Bob says.

Mat remembers his trophy lion moment. How he shot a terrific male with the Remington and how the other male and the nine females, instead of running away, began circling him and Paulo, his personal guide. How they counted the cartridges between them and realized they were three short of ten, and even when the tracker and driver arrived, blowing the Jeep's horn, the lions were not easily driven off.

But tales such as this—an airplane crash and a miraculous or lucky escape, hours lost and alone in the African bush, the charge of an aggressive or wounded buffalo, tense moments when the lion pride is undecided whom to kill next—are standard fare in books about hunting in Africa. It is impossible for the brain of a lion or an elephant or a kudu to adjust to the new reality of disappearing habitat and the aggressive overpopulation and dominance of *Homo sapiens.* The neuron linkages in their brains are simply not capable of making the same kind of sophisticated assessments and adaptations that have allowed weak, hairless men to climb to the top of the food chain.

The Most Unusual Hunting Adventure

Mat Dunaskiss successfully hunted lions and plains game on his one trip to Africa, but many hunters have done that. It is not unusual for a hunter to have a great, snarling lion head over his or her office desk or, if the individual is not married, mounted over the bed.

Mat, however, did something that no one you know or ever will know has done. This is either one of the most foolhardy stories ever to come out of Africa or one of the most profoundly courageous. It has the extraordinary advantage of being true. Mat wrestled a full-grown black mamba and lived to tell about it. In fact, without being bitten, he killed it, and he now has it mounted, in all its astonishing twelve-foot glory, in his office. Here's what happened. . . .

The second bush plane (you will recall the first was demolished) deposited Bob's hunting party safely in the Moyowosi bush, where the men were immediately set upon by biting tsetse flies.

"It was awful," Mat says. "We hadn't gotten off the plane before they attacked. It was hot, and, on top of that, we climbed into an un-air-conditioned truck and drove eighty miles—at eight miles an hour—with those little buggers biting and swarming around us. That ride was as close to hell as I ever want to get. About a mile from camp we crossed a tiny stream—no more than a two- to-three-foot ditch, really—and instantly the flies disappeared. It was like magic."

Everything was magic to Dunaskiss. The camp, beautifully situated. The food, delicious. The tin-can showers, luxurious. Even the machans—Mat calls them "tree stands," betraying his Midwest hunting roots—were situated over magnificent water holes. For a first-timer in Africa it was all extraordinary, exotic.

On the first day, Paulo positioned Mat on a machan over a water hole, but, dry as it was, no big game came to water. All morning he sat beside his African tracker and a driver, and they saw nothing, heard nothing, smelled nothing, until they noticed a rustling in the tall grass behind their position in the tree.

"It wasn't a stealthy sound," Mat says. "Whatever was coming wasn't afraid or expecting trouble."

Mat picked up his bow and nocked an arrow. He stood up and carefully looked for the source of the sound. There was nothing to see, but the noise continued. In an environment where most animals are cautious about the noise they make, and are continually snapping their heads up to watch for lions or leopards or hyenas or wild dogs, the noisy approach to water suggested some cocksure predator.

Just when the bow hunter thought he couldn't stand another moment of anxiety, a narrow gray head emerged on a gray stalk several feet above the level of the grass. It was just a dumb old snake, and the senator thought, "I'm going to bust this snake."

What he didn't know at the moment was that the cold-blooded reptile was one of Africa's most successful and dangerous predators, a snake that could outrun a man, a snake whose venom was universally feared as the most toxic in the world, an aggressive snake that wouldn't back down from a fight. It was a black mamba, a snake that brave and intelligent men feared, but Mat didn't know that.

When a mamba bites, its victims often panic, and this pumps the snake's neurotoxin through the bloodstream. Victims sweat and cough. They have trouble breathing. The heart races. The poison begins to paralyze muscles. Within the hour, sometimes within the half-hour, the victims suffocate and die. Even if they survive, they are left with unpredictable and debilitating nerve ailments and a shortened life expectancy. If Mat had known this, if he had remembered he was deep in the bush and far from sources of antivenin, it might well have changed his actions that day.

With twelve feet of poisonous snake curling below the machan and headed toward the water hole, Mat thought of the trophy python in Bob's office. So he drew an arrow, sighted, and shot.

A mamba is relatively thin for its length, not as thick as a fat man's thigh, like an anaconda or a boa constrictor. Not an easy target for an archer, but Mat hit it. The broadhead struck off-center, though, and did not slice it in half.

The snake recoiled and struck repeatedly at the arrow, its venom dripping down the shaft and spraying onto the dirt. It writhed in a fury that made Mat shiver and, pulling loose from the arrow, slithered toward the water. Mat and his tracker, an African nicknamed Mile Eye because his eyesight was superb, quickly climbed down from the machan. Mile Eye had no teeth, so he spoke with a lisp. Mat had been surprised to learn that he knew a few words of English.

"Cobra, bwana. Cobra," muttered the tracker. (Bwana was no longer the term for "white master" but carried more of the East African suggestion of "boss" or "big man," or maybe only "the guy who's paying me.")

The snake paused on the edge of the pond, and Mat shot again, missing. He shot again . . . and missed again. The mamba went into the water, but Mile Eye ran to the opposite side and threw rocks to turn it back in Mat's direction.

The American bow hunter recalls the instant when he realized there was more to this creature than "just a dumb old black snake." When the mamba slithered up over the bank, its head rose up two or three feet off the ground. Mat says their eyes locked, and he momentarily froze. The mamba came over the bank in that fluid, no-hands motion peculiar to snakes and, only four to five feet away, began to curl. Its head rose higher and higher.

"Bwana!"

Mile High's shout may have saved Mat, who drew his bow and shot again. This time the arrow hit the mamba squarely, though well back in the body, and the snake again went through the fantastic dance of twisting and biting the arrow, the same dance that had fascinated and horrified Mat the first time he shot it.

The arrow tore out of the gaping wound, and the snake, undoubtedly sensing how badly it was hurt, raced for a hole in the ground. When its head disappeared, Mat picked up a stick and hit the snake as hard as he could, but that didn't even slow it down. As it rapidly disappeared into the hole, Mat grabbed the snake with one hand and, taking his last arrow, jammed it through the snake's body, pinning it to the ground.

The situation was similar to the condition of the man who succeeds in jumping onto the back of a lion and holding on. He's fine as long as he rides, but the moment he climbs off or falls, he's in trouble.

Mile High ran up cautiously, and the men conferred above the snake's tail with sign language, grunts, and a great deal of excited conversation that neither man understood. The driver, who proudly considered himself multilingual, was completely confused. Finally, the driver's sensible suggestion was to get the hell away from the snake, but Mile High, realizing Mat wanted this snake for a trophy, suggested making rope from a native vine, tying it to the snake's tail, and pulling it out so that Mat could kill it. When this trick didn't work, they used a T-shirt, tying one corner to a long pole and the other to the snake. In this manner they pulled the mamba out of the hole, beating it with a log as it came.

The snake died not so much from hemorrhage, as when a whitetail or a zebra is struck by a broadhead, but because the men simply bludgeoned it to death.

When the twelve-foot mamba finally lay still at their feet, the photographer arrived. Snapping shots from all angles, he lay on the ground for a close-up of the dead reptile's black mouth at boot level. Suddenly, he screamed and jumped up, holding his arm. Mat hit the snake over the head with a terrific blow of the stick. Just as quickly, he realized the mamba was already dead.

There, where the photographer had lain, was the largest scorpion Mat had ever seen. He took his last arrow and, by hand, stuck the arthropod through its chitin shell. Within minutes, the photographer's arm began to swell, and he began to perspire heavily and shake with a chill. Mile High spoke to them excitedly in his native language, but the Americans understood nothing, so it only made the situation worse. Then this most serious of Africans gave them his most serious, toothless smile and held up four fingers.

"Now what the devil does that mean?"

* * *

Now Mat had a snake trophy, just like Bob. To this day, he is the only man in the world to have seized a wild black mamba with his bare hands to prevent its escape and lived to tell about it.

Mat knows that if the snake had bitten him, he would almost certainly have died there at the water hole in the Moyowosi.

"Adrenaline makes you do crazy things," he says.

Everyone who knows him says it wasn't that naturally occurring chemical that saved the day. It was just the Lithuanian in him. Tough. Stubborn. It's probably a good thing Lithuania is such a small country.

Remember that when you face a gang of bullies at the next Sunday school picnic. Look around for just the right guy to watch your back. Look for a Lithuanian. You won't be sorry.

Dad. Son. Buffalo.

1991

Chapter 10

When a buff comes he comes with his head high and thrust straight out. The boss of the horns covers any sort of a brain shot. The only shot is straight into the nose. The only other shot is into his chest or, if you're to one side, into the neck or the shoulders. After they've been hit once they take a hell of a lot of killing. Don't try anything fancy. Take the easiest shot there is.

The Short Happy Life of Francis Macomber[1]
Ernest Hemingway

Erik Eastman, Bob's youngest son, is thirty-three years old and married. At this writing, in the fall of 2008, he and his wife, Yi-lan, are expecting a baby. And so Erik will be awakened at 2:00 AM to change diapers and at 3:00 to take the newborn to its mother for a feeding. He will walk it—of course, the baby will have a name by then—for hours, lovingly pacing and cooing and stroking its head as it cries with colic or groans in night terror. Then he will drag into the office late, his hair a mess, and he will need a second or third cup of coffee.

Erik and Yi-lan are going to make Bob a grandfather. He may be one of those granddads who hand the baby back when it cries or soils its diaper in public. He may be the relation who baby-sits when the child is cheerful and needs little attention; the one who shepherds it on the swing, where all that is required is a gentle push. Bob will be a typical granddad, except that he has one hand on the swing and in the other

[1]Page 152.

some new book about leadership or economics or business. Bob will buy the baby its first book about business leadership, too: The Three Little Pigs on Business Location or perhaps Peter Pan: Never Fly Coach.

I believe Erik may have an easier transition than his father. Erik will only move to father status; Bob will find himself in that waiting room where one's life pivots and faces the sunset.

We are led to believe that the process of aging is normal, so everyone who is "lucky enough" to live to old age must endure its universal brand of physical and mental deterioration. We are told we ought to accept, with dignity and grace, that which we cannot change. We read that if we do not welcome the age spots on the backs of our hands, the thinning of our hair, and the slower metabolism that turns a simple homemade cheesecake into cholesterol dynamite, threatening not only to add a roll of fat to our waist but to clog the freeways to our heart with sludge, we should learn to endure these things with relative forbearance, if not utter happiness. We should accept the inevitable, the unendurable, with as much poise as we can courageously muster.

Baloney.

What the Dad Wanted

Eighteen years ago (at this writing), Bob Eastman took his sons, Erik and Rob, to Africa. Erik was sixteen years old; his older brother was pushing eighteen. They were smart, robust, playful kids, everything Bob wanted sons to be. Erik was sturdy and powerfully built. Rob was lean, with the physique of a distance runner. Bob wanted to give them a wonderful, unforgettable experience. He wanted to enrich their lives, to challenge them with the unknown, the unexpected.

Eighteen years ago, Bob wanted his boys to learn a valuable life lesson, although he does not recall having a specific plan or knowing what that lesson might be. What would happen, would happen. Nevertheless,

Bob Eastman took this Kirk dik-dik in Tanzania in 1997.

he wanted to provide an opportunity for them to learn something. About Africa, because it was his passion. About themselves, because they were his passion as well. Perhaps they did, Bob included.

The operative thought in the above paragraphs—indeed, it was inherent in the safari from its inception—was what Bob, the dad, wanted. Bob wanted something from Africa. He was paying a lot of money for the experience and did not expect that this "something" might actually have been available closer to home. In the secret, innermost part of this dad, he wanted to be the boys' hero; he wanted them to respect him and his work, his experience and knowledge. In short, he wanted to be their real Dad, with a capital D, like the great dads of his youth, Ozzie Nelson and Ward Cleaver and perhaps Bob Sr. It's understandable and natural. It's even laudable. He wanted his boys to love him.

Whatever Bob's sons learned on that exotic trip, no teenager would readily confide it in his fifty-year-old father, certainly not in a straightforward manner that an adult would understand. What Bob took away, however, was the recollection of a near-fatal error in judgment, and, of the many errors he has encountered and survived in his business and hunting lives, this one was of his own making.

Trying very hard to be the perfect dad, he placed Erik in mortal danger. What everyone in the hunting party experienced was a lesson not so much about Africa, about buffalo—although a buffalo played a central role—or even about Erik. That kernel of knowledge was about Bob himself and the truth of being a father.

* * *

Well-considered scientific speculation indicates that all that happens to us—everything in our entire lives, everything we say and everything said to us, everything we read and hear and observe—is recorded in the cerebral cortex. It's as if the brain were partly a thinking and planning machine and partly a memory storage device, a giant sponge with an attached video, which may at times be faulty.

This line of investigation suggests that all we have to do to prompt a flood of memories, surrounding us with other places and people of the past, is to think very deeply. All we have to do is concentrate, and we will see our dad teeing one up on a freshly mown golf course or our wrinkle-free mom baking a pie. We will be transported to a time when we could roam the neighborhood with our Red Ryder BB guns and the neighbors would not call the SWAT team. Such memories will come flooding back under hypnosis, during meditation (or medication), or at some moment of great stress.

In such a moment our entire existence—our good and bad deeds, our hating and loving, our ticker-tape parades, and our inevitable deceits—flickers to life, and it is possible to relive, although not to alter, angry words with our brother, the passion that begot children, the business maneuvering that made us wealthy or sent us to jail.

It is fine to be a skeptic about this "new-age" science because most of the time, it seems, we live as if we are drifting along through a fog; the farther any particular day or event recedes, the more impenetrable the fog becomes. We remember, but relatively little: patterns, incidents, occasionally an emotion or a motive. Snapshots, really. Frames randomly pulled, and sometimes not very honestly, from a continuous thread of breath.

On balance, a little fog is not a bad thing. The talent of total recall, remembering every minute of every day, surely could not make one happy. At some point in a life of care, we earn the gift of forgetfulness; we deserve to drop the burden of the past and just get on with our sunrises and sunsets, for they will not last forever.

Which brings us to the day in Africa when Bob Eastman nearly lost Erik, his youngest son. It is a day he cannot perfectly recall or entirely

One of the Big Five, Africa's Cape buffalo can be extraordinarily difficult to hunt, especially by bow. Campfire stories about aggressive buffaloes almost certainly predate gunpowder. Bob Eastman took this superb buffalo in the grasslands of the Moyowosi region of Tanzania.

forget, and the dad's recollections differ in detail from those of the son. Through the distorting lens of time the details may no longer matter, or perhaps they are all that does matter.

Still, Bob stands at the threshold of becoming a grandfather, and his sons have become grown men. They are perfectly formed and ready to become fathers if they choose. And Bob is both excited by that prospect and stunned that it almost did not happen.

A Buffalo Intervenes

Shimmering waves of heat fled across the veld of Tanzania. Only the tropics can produce such searing heat and humidity—the tropics below the equator and south of the Horn of Africa, where the rivers and ponds either choke and gurgle in torrential flood or cry out for water. There is no middle way, no moderation, until one reaches the temperate zones. Thus, each step the Eastman party took on that inexplicably hot winter day was oven ripe.

Black buffaloes grazed in the distance, however, and the hunting party carefully made its way in their direction. Downwind. Alert for movement or the other predators that often shadow the herds. Mindful of anything that might alert the fierce bovines. Careful of birds and lions, especially lions. But on this day there was nothing except heat and biting flies.

Erik plodded ahead with Paulo Shanalingigwa, the professional hunter. Bob had pushed Erik forward, toward the buffalo, encouraging him to take the lead.

Bob was like his own father now. Wasn't it his job to bring the boy face to face with challenges, opportunities to grow? Opportunities to become a man. Or so Bob may have figured at the time. The boy was sixteen. Soft American kid. An experience with a buffalo ought to toughen him up.

Cape buffaloes, of course, have a reputation. Tough beyond our usual expectation. Aggressive. Calculating and mean. Able to absorb shot after well-placed shot, arrow after arrow, and still kill you. This is a fighter that does not even try to duck your stinging jab, but takes the punch and closes with a series of crushing body blows.

A buff, like an experienced guide or tracker, takes the measure of a hunter quickly. Not that the animal does this in a personal way. A buffalo does not care. A buffalo measures the distance, your speed, and

Bob's son, Erik, poses with professional hunter Paulo Shanalingigwa and the Cape buffalo they took together in Tanzania in 2008. Erik is wearing a Bug Tamer jacket to protect himself from swarms of biting tsetse flies.

the angle, calculates the ground and the cover, because it simply wishes to crush you. It isn't personal.

Hemingway and Ruark wrote about high-power rifles, but the Eastmans—Erik and Bob and their dad—carried recurve bows, stick bows, hardly "stoppers" in the shooting sense. This meant the first shot, Erik's shot, had to be nearly perfect. It was a lot to ask of a sixteen-year-old squirrel and whitetail hunter on his first trip to Africa. But Bob, remember, was filled with a dad's ideas and responsibilities.

Now they were moving through curtains of hundred-degree heat and humidity toward the thickly muscled animal that American professional hunter and writer Peter Capstick respectfully nicknamed Black Death. Bob recalled Ishmael's words when, upon boarding the whaling ship *Pequod*, he at last beheld the intense, perhaps mad, one-legged Captain Ahab. Even after listening to the seamen's tales from wharf and tavern, "reality outran apprehension."

Erik's long-ago confrontation with the buffalo may not have been so much about him as it was about Bob. Less about the son than the father. Blind when it came to his magnificent but untested kids. Stubborn on the point of "growing up to be a man." Oblivious to his own father's long shadow.

That day they paid attention to the small things. Blackened the sharp broadheads to prevent them from shining in the tropical sun. Lightly lubricated the head and arrow shaft with Vaseline for better penetration of a buff's leathery, inch-thick hide.

"Place the head of a straight pin against the fleshy side of your thumb," Bob said. "Now, push it through a thick rawhide boot. That's a buffalo hide."

That's what Bob told his boys.

Erik said he understood the gravity of hunting buffalo on foot with a bow, though Bob wasn't so sure he did. After all, what the father preaches and the children hear . . . it's a story as old as mankind.

What, really, could an American middle-class teenager possibly understand about a buffalo? On a good day an old buff is one of the most disagreeable and dangerous animals on earth, a thousand-pound pit bull. It has fought lions all its life and, for pure toughness—a bush-bred will to live—it can be categorized with Komodo dragons, certain aggressive poisonous snakes, and great white sharks.

It might have been lost on the boy that one needed to make special preparations, take extra precautions. But his father—who, after a dozen bowhunting safaris, considered himself an old Africa hand, a man who knew how things worked—surely knew better.

It was useless to reflect. Memory distilled through eighteen years of review and justification . . . and perhaps a little self-recrimination. As he thought through it, Bob could feel the memory slipping. Was it really so hot, so humid? Hadn't the boy been as excited as he expected? And did their PH express any misgivings?

It is as if the movie camera were old, so frames rush herky-jerky through the clacking projector of memory. The Zapruder film loses its crispness as JFK slumps forward, suddenly beyond action and into myth. The old films are retouched, restored, re-colored until one wonders what is real. What is real? Is that a shadow behind the fence on the grassy knoll? Does the shadow have a gun?

He Never Flinches

Four men are walking in loose formation. Keeping an acacia or a clump of high grass between their panting, sweating bodies and the dark shapes looming ahead. Erik strides forward with Paulo. His father follows with the tracker.

Suddenly, in the low glare of afternoon sunlight dipping toward the green hills of the Selous, with no doves calling and no jackals yipping, with only the silence and the ground crunching under their boots, Paulo stops. The black hunter turns to Erik and says, in a voice as soft and confidential as a breeze through the grass, "Shoot. Now."

The buff lifts its head. A scarred old bull. And though it is not a world record, the men can see that it has fought for its life, fought for its place in the herd. This bull is wise in the ways of the veld, and maybe it knows a little about men, has been hunted before. No gleam brightens its mysterious depths; no light reflects from its lidded black eyes. The thick, boned horns are wickedly curved, black except at the tips, where they are polished like ivory. The tips that hook you, disembowel you, rip you open like a gutted matador in the bullrings of Madrid.

"Shoot," Paulo says once more, this time forcefully, seeing that the teenager is struggling to get an arrow onto the string of his recurve and that when he does, it will not stay in place next to the nock. The boy is trembling.

And then the instant when Bob startles from some waking dream place—that lull induced by heat and a tiring walk—and hears or feels pounding. It is his own heart. The buffalo snorts. The sound is not loud but deep, a warning, as if the bull understands some core value. It turns to face the men, and so, head to head, it is too late for the bowman.

It's coming now. The buffalo is loping, running. Immeasurable, unstoppable as the end of the world; Vandals at the gates of Rome. It is too late for Erik to shoot. Maybe too late even for them to run, but, weaponless, the tracker turns and flees.

Bob recalls backpedaling, as if that would save him. And the throb in his ears is, he knows, simple, elemental fear. Still, that is his son, his child, out front, and he has pushed him there.

Erik stands quite still as the bull rushes toward him, lowers its head to crush him. Bob recalls that Erik does not throw away his bow or turn and run. Perhaps he is immobilized by fear or fascination or incomprehension, because a train wreck is about to overwhelm him. Bob sees his child holding the thin bow, with the arrow crooked and flopping at an odd

The charge of a buffalo can be terrifying, and a wounded buff in dense grass is the stuff of legends. The help, the trackers and skinners, will flee, but they are unarmed. It is the responsibility of the professional hunter to then place a bullet into the running buff's forehead and drop it before someone is killed.

angle between the wooden riser and the index finger of his right hand—it is still not on the string—and he tries to shout: "Erik! Run!"

Eighteen years later, he still wants to shout into that memory. Make changes. Rearrange the events, the intention. Bob wants to tell Erik how desperately he loves him and that he is sorry for what is about to happen, for so many things.

Instead, he stumbles backward as the buffalo reaches its half-ton of long stride, and no words come out, although he believes his mouth is open.

Paulo snaps his rifle upward and fires, once, racks the bolt and fires again. The surging blackness crashes at Erik's feet. The boy still does not move. The buffalo's legs twitch powerfully, and then it is dead. Bright red blood drains out of its forehead, nose, and mouth, seeping into the thirsty soil, seeking Mother Africa, the soil that has soaked up so much blood that it likely will not heed this little bit more.

* * *

And so, on the occasion of becoming a grandfather, Bob is doubly thankful and proud. His boy did not run or stumble, did not scream in fear and collapse. He did nothing that might hinder his hunter's shot. Perhaps he froze in terror or simply could not process the facts when he faced an alien dilemma; perhaps he froze from the conscious realization that his dad and the professional hunter would not let anything happen to him—that freezing, not running, was the best thing to do, an act of faith. Bob could never be sure.

The dad is only thankful that there is no more to remember of that day, and that this son, Erik, has allowed him to cross the threshold and become a grandfather. Soon enough it will be Erik's turn.

Going With the "Flo"

1997

Chapter 11

We know that the life of dinosaurian hunters was hard. Most skeletons we excavate have clear marks of old wounds—broken and healed ribs, cracked limbs, and lower back vertebrae fused together by injury. To survive and raise their young, the predators needed more than sharp teeth and strong claws. They needed social bonds.

Raptor Red[1]
Robert T. Bakker

If you were asked to draw cross hairs through Africa, north to south and east to west, your lines would probably intersect over the Central African Republic (C.A.R.), a nation so poor that Haiti sends it aid. The C.A.R. is so poor that it has adopted French, the language of its former colonial master, for its official language. Although this may not seem politically correct in the revolutionary New World Order, it is certainly practical. The landlocked state on the Ubangi River is composed of at least eighty quarrelsome ethnic groups and dozens of political parties, many of which exist in a limbo of perpetual revolt against any central government.

According to the Central Intelligence Agency, the C.A.R. has serious environmental problems that threaten its survival as a nation. Available tap water is rarely potable; the growing population has drawn down the fragile water table, especially in the north, and this causes desertification. The Sahara is creeping south toward the great river; the few remaining virgin forests are being cut at an alarming rate; and poaching, usually

[1]Page 240.

Bob Eastman with a new friend in the Central African Republic in 1996. Homemade, native crossbows are not powerful enough to knock a monkey out of a tree, but the tiny homemade arrows are tipped with poison.

blamed on the Sudanese, has diminished the country's reputation as one of the last great wildlife refuges.

France, a country with which the United States has such a love-hate relationship, remains a dominant element in the social, political, and economic life of C.A.R. The French saved America's bacon in our own War for Independence, but only because they hated all things British, not for any love of British colonials. And a graphic recounting of French atrocities in Central Africa (and those of their Belgian, British, and German cousins) during colonial rule would cause modern sadists to blush with shame.

Nevertheless, this deeply divided African country is apparently making progress toward the French ideal of liberty, equality, and fraternity, with a great deal of international aid, which some argue is persistent and excessive.

A small part of that aid is devoted to saving the C.A.R.'s natural habitat. Although the international community is certainly squirrely about its commitment to the tradition of big-game hunting, a few foreign companies, such as Safaria (www.safaria-car.com), which is headquartered in Paris, are both managing the wildlife resource and enabling a trickle of foreign currency to escape the incompetence, graft, and perpetual hostilities of that nation's fledgling bureaucracy so that the currency can flow to the people. Such companies' management not only involves culling but also encouraging and shepherding.

Safaria

Simply looking at the Safaria catalog, its big-game hunting diary, makes one want to call the office and book a trip to the C.A.R. Luxuriously produced and illustrated, the catalog highlights the company's fifty-eight hundred square miles of hunting territory, contiguous miles spread across the center of the country. Thus, studying the cross hairs you have placed atop the continent to locate the C.A.R., you have also located Safaria's five enormous game concessions.

Florent Mathieu (or Flo, as clients call him), the manager of Safaria, has been a professional hunter for more than twenty-two years.

"Our concessions are mainly shrub savanna," he says, "interspersed with small plains and forests—*bakos* in Sango, the primary language of the C.A.R. Plus there are many natural salt licks. In the center of Africa, the wet season is May through October; the dry season is November to April."

While countries to the south and east have a well-deserved reputation for big-game habitat—Kenya, Tanzania, Mozambique, Zambia, Angola, Namibia, and even South Africa—the Central African Republic was created at an intersection of biozones that allow many types of animal communities to flourish. To the north, the dry Saharan waste spreads into Chad; to the east is the hill country of a dry and restive Sudan; to the south and west are the wet habitats of forest and jungle in Cameroon (which means "shrimp" in Portuguese), the Congo, and Zaire.

Thus, C.A.R. has almost one of everything, from plains herds of African savanna buffalo to jungle-dwelling chimpanzees and even, in the most remote sections of high forest, a threatened population of gorillas. For hunters, however, Safaria recognizes these top five opportunities, along with its herds of buffalo, roan antelope, duiker, and sitatunga:

- Lord Derby eland. The C.A.R. is home to about three-quarters of the total population of this world's largest antelope and has spiral-horned trophies to match the numbers.
- Leopard. Although the versatile leopard is mostly hunted over bait, as in other African areas, Safaria's PHs and trackers are also skilled at still hunting and even calling.
- Lion. In the C.A.R. the lion is traditionally hunted by tracking and calling—"imitating its roar," says Florent Mathieu, perhaps unnecessarily. This generates moments as exciting as finding one's first love, an airplane crash, or an earthquake. "Few hunts in the world generate more emotion," notes the Safaria brochure, also in astonishing understatement. "The two techniques can be used together, leaving imperishable memories for those who have experienced it. Tracking a lion is a true challenge, requiring experience, endurance, patience and perseverance." The brochure fails to mention teamwork and courage.

• Bongo. Florent Mathieu reflects that the beauty of the bongo is matched only by the extreme and even tedious difficulty in hunting it. He notes that although he has sat with clients in blinds, the preferred method, the one that pays off most often is tracking and stalking, which is more arduous.

• Pig. "Our hunting grounds are one of the only areas on the continent where three of the four species of African pig can be found," Mathieu says. In very dense areas, the diurnal giant forest hog may grow to five hundred pounds. The red river hog, cousin to the European boar, and the warthog are also found in large numbers and can be taken by still hunting.

Safaria calls its stone cabins "bungalows." Each is equipped with a bathroom with a flush toilet, a shower, and a sink. In addition, each camp has a power generator to provide lighting, hot water, and equipment recharge.

"A camp is manned by sixteen staff and one professional hunter," Mathieu says, "and we have four camps. Eight men provide camp services (majordomo, chef, waiter, laundry boy, mechanic, camp boy, gardener, and taxidermist), and eight are trackers.

"Our catalog must represent us to the world," continues Mathieu; "therefore, it must show who we are, what we do, and the chances for guest hunters in central Africa. It must also show the high quality of our camps and services."

Mathieu, like many PHs who have served long months in the bush with a variety of international clients, has a special passion for the people and wildlife of the C.A.R.. This is evident not only in his catalog but also in the way he talks and writes about hunting and tracking big game.

"We work very hard for our clients," says the Frenchman, who has passed up the perpetual glamour of the City of Light for stone cabins in the hard and sometimes dangerous countryside of Central Africa. "And we treat everyone as if he were a billionaire. After all, coming to the C.A.R. to hunt bongo or lion is very expensive. So we give 100 percent."

Giving 100 percent means that the PH and his crew will work as hard as the client—harder, if they can legitimately help a hunter take his or her trophy.

"When we organize a stay," says Mathieu, "we guarantee that the most common animal is in the chosen area. We use all possible

Bob Eastman hunted in Central Africa with Florent Mathieu of Safaria. "You just can't imagine how difficult the area is," Bob says, "how hot and steamy. The moment you exert yourself the least bit, you're drenched with sweat. It was hard and I'm proud of the game I took there—from Peters duiker to bongo to sitatunga."

means to allow good progress, but we have no obligation to guarantee a result, which depends on luck and weather, plus the shooting skill, physical condition, and enthusiasm of the client. No bag is guaranteed." (The term "bag" is particularly European, but it is understood internationally by hunters.)

For all of these reasons, and because few bow hunters had ever taken the highly sought-after bongo (1994), the diminutive duiker (1996), and the sitatunga (1998) in their wild and native forests, Bob Eastman chose Safaria as his hunting outfitter. In those days, Safaria hunted in the C.A.R. and in Cameroon to the southeast.

Of Dogs and Men

"They were very difficult hunts," Bob says, shaking his head, as he recalls the adventure and the misery and his ultimate successes, "very difficult. Before you go, everyone talks about the heat and humidity, but nobody really dwells on it. But they are the first obstacle, because your inclination is to stay inside, where it's cool, or sit in the shade by a hotel pool. As soon as you exert yourself, even a little bit, you begin to sweat, and your body doesn't stop until you're soaked. But staying cool and dry isn't what you went halfway around the world for; it won't help you get close to the animals."

When the Michigander's plane landed at Yaoundé, Cameroon's capital, the heat and the stifling humidity hit him very hard. It was like home during those one or two weeks of late August and early September, prior to archery deer season, when the smothering air lies like a blanket across the Great Lakes. Nothing moves in the woods without a great effort, and in vehicles and offices people who normally disdain such a thing as air conditioning turn the thermostat toward lower and lower temperatures. In Cameroon, however, this is the climate year-round, and air conditioners are few and far between. In other words, it doesn't get better.

No archer (and few riflemen) had bagged a sitatunga before Bob Eastman took one in Cameroon with the French-based Safaria. "Without the Pygmy men and their tracking dogs," Bob says, "we would never have found a sitatunga. The forest is incredibly dense. The Pygmy men went barefoot and never stumbled, even in the dark."

The wilderness of Cameroon's dense, dripping forests holds heat like a well-insulated oven, trapping it under leaves of hundreds of types of trees and giant shrubs in overlapping, multi-storied canopies designed to hold in the darkness, to prevent more than a momentary ray of sunshine from striking the earth. And when a rare breeze stirs the mosquitoes and biting flies, the hunter looks momentarily upward and is amazed that a thousand tiny, flapping hands are waving the sun to be gone, warding it away from his particular square foot of jungle.

Yet sun does leak down, filtered through the giant trees and the countless snaking vines to the leaf-covered ground, and whether the occasional spot of light helps a sweating, insect-swatting hunter avoid stumbling over the overlapping, interconnected roots is an open question. Perhaps a perpetual green-brown gloom would be better for Western eyes. Imagine the forest is an active participant in cloaking its creatures, inhibiting the foreign hunters, as if to say, "You may hunt here, and you may succeed in taking one of my bongos or a sitatunga from the swamps, but I am going to make you pay."

For Bob's hunts, Mathieu enlisted specialists in tracking, men so skilled in making their way effortlessly in the wild that they seemed to be a separate species altogether. These men were lightly clothed, dressed in garments that would embarrass Americans and Europeans, even in the quiet privacy of their own homes. They wore rags, really, shirts and pants that were cut from cloth of limited thread count and questionable durability, then pasted more than stitched together.

These men were the Pygmies, the celebrated little folk of the African jungles, a people who have subsisted in areas in which white people and black people alike would quickly perish, if they were lucky. Indeed, when left to their own devices, when their game has not been poached and their land cut over and their tiny gardens trampled, the Pygmy people have thrived.

In their homelands, the Pygmy men are the greatest trackers in the world, and when employed in tandem with their dogs, a hunter is certain to find a bongo or sitatunga. Bob Eastman found the Pygmy men to be both tough and friendly, unaccountably clever in the ways of the deep woods and its creatures. Without them and their dogs, he would never have seen an animal.

"The Pygmy men," Bob says, "went barefoot and never stumbled. Even at the end of the day when it was pitch black and Mathieu wanted to turn on a flashlight, the trackers were almost running ahead of us. It was hard to keep up with them. I was always thirsty and swatting flies, and they never were.

"After the first half-hour, I was soaked with sweat, and by the end of the day I was exhausted, but these guys were smiling and relaxed and still didn't seem to drink much water. I don't know how they did it. I'm still amazed."

Since the mid-'90s, every foreign hunter, bow or gun, worked with outfitters who hired local Pygmies and their dogs. Few bow hunters wanted to tackle bongo or sitatunga—indeed, there have been very few reports out of Cameroon that bongos have been taken without using dogs. There have been two or three, at most. It could happen, if one hunted long enough from a blind.

"Our trackers brought dogs that helped find bongos," Bob recalls, though whether they were trained to hunt this single species he could not say.

He did say the pack seemed to have natural leaders, perhaps those dogs that had fought their way to the top of the social hierarchy, but there were no shiny collars or round bellies or distinctive breeds. These were skinny working dogs. While they were not mistreated, they were not overfed, either, and none of them would ever see a veterinarian during its short life. It was easy to imagine the existence of these dogs with the people of the jungle, perpetually foraging for a bite of food, begging for that rare bone, and living with everlasting fleas and a variety of internal and external parasites that would land them in emergency medical quarantine prior to entering any civilized nation.

"When it came to hunting those jungles, though, the dogs were as tough and unstoppable as the trackers," says Bob. "Whether the men led the dogs or the dogs led the men I can't say. But for a bow hunter to get a shot of any kind in the deep forest without using dogs to find a bongo, and then surrounding it to keep it from running when you approach, would be a miracle. I don't think that's ever happened. With a gun, maybe . . ."

Bob could have taken the easy way and hunted from a stationary blind in an area in which a bongo would likely wander through, although this probably would not happen within his lifetime. He could have hunted the natural salt licks, but instead he chose to run with the dogs and the Pygmies. And that wasn't an easy choice for a man carrying a

Bob Eastman took his bongo in Cameroon with Florent Mathieu of Safaria in April 1994. It scored 84⅞ and ranks as the No. 1 bow-hunted western bongo in the world.

recurve and quiver of arrows, a man accustomed to a desk and telephone, a secretary and—in those days—an evening cocktail or three, with perhaps a long walk along a paved road at lunchtime. At one hundred and sixty pounds, Bob has never been overweight. Lean, yes—stout, never. But he knows that no matter how much he ran, how far he walked carrying a pack loaded with rocks, or how much he lifted weights and fasted, he could never have kept up with the Pygmy trackers, and staying close to the dogs in the jungle was simply out of the question.

Bob Eastman's first forest safari took him to the C.A.R. Two years later, his second safari with Mathieu's Safaria landed him in Cameroon.

Eventually, he took his bongo with the recurve bow, the animal's yard-long horns spiraling upward, to end in polished ivory tips. Its red-brown coat had glorious white stripes almost circling its trunk, like rays of sunshine seeking a path through the dense overhead canopy.

* * *

The sitatunga is an antelope similar to the bongo but smaller and darker. Its horns are similarly spiraled, and its coat retains the thin striping. Also called a marsh antelope, the sitatunga is found in the papyrus and reed swamps of Central Africa and takes readily to the water when pursued by leopards or lions. Some sources even claim that sitatungas can sleep underwater, which is not a bad habit when the water is crocodile-free, and when hunters can legally collect a trophy from a river boat with a high platform to permit vision above the swamp.

Bob hunted northwestern Tanzania and then Cameroon for his forest sitatunga, taking it in West Africa in January 1998. Its total SCI score of 45⅛ qualifies it for a number one listing in the record book. The fact that, until recently, it was the only one of its subspecies taken with a bow testifies to the difficulty of hunting these secretive creatures.

Regarding the sitatunga, Bob recalls that he and Mathieu and the band of Pygmy trackers hunted hard for eleven days. It was often exhausting, usually miserable, and eventually rewarding.

A Note about Bongo and Sitatunga

The International Union for Conservation of Nature (IUCN) lists the western/lowland species of bongo as "Near Threatened." This is almost certainly due to poaching; illegal logging; diseases from domestic cattle, such as rinderpest; and loss of habitat because of increasing human population. This was the bongo subspecies Bob Eastman capably hunted in Cameroon with Safaria in the '90s. The listing reads as follows:

Listed as Near Threatened as the species faces an ongoing population decline as habitat loss and hunting pressures increase with the expansion of human settlement and commercial forestry. It is estimated that this decline will exceed 20 percent over three generations (twenty-one years).

The Convention on International Trade in Endangered Species of Wild Fauna and Flora (CITES) lists bongo as an Appendix III species. This listing regulates its exportation from a single country, Ghana. Otherwise, bongo is not protected by the U.S. Endangered Species Act and is not listed by the U.S. Fish & Wildlife Service. The International Union for Conservation of Nature (IUCN) considers the eastern or mountain bongo to be endangered only in Kenya.

Although the IUCN says the population of sitatunga is decreasing, it is difficult to arrive at a scientifically valid count of its numbers or population. Unfortunately, it makes sense that in today's Africa the sitatunga population is decreasing from land encroachment and poaching by hungry residents, but the (IUCN) nevertheless awards the sitatunga a status of "Least Concerned":

Total population numbers have been estimated at 170,000 (an overestimate), of which 40 percent occur in and around protected areas.

It is now rare and localized in West Africa, and widespread and locally common in Central Africa and some parts of Central, East, and southern Africa. Numbers are considered to be generally declining except in some core areas, but the extent of this decline overall probably remains below the 20 percent threshold that would indicate a category of "near threatened." Given continuing habitat degradation and intensive meat hunting in parts of its range, if present trends continue, the sitatunga may disappear from many areas where it still occurs, and viable populations will eventually be largely restricted to those regions which currently support substantial, stable, or increasing populations.

Notes on the chapter:

1) Just how poor is the landlocked Central African Republic? The United Nation's Human Development Index, which takes into account such standards as life expectancy, literacy, and standard of living, ranks the C.A.R. as one of the poorest countries on earth, #179 out of #182. The only countries worse off are Sierra Leone, Afghanistan, and Niger. By comparison, Haiti, the poorest nation in the Western Hemisphere, ranks a relatively comfortable #149. One would think that a deprived country, about the size of Texas and with four and one-half million inhabitants, such as this ought to beg for development and business opportunities other than its exploitative diamond trade, a few oil wells, timber harvesting of its rapidly disappearing forests, and Sudanese poaching. The World Bank Group, however, ranks the C.A.R. 180 out of 181 on "ease of business." (The ranking uses a composite index on regulations that enhance business and those that constrain it.) The U.S. Central Intelligence Agency estimates that 13.5 percent of the population is HIV positive. The C.A.R.'s eighty ethnic groups are 50 percent Christian, 35 percent indigenous religions, and 15 percent Muslim.

2) Cameroon is tucked into a distinctive fold on the shoreline of the Atlantic Ocean. Barely one hundred miles north of the equator, Cameroon is a collection of miseries called a nation-state. With two hundred or so separately identifiable ethnic groups and dialects, the country has not displayed much promise or progress for its twenty million inhabitants in the half-century since it shed colonial rule.

Learning to "Polish One's Mouth" 2006

Chapter 12

It is one thing to write as a poet and another to write as a historian: The poet can recount or sing about things not as they were, but as they should have been, and the historian must write about them not as they should have been, but as they were, without adding or subtracting anything from the truth.

Sanson in Don Quixote[1]
Miguel de Cervantes

Doves are everywhere on the great plains of the Selous, that fabulous wild game reserve in the south of Tanzania: nesting near the hippo pits along the Chinese railroad, the Uhuru or Freedom Railway; atop dry, rocky ridges rising abruptly from the tall-grass veld; in the shade of scattered *miombo* trees throughout the safari plains.

"O-Paul-O. O-Paul-O."

They coo all day, the delicate, emerald-spotted wood doves.

"O-Paul-O."

What are they saying? Whom are they calling? What is their meaning? Do they have a meaning? Doves are ubiquitous on the plains, regardless of who or what is stalking through the grass: lions, wild dogs, or human hunters.

At lunch we rest in the shade of a tree. Heat shimmers around us, and the great, broken plain dissolves; distant details flutter and become

[1]Page 476.

indistinct. Abel Shana and Ramadhani Juma, the driver and the tracker, set our table and chairs in the shade of a giant mimosa. Then they go to the opposite side of the truck for their own lunch in the company of the government man, the black Muslim Saidi M'tile, who carries the antique, German-made .458 Winchester Magnum. M'tile the watcher, the silent note-taker. M'tile, who slits the throat of the downed antelope destined for the table.

Enveloped by the heat of midday, we chew cold impala with white bread and hard-boiled eggs, washing the food down with warm Coca-Cola or bottled water that must be flown from Tanzania's disaster of a third-world capital, Dar es Salaam. It is a simple meal, but an expensive lunch.

And so we tease our professional hunter, Paulo Shanalingigwa, that the doves are calling him: "O-Paul-O. O-Paul-O."

"No," he says, as if he is gullible, though he is not, or as if he does not get the joke—he does. "They are only talking to others of their own kind and pay no attention to us until we burn the grass. Then they pay attention."

This year the rains came early, and storm clouds lingered over the Selous. Even in mid-July, the middle of winter here below the equator, the grass is wet and will not burn; water puddles in the rutted trails. It is the African story. Too much rain or too little. Too early or in the wrong place. One way or the other, the people suffer. The grass is tall and thick and dangerous.

It is not, of course, that the grass itself is dangerous, only what it may conceal. . . .

Politics: The Timeless Story

At fifty-six years of age, Paulo is a natural leader on a continent that desperately needs leaders. Six feet tall and two hundred and twenty-five

Dining in the bush is an unforgettable experience. At the base camp of Tanzania's Pori Trackers on the banks of the Greater Ruaha River, professional hunter Paulo Shanalingigwa entertains hunters and guests with impala steaks and locally grown vegetables.

pounds (two hundred and ten, he insists), he is an imposing but not overpowering figure. Serious; intelligent. His hands work the lever of a rifle as deftly as they wielded a pen in his student days. We have followed him for days across the veld, searching for elephant spoor. And we will follow him again before the trek is done.

Paulo says he learned the craft of leadership from his father, Abel, who was a teacher in Singida province. There, in the central north of Tanzania, not far from Mount Kilimanjaro and the Ngorongoro Crater and the Serengeti, which attract so many thousands of tourists each year, Paulo was raised in a home that valued learning, in a village that honored his father's profession.

A teacher in Africa has a status unlike that of a teacher in the United States. In America teachers—even university professors—may be esteemed by a few students, but the reward for their service is small, and, if their pay and incentives are any indication, their social status is rather low. In Africa, especially in the countryside, a teacher is valued and respected, and if he is patient, kind, and knowledgeable, and if he is not a tyrant, he may become a role model for his village. It is a duty and a blessing, and it carries obligations.

So, as the nation of Tanganyika lurched into independence, bankrupt and structurally ill prepared, Paulo's father stood for a seat in the new parliament. He won and ultimately served his district for a decade. His family assumed that Paulo, who showed wit and energy, would also become a teacher or perhaps even a doctor or a government official. At eighteen, however, an age when local young men usually took wives and a plot of ground to raise chickens and plant a garden, Paulo was uncertain about his future. And then a fortuitous event, although it did not seem especially fortuitous at the time, occurred during his six months of compulsory military service.

One day, a Tanzanian army officer lured him into a local tavern and brothel. Paulo found himself paying for drinks he could not afford. When the officer's attention was diverted by a woman, Paulo struck up a conversation with the only white man in the bar. The man's name was Keith Comack.

Comack, as it turned out, was a professional hunter in the employ of Tanganyika Wildlife Safaris, or TAWISA, and it was headquartered

Archer Bob Eastman discusses tracking his impala with rifleman and professional hunter Paulo Shanalingigwa The differences in effective range and energy delivery of their chosen weapons often cause guides—who are usually trained in a traditional manner with traditional expectations—to begin a relationship with a modern bow hunter as a skeptic.

not far away in Arusha. In an ultimately unsuccessful attempt to shield the company from the socialist passions ignited by revolutionary-turned-autocrat Julius Nyerere throughout the recently independent Republic of Tanzania, TAWISA was naturally looking for capable and willing black faces to front its established safari business.

By the time their conversation ended, Comack had recruited Paulo for TAWISA, promising that the safari company would help him earn his wildlife certificate, the first step toward becoming a full-fledged professional hunter. Paulo had found his passion.

Could he come for an interview? Comack asked.

The army refused his request for leave, but Paulo made the trip anyway. Upon his return they punished his disobedience with solitary confinement. For five days he stood ankle-deep in cold water in a cell where turning around was difficult and sitting or lying down was impossible. When the door finally opened, most prisoners collapsed from exhaustion and muscle cramps. Paulo swore he would walk away under his own power and without assistance. He did.

Nationalization

TAWISA proved true to its word. Paulo Pribo Shanalingigwa attended the African Wildlife College in Mweka from 1971 until 1972 and, eventually, the University of Dar es Salaam. After that, his rise to the status of Tanzania's first black professional hunter required a genuine feeling for the East African hunting environment: the animals, the clients, and the volatile politics of *uhuru*, freedom.

Years before Paulo earned his independence in the field, Nyerere, the nation's first president and the man for whom Dar es Salaam's international airport is named, nationalized the tourist industry, including the safari business.

On 7 September 1973 TAWISA and dozens of other foreign-owned companies were placed in communal ownership. Their assets—tents, trucks, cookware, and especially aircraft—were appropriated, sometimes with little notice and never with compensation by the new people's government. Upon hearing the news of nationalization, Stanley Lawrence-Brown, of the long-established and highly regarded Lawrence-Brown Safaris, collapsed and died from an apparent heart attack in his Arusha office. Nationalization marked the end of one safari era and the beginning of another.

Paulo Shanalingigwa, owner of Pori Trackers, was Tanzania's first black professional hunter. On the verge of retirement, he remains cautious when speaking about the difficulties of operating a safari business. He has learned, he says, to "polish his mouth."

Some have written that overnight, thousands of tourists—hunters, mountain climbers, photographers, and even honeymooners—were rounded up by the police and driven to airports or to the northern border with Kenya.[2] Apparently some were; others were not. The times unfolded with a destiny but without a direction.

When that calamity unfolded, Paulo simply went home to his village, Kinampanda, a hamlet of five thousand mostly Christian Africans in the Iramba district of the Singida province in central Tanzania.

"It is an old village," Paulo says. "It was not created by Nyerere's efforts to concentrate the people into communes."

Like the nationalization of private industry, Nyerere's village-level communal movement was a rejection of the European capitalist model of building wealth employed by Britain, France, Belgium, Germany, and Portugal. After all, they had been the oppressors, the occupiers, across the great continent.

Nyerere's plan to centralize the population in extended families on the land for the most efficient economic production (and political control)—a plan based on the concept of *ujamaa*—was inspired by the socialist systems of the former Soviet Union and the People's Republic of China. It was a bold but ultimately disastrous move that crushed the nation's fragile middle class and, in combination with war and drought, delivered Tanzania to the brink of social and financial collapse. It

[2]Paulo, who certainly should know, says it is not true that thousands of foreigners were forced to walk to the border. While that may have happened elsewhere, in Mozambique, for instance, such talk, he says, is a slander against Tanzania spread by people with some personal ax to grind. According to Paulo, the era of nationalization proceeded in an orderly way and with respect for the lives and property of people affected. On the other hand, Julius Nyerere's efforts to mold a communal Tanzanian countryside on the model of that forced upon the people of the USSR, was a tragedy both for the country and its people. And to justify collectivization as a return to *ujamaa,* or extended family roots, was simple tyranny veiled with cheap philosophy.

struck like a torch, searing the heart of thousands of years of African family ties.

Kinampanda was poor then, as it is today—farming, cattle, "a little of everything," Paulo says—but, half a century after independence, it at least has schools, and the schools have water wells, as do the other institutions. Only the poor must stand in line for water. Some things never change.

The family opposed Paulo's interest in a wildlife career. At the time, Tanzania's wildlife business was on the ropes, but Paulo determined to look to the long-term future of hunting and conservation and to his own self-interest. Big game was naturally abundant, and, with little else of export value, his country suffered from a chronic shortage of foreign capital. So Paulo hung on. Patience became a cardinal point on his instinctive moral compass.

Eventually, the wheels of an inefficient and corrupt bureaucracy sputtered once again to life, and the safari business began to recover. Paulo worked his way up through the hunting ranks from a humble skinner and tracker to driver and game scout. It affirmed his vision and his education that in 1978, just as Uganda's notorious Idi Amin[3] led his army across the border into Tanzania, Paulo was promoted to director of hunting for the TAWICO Hunting Corporation. Within a few years he became Tanzania's chief of hunting, from the Serengeti and Lake Victoria in the north to the Selous and Lake Malawi in the south.

[3]Idi Amin (Dada) led a military coup in January 1971, deposing Uganda's elected president, Milton Obote. Amin's rule was characterized by extreme human rights abuses, violent political repression, ethnic persecution, extrajudicial killings, and the expulsion of Asians from Uganda. A charge of cannibalism was also laid at Amin's door. Estimates of people killed as a result of his regime are as high as five hundred thousand. Dissent within Uganda and Amin's attempt to annex a section of Tanzania in 1978 led to the Uganda-Tanzania War and the collapse of his regime in 1979. Amin fled to Libya and then to Saudi Arabia, where he lived until his death in 2003. One of Paulo Shanalingigwa's brothers was killed in that war.

"I learned to polish my mouth," Paulo says of the politics that often determine wildlife management decisions, as in the United States.

It also helped that his friend and, ultimately, his mentor, Saidi Mfaume Kwawa, was the brother of the prime minister.

In other words, the hunter and game scout, the humble skinner and driver, learned the skills of politics and practiced them successfully, both within the Tanzanian bureaucracy and within the traditionally white hunting establishment. Paulo learned moral or tactical flexibility, while looking to the best interests of the leopard and the wildebeest and his own family in the long term. He learned to give and receive *takreema*, "thank-you gifts," the upscale term for bribes and goods and services that make the world turn, not only in Africa but almost certainly, if more subtly, in America as well.

Eventually, through his own hard work and the efforts of friends, and because East Africa is blessed with big game, Paulo rose into the world spotlight. Just as predictably, he fell victim to the petty bureaucracy and the politics, the whispering and backstabbing, the wolf behind the door—all the things that come naturally with high office, especially in a poor country. He was dismissed as chief of hunting. When the prize is small, the struggle is especially vicious.

Paulo's political enemies made certain he knew he was in disfavor, and they blocked his subsequent application for certification as a professional hunter. Thus, the man in charge of accreditation and education for the nation's wildlife professionals was turned away. It would be natural to say that it was not personal, just politics, but it was personal.

"This line, right here," some low-level clerk would say, pointing to a misspelled word, an insignificant line accidentally left blank, or an ambiguous question. "I'm sorry, but I will be unable to process your application. Please come back next year."

Paulo was blacklisted; his reputation and career were in ruins. For a while, his parents' desire for Paulo to become a teacher or a doctor

Webster (red shirt, blue slacks) shops for fresh vegetables for the Pori Trackers safari camp. The village of Kisaki is near the Greater Ruaha River in Tanzania's immense Selous Game Reserve.

seemed prescient. Instead, Paulo opened a game capture business and bided his time. With this license, he caught wild animals and shipped them to zoos or smuggled them into the villas of rich Saudis. At times he operated openly and legally; on other occasions, however, his business was beneath the radar of both governmental authorities and international nongovernmental organizations. And all the while, he kept his family at a distance from the political wrangling.

Eventually, those with personal vendettas, those whose brothers-in-law wanted Paulo's position, men who needed more and more *takreema* or jobs for their children also fell victim to the knife in the back, usually in a political sense but not always. With the same calm he would later exhibit when facing charging elephants, Paulo won over his critics. His first hunting concession was part of the Moyowosi Game Reserve in the west. That first year, it was a remnant, not the whole cloth, of a sustainable business, but it was a beginning.

Then, Reno

Completing his first safari in Tanzania, Bob Eastman looked out the window of his airport taxi and realized he was a white speck in a black flood of humanity. On impulse, and with little expectation, he tapped the cab driver on the shoulder and handed him a business card.

"Does Tanzania have any black professional hunters?" he asked. Despite his experience with big-game hunting, he was not familiar with the nascent black hunting establishment.

The driver took Bob's card, mumbling politely that he thought he knew of one. That was the last Bob ever expected to hear on the subject, one seed casually flung into the wind. Within weeks, however, he received a letter from Tanzania.

Bob met Paulo at the Safari Club International Convention in Reno, Nevada, in 1989. SCI had convened in Las Vegas since 1972, but there it was a small fish in a big pond. Reno dusted off the red carpet for the growing club of international big-game hunters, and SCI signed a multi-year contract with the Reno-Sparks Convention and Visitors Authority. Bob's meeting with Paulo "felt right," he says, and he booked a hunt for two years later.

That booking was an endorsement that most SCI members hesitated to proffer. Conventional wisdom held that to book a hunt with a black professional hunter would mean endless frustration and delay. Word on the streets of Reno was that black professionals were inevitably undercapitalized. Equipment would break down, and no one would be able to make repairs. Problems with licenses and permits, even visas, would arise. Unused to enforcing discipline, and perhaps exercising tyrannical powers in the deep bush, the men who make a safari successful—the cooks, the trackers, the skinners—would be lazy, mouthy, thieving. The camp would be dirty and the food would be poor quality. Hard-won trophies would vanish. African hunts have always been expensive, and in those years, few SCI members—certainly not the most competitive, most demanding members—would risk hunting with Paulo Shanalingigwa.

When asked about his difficulty in breaking into the ranks of the traditional "white hunters," Paulo shakes his head and keeps his memories to himself.

"That was a long time ago," he says, perhaps polishing his mouth.

Though he did not allude to it at the time, Bob Eastman realized there were undertones in the white hunting community in both the United States and Europe that had not kept pace with the times. Paulo swore there would not be problems in his camp. He also vowed that if he found any of the normal objections to black professional hunters to be justified—disorganization, delay, poor food, insolent service—he would refund Bob's money, on the spot in the bush.

"That was good enough for me," Bob said. "Paulo spoke with sincerity that made me a believer. There was no sales pitch."

Now, after seven safaris with Paulo as his guide, Bob would not hunt Tanzania with anyone else.

"We've become friends," he says. "When Paulo comes to the United States, he stays at my home in Michigan."

Without hesitation, he refers his friends to the black professional.

According to Eastman, it is in the field, far from lawyers and doctors and shopkeepers, where Paulo's qualities as a guide and leader, a "real professional," are most evident.

"Not only has he made quick shots that saved my life, but on a day-to-day basis, he communicates easily with his staff and with local people," Bob says. "They obviously respect him, and so do I. Because of his experience and his political savvy, he smoothes out bureaucratic wrinkles. And even though we have tracked through some of the damnedest bush on the continent, Paulo has never once gotten lost . . . or never admitted it."

Erik—Another Point of View (1995)

East Africans may always have burned the veld during the winter. Of course, flames don't consume the entire continent at once, but enormous areas of dry, dead grasses are torched, bit by bit, each year. The roots do not burn. What rises from them, in place of the heavy top mats of brown thatch, are tender shoots that cover the valleys with spring green. (The East African spring is the seasonal opposite of ours in the Northern Hemisphere.) Once rains begin, the plains become green again almost overnight. Succulent new grasses provide for elands and wildebeests, baboons and zebras, which, in turn, provide food for lions and hyenas and leopards. The doves, too, must benefit because each year they seem more numerous, and their calls become more insistent.

The expected spin-off of a burn is that plains game becomes visible. Prairie grasses range in height from just inches to a dozen feet or more, but when the grass is burned and new life springs upward through the ashes, one can see what is on the ground. Usually, this is a good thing.

In 1995 Bob took Erik, his youngest son, to hunt with Paulo and his son Lyanga. Lyanga was considering following his father into the hunting and wildlife business. In early winter that year, much of the grass was burned, and the party scouted both from the Land Cruisers and on foot through the black ash that would, in a few short weeks, fertilize luxurious new tropical growth.

Numerous *mbogos*, or Cape buffaloes, were visible from the first day—black hide against black ash. Stalking a herd, Erik noticed that one bull was separate and lying down. It seemed perfectly positioned for a close approach and a deadly shot from his recurve bow. A slight breeze blew in the young hunter's face, and a termite mound, followed by a tall tuft of unburned grass, could shield his final approach. The setup was almost too good to be true.

No American hunter stalks alone through Africa, no matter how experienced he or she may be. There is always an entourage, and in this case Erik was accompanied by Paulo with his favorite .375; Bob with a camera; Lyanga, learning his father's craft; and a native tracker. It was just too many people to move unseen and unheard within bow range of *mbogo*.

Right away, Paulo was concerned. Something just felt wrong. It was "a feeling," he said, nothing more. And the tracker kept muttering, *"Mbaya, bwana. Mbaya."* (Bad, boss. Bad)

Something was almost certainly wrong with this buffalo. From a distance, there was no telling what that might be, and to become too curious too close, instead of going directly for the kill, would surely provoke a charge. So the group walked toward it, maintaining the illusion of silence and invisibility.

Keeping his head low during the stalk, at fifteen yards Erik finally nocked an arrow and, stepping around the clump of grass for his shot, was stunned to see that the buff was already on its feet. Not only that, but it was whirling in his direction, head down and gaining speed.

"It happened so fast, I couldn't shoot," Erik later said, "and besides, it was coming right at me."

Erik froze. Although it sounds less than courageous, it was precisely the correct action because, acting on reflex and without thinking, evaluating, judging, or consulting anyone in the group, Paulo had to make a perfect shot immediately. As Bob gasped, a single crack of the

.375 dropped the charging bull, and it came to rest, nose first, only five yards from the boy. Like so many hunts, following months of preparation, hours of expectation, and moments of panic, the episode was over in seconds.

Years later, Paulo remembered that hunt.

"It was unusual to find a buffalo lying down within sight of a herd. After I shot and the herd ran away, we found that the bull had been attacked by lions. Scarred and bleeding, it was weak, but it could still have killed someone.

"Fortunately, Erik stood perfectly still, and that gave me the shot. If he had panicked or run, the shot would have been more difficult."

O-Paul-O, O-Paul-O indeed.

The Leopard and the Law

2006

Chapter 13

Therefore the laws of biology are the fundamental lessons of history. We are subject to the processes and trials of evolution, to the struggle for existence and the survival of the fittest to survive. If some of us seem to escape the strife or the trials it is because our group protects us; but that group itself must meet the tests of survival.

The Lessons of History[1]
Will and Ariel Durant

As hunters, we speak glibly about "the law of the jungle" because it is to our advantage, in our best interest, that we and our prey understand that the universe is simple and cold. One kills and is killed. One eats and is eaten. When we are in pain, it feels personal, yet it is not. When we are alone and frightened, it feels very personal, but even then, it is not. Nevertheless, in Africa, the law—ageless, inexorable, and impersonal—is changing.

* * *

Leopards come to bait so softly that professional hunters occasionally must wake their clients to make the shot. Being cats, spotted and wild, leopards are so naturally stealthy that, by comparison, bears tiptoeing across dewy North Country moss seem clumsy. Ancient white-tailed bucks in heavily hunted zones might as well wear funny hats and blow noisemakers, by comparison.

[1]Pages 18–19.

What makes the cat such a superb African hunter? It is not that a cat's feet are especially padded, although they are; it is the biological imperative that to survive in Africa, an animal must possess astonishing qualities, naturally and unthinkingly. The intricate articulations in the legs and feet of this feline, its knees (if you will), bones, cartilage, and all the connective tissues, operate so fluidly that they are positively delicate—a network of silk and bone china, light as a canary's breath, more precisely balanced than a computer chip.

Beginning with its miraculous feet, a leopard is the total package.

An Evolution of Deadly Grace

Of course, a leopard cannot select its various body parts, take them for a test drive. Nor does it choose how these parts are employed—at least, not in the sense that we understand choice. It must use them—fangs and claws, strength and speed, stealth and merciless ferocity—to kill. Otherwise, it will starve; its cubs will starve. Such facts may seem brutal, but this is the law, and the law of the plains is undeniable and absolute. Every leopard—indeed, every impala, every warthog and wildebeest—must conform.

On the vast plains along the Great Ruaha River in Tanzania's Selous Game Reserve, the rule of law is intense and unremitting. Law is as present in the formidable heat-strangled, water-starved thorn trees as it is in the succulent euphorbia. And in the hunter's blind. And in the bone-crushing bite of the crocodile. And in the dried remains of a carcass, so unappetizing that even the maggots eventually abandon it.

Books could be written about the leopard and the law because everywhere on the plains of Africa there is law. Before men appeared,

Hanging an impala carcass as leopard bait, the men of Pori Trackers cover it with thatch. This, says professional hunter Paulo Shanalingigwa, keeps the direct heat of the intense tropical sun from drying the carcass and keeps sight-feeding carrion birds away.

Bob Eastman (carrying 150-pound crossbow) and professional hunter Paulo Shanalingigwa (carrying

a .375 rifle) work their way through the undergrowth while circling a group of impalas.

there was law. From the intricate design of a leopard's foot to the nightmarish wrangling of vultures and hyenas once they have eaten their fill, the law is eat or be eaten, and every aspect of every plant and animal is designed to fulfill that law.

The law is killing; and because universal forces tend to balance–creation and destruction, the yin of earth and water with the yang of fire and wind—the law is submission to being killed. Kill and be killed, eat and be eaten. This law is omnipresent and inescapable. Even for leopards. As we shall see.

* * *

Torsten Rademacher, the German rifleman, has killed a leopard just two days before. One shot. A fine, healthy cat. A hungry cat. Perhaps a lazy cat, although it is unnecessary, even redundant, to describe any cat in such a manner.

It is a surprise, then, when our professional hunter suggests returning to Torsten's blind, for there is a mystique surrounding cats, especially big cats. Or maybe it is only myth that they are intelligent in ways we do not understand. Watch a house cat as you tease it, pretending your belt is a snake. It rubs against your leg, purring. It attacks. It knows you are playing, and yet it is deadly serious. Five minutes later, that same purring kitty captures a lizard and tortures it to death before laying it on your doorstep. Is it a gift or a bribe, an offering or some feline sleight of hand?

So when Paulo, our PH, says we should return to Torsten's blind, Bob Eastman naturally has questions. After all, both of these men are professionals and experienced in the ways of big cats.

"Abel says there is another leopard," Paulo tells us.

He always relies on his own best judgment, but he considers the advice of his African scouts. Thus, he assesses the blind's continuing

Michigan's Bob Eastman (center with crossbow) poses with his Pori Trackers outfitters: (left-to-right) owner and professional hunter Paulo Shanalingigwa, Abel Shana, government game scout Saidi M'tile, and Ramadhani Juma (kneeling). The leopard Bob shot is high in the tree where it was apparently carried and partially eaten by another leopard.

potential. Abel Shana, Paulo's nephew, who is occasionally his driver and sometimes his tracker and skinner, is quiet. Observant, like his uncle. Thoughtful, when he is not shivering with malarial fever.

"But Paulo," Bob objects. "Won't the area be disturbed? Hasn't human scent contaminated the bait?"

Bob has hunted Africa many times in many countries, always with a bow. A rifleman could afford the luxury of a hundred yards between blind and bait, but the archer must be close. Blindingly close. This, too, is the law, although a different law.

"I don't think so," Paulo says.

He is always patient, predictably thorough, and emotionally controlled. One might almost say, distant.

Our black professional hunter runs a hand over his bald head. Turning fifty, he no longer possesses the stamina of youth. He has put on a few pounds as well. Now he is puzzled . . . and tempted.

"A leopard was on that bait last night," he says.

Less than twenty-four hours after the German made his kill, another leopard appears. And a leopard often does not eat every day. When its stomach growls, it kills and eats. Or simply eats . . .

If we hang fresh bait tonight, Paulo thinks aloud, it might come back again.

* * *

Paulo has been involved with wildlife his entire adult life. Unlike the cat he is hunting, though—a cat born to subdue and consume lesser grass-eating creatures—Paulo clawed his way up the food chain to become Africa's first black professional hunter.

In East Africa, trackers are black, as are drivers and skinners and cooks. The men who wash the underwear of American businessmen and the snotty handkerchiefs of Indian politicians, who fold the socks of

Arab playboys, are all black men. And they are poor, so poor that simple poverty would be a step up. This is or has been the law for generations, and Paulo has performed all of these services and more.

Traditionally, the PH is white, which is the way it has always been, but that tradition is evolving.

So, law changes. Should that come as a surprise? Shakespeare knew the law, but mistakenly thought it was love. And these days, not every client is white. Oil-drenched Saudi princes show up with a half-dozen Eastern European prostitutes and cases of booze, the Quran under one arm, a bag full of cash under the other. There are Japanese businessmen, Argentine cattle barons, Russian mobsters, and Persian carpet salesmen.

Because he is bright and affable and hardworking, because he has been lucky, Paulo changes the law or is, perhaps, simply a tool in an evolutionary process that no single human can fathom. It has been no easier for him than it is for the leopard he hunts. Patient. Steadfast. He knows what he knows and holds his cards close. Like a leopard, what he sees he rarely reveals. What he thinks he acts upon, however, with human deliberation and sometimes with surprising speed.

In Paulo's camp it is, "Do this" or "Please go there" or, at most, "Not like that. . . ." This unassuming manner works for him and his staff and clients because he is a professional, and, on safari on the lonely plains of Tanzania, he is the law.

* * *

Although Bob has misgivings about the bait site and is aware that, except in matters of life and death, the client's wishes can trump the PH's recommendations, he consents to Paulo's plan. A client can almost always have his way if he argues long enough. And threatens. Pouts or throws a temper tantrum or bullies. Lord knows, Paulo has seen plenty of that.

Clients pay so they can have the last word. That is law, although that same law says a client, no matter how experienced, is usually wrong, and in the end he loses. Bob Eastman knows this, understands the law. After all, this is his twenty-fourth safari—or twenty-fifth; he cannot remember exactly. And so, he relents. Smart.

The next morning, two days since the German shot his spotted cat, Bob arrows an impala. The sweet little antelope becomes fresh leopard bait. Its large, incandescent eyes, greasy guts, and black-ringed horns hang in a tree beside a dry, no-name creek bed less than twenty-five yards from the archer's blind.

Paulo's plan is simple, but its execution takes hours. Cut down the stinking hindquarter of zebra over which Torsten shot his leopard and drag it away, miles away. Replace it with the impala. Cover the little antelope with thatch to keep Africa's multitude of buzzards away—although all the buzzards in the world would not hinder a hungry leopard—and keep the carcass fresh and out of the sun.

With Paulo's grudging consent, Bob moves the fully enclosed, portable blind closer to the bait so that, if he gets a shot, his crossbow bolt will fly level to impact. The law says that, kill or wound, a hunter is only going to get one shot, so Paulo lays his rifle aside and loads the 12-gauge pump with aught buck. At close range, the shotgun gives some small margin of error, of safety.

If Bob misses or only wounds the leopard and it charges, someone could die or become horribly disfigured. The cat could slink through the grass and be on top of them from behind in seconds, or minutes or hours. No one can predict. It's not a lion. The double-aught should be enough.

Paulo knows the men would not see the leopard before it tore into them, its raking, disemboweling claws reeking of bacterial decay, its magnificent yellow incisors plunging and holding, searching for the spinal cord. *Le griffe et le dent.* Tooth and fang. Silent, except for the

African thorn trees are a formidable obstacle to moving quietly through the bush. It was one of these smaller bushes that seized Bob Eastman's hunting buddy George Gardner by his faux-wool camo and held him face-to-face with an angry hippo. All ended well, but his camo was ripped to shreds by the time the episode was over.

men's choked screams. Paulo would yank the gun upward and pull the trigger and keep pulling it until one or the other, leopard or man, hurt so much that dying was preferable to living.

So in the morning they shoot the impala, and Paulo's men hang it in the tree and reset the blind. No one takes special pains to work quietly. The leopard will know they have been there, and it may or may not matter. Then, returning to camp by way of the river, by way of the neighborhood of grunting, quarrelsome hippos, they wait for early evening.

Dragging the reeking, fly-besotted zebra haunch behind the truck, Abel Shana and Ramadhani Juma cut it loose in a copse of *miombo* trees. This is Africa. Nothing is wasted. There is too much hunger. Too much need, even though the men do not often see it or hear it. Still, it is a need that presses in on them from all sides. Hems them about. Ensures that the Selous's top predator understands that without his technology he would be helpless. That is also the law; and it has always been that way.

Into the Gloom

That evening, Bob, Paulo, Abel, and the government game scout—the Muslim Saidi M'tile, who, because it is his religious ethic or because he enjoys it, slits the throat of animals bound for the cook pot—leave camp in the white four-wheel-drive Range Rover.

The hunters climb down from the truck's high open seat and send Abel, Saidi, and the truck away to the limit of radio communication. Paulo and Bob, who planned the evening prior to leaving camp, circle to the blind without speaking. There is no wind, but whether wind direction is important when hunting leopards is an open question. Paulo says a leopard knows humans are present or were recently present and, arrogant in its power, its snarling insolence, simply does not care.

And so, unaware that the law of tooth and fang has given way to the law of broadhead and bullet, the leopard commits a fatal error.

Inside the blind, the men make themselves comfortable, as comfortable as two men can be sitting side by side on low stools, one with a loaded shotgun, the other with a cocked 150-pound draw-weight crossbow. And so they wait, neither expecting nor hoping. As twilight condenses around them, barely a pink flicker in the wide evening that is Africa, a leopard appears in the tree. Its yellow, spotted body is brilliantly silhouetted against the dark.

Paulo picks up the short-barrel shotgun. He wipes his sweaty palms continually on his shirt and nudges his client. Alert and aware of the cat, Bob places an arrow on the rail of the crossbow and engages it against the string. He pushes the safety forward to the off position, lifts the eight-pound horizontal bow, and sights through the red dot scope. When the dot is centered on the leopard's shoulder, the animal vanishes.

Bob lowers the crossbow and looks at his professional hunter for some explanation, reassurance that he has not somehow screwed up. Paulo only shrugs. There is no knowing why the big cat appeared and no explaining why it disappeared.

Choose one, Paulo thinks.

It was uncomfortable. It was not hungry. It was distracted. It was curious. . . . The men shrink onto their stools again and wait.

"It won't come again this evening," Bob offers, "or will it?"

Before dark, though, before full blackness envelops them, another silhouette appears, and this time Bob pulls the crossbow trigger. A muffled thwack, like a hammer driving a nail into a soft board, briefly overwhelms the blind and the evening's peace. Once again, the cat disappears.

But what had made it return, if indeed it was the same cat? Perhaps it was some waking dream, if leopards dream. Perhaps it was only the thrill of its own raw power or some sneering cat disdain that dismissed the multiple man-scents, or maybe its groaning hunger overwhelmed its sense of danger. That must be it, basic hunger and nothing more. Here was something good and fresh and easy, and it was willing to take a chance, roll the dice. The cat lives first of all within its own law, and when the law of belly overruled the law of caution, it chose to eat.

So Bob pulls the trigger. The cat leaps off the branch and is instantly lost in the high grass, for it is July and wet, and the grass is not burnt.

Abel Shana (left) and Ramadhani Juma hold up Bob Eastman's 2006 leopard. Bob took the cat in the evening with a crossbow from about 25 yards while hunting from a portable pop-up blind with Paulo Shanalingigwa's Pori Trackers.

Paulo keys the radio for the truck to come, and the men wait, quietly dissecting the shot and the angle, though there is no need for quiet now. They note the time and unzip the blind, step outside and stretch, and that feels good. Only in the government man's report, a thing of straight lines and right angles, will there be no blood, no sweaty palms, no hunger or need or pain. Only a man, a shot, and—they will know in the morning, because no man wants to track a wounded leopard at night—perhaps a kill.

"I Have Never Seen Anything Like This"

Before noon the next day, Bob has recovered his leopard. It did not run a hundred yards. The arrow hit hard, angled slightly forward, and sliced through the cat's vital organs. It could not have gone far. Practically everyone in camp has traipsed to the site to take up the trail, but, to everyone's dismay and delight, the sandy creek bed contains a mystery. Blood has gushed onto the ground where the leopard jumped after being shot. Blood has splattered the grass and darkened the sand. Blood has squirted heavily onto the side of the bank, and then, suddenly . . . blood and leopard disappear.

It is odd. Law suggests that a leopard, hard hit, should sprint a short distance and die, even as it runs. Bleeding heavily, it must be nearby, but where? Five, ten minutes the party searches. A quarter-hour passes, and still there is no trace. Bob is anxious.

Paulo begins to yawn. The emerald-spotted wood doves begin their call, a sweet monotony that echoes throughout the day as heat waves rise across every corner of the Selous plain: "O-Paul-O. O-Paul-O." It is hypnotic and endless.

The professional hunter yawns, stretches, and glances up.

"*Ahh.* There is your leopard, Bob," says Paulo, softly authoritative.

And there it is, indeed, nine feet off the ground, hanging in the fork of a scurvy oak, very dead.

"I have never seen anything like this," Paulo says, and the men shake their heads in agreement, even those without his thirty-two years of managing, capturing, and hunting African big game.

"How do you suppose it got up there?" Bob asks.

Abel and Ramadhani climb the tree and bring the cat down. Or what is left of it. It is not pretty. Something has eaten Bob's trophy practically in half, beginning with the stomach and intestines. No one knows for sure, but everyone has an idea, and they all speak at once.

Lions would have dragged it away and devoured it completely. Hyenas would not have dragged it at all, but would have gobbled it up on the spot, as would a pack of wild dogs. But neither hyenas nor wild dogs can climb trees.

Finally, Paulo says, "I believe the leopard was badly wounded. It ran and climbed this tree to be safe. It died here. Another leopard smelled it, climbed the tree, and began to eat it. It could only have been another leopard."

Paulo had spoken, the pro weighing the evidence and offering a summary. The great cat's delicate feet, its ripping claws and extraordinary cunning could not protect it and indeed may have led it into the trap of pride. That, too, is the law, and somewhere there is a lesson. Everyone nods in agreement.

Confrontation in Tanzania—Elephant

2006

Chapter 14

. . . the unselfconsciousness, the authority, the completeness of a wild animal, a great strange creature who looks straight at you out of his eternal present . . .

The Left Hand of Darkness[1]

Ursula K. Le Guin

He had missed, the arrow flying unseen at two hundred miles an hour or more, wide of the mark, leaving his target unscathed. The errant shot resulted in a complicated but inevitable series of events that culminated in blood and death. First came the discovery of the lone bull. Then, a tense hour of tracking, suffering the heat and the flies, and the sudden, stunning apex moment when everything went wrong. All but one small thing. . . .

Was it a character flaw, a physical disability, or simple fear, being that close to the bull? Was it loss of nerve in an archer who was no longer a young man? Or was his eyesight failing, as eyesight does, taxed by the strain of late nights, continuous worry, long reports, and the simple accumulation of years?

Perhaps it was equipment failure—the crossbow trigger stuttering or the arrow improperly seated against the string. After all, the man was an experienced bow hunter, a leader in Safari Club International, a player in the archery industry and in Great Lakes outdoor issues. No one would have been suspected of undue flattery if he allowed himself to imagine a mechanical malfunction.

[1]Page 71.

Amid the speculation one fact is certain, however. When the elephant turned and began to race in our direction, only twenty yards separated a man from utter disaster. Twenty yards, two seconds.

Now, two seconds, on the face of it, seems like such a tiny, almost useless, period of time. But two seconds to a sprinter is twenty yards; two seconds in the family car is sixty to eighty yards; two seconds in the jet that deposited us at the ramshackle third world airport west of Dar es Salaam is five football fields. Two seconds can be an eternity . . . or lead to one.

Facing an enraged elephant, two seconds is time enough for a single gasp during which one must decide which direction to lunge. Not that it will matter. A terrified man stumbling through the forest cannot outrun an elephant, bull or cow.

So in less than two seconds our professional hunter made a decision, threw the rifle to his shoulder, took aim, and fired. The heavy bullet crossed the space in a microsecond, and the bull elephant dropped literally at our feet without so much as a twitch.[2]

An apex moment. Writers lazily refer to it as the "moment of truth," as if it were a bullfight or a wedding ceremony. Whether there is an unfolding truth in some apex moment is always debatable. Witness descriptions of a crime or some instant of inspiration invariably differ. Was it murder or was it self-defense? Did the professor or her student initiate the reaction, or was it just a fortuitous accident? Who gets

[2]Gladwell, *Blink: The Power of Thinking Without Thinking.* This eminently readable book is about those two seconds when critical decisions are made instinctively. Demonstrating with a variety of current situations, Gladwell argues that decisions made very quickly can be just as good as decisions made after hours of agonizing study and debate. While not infallible, Gladwell says, these frequently superb snap decisions can be informed and controlled. Successful professional hunters like Paulo would surely concur. They and their clients sometimes live or die based on instinctive judgments and snap decisions they must make and then act upon in just seconds.

credit? Who gets blamed? The truth is always present and, like wrestling with a dream, always difficult to interpret. As if by witnessing it, the circumstances change, shifting shape and color like a cloud or a nuclear particle, subtly but certainly, and confusing the truth with doubt.

A man's life has only so many moments, and few of them are pinnacles of excitement or fear or inspiration. Life proceeds along a continuum, a slide, an easy and inevitable path to obscurity. Einstein rebels against his bohemian inspirations. McNamara excuses his culpability. Hemingway realizes his dementia is unavoidable. Thus, real apex moments, those two seconds when destiny turns and stares unblinking at us from twenty yards, cold and detached and deadly, must be rare. In an instant, one sees life differently. Something is born; something may die. The shadow of truth emerges.

Thus, because of its rarity, even when an apex moment ends in failure and tragedy, it is worth holding tightly, until the instant of one's own final calamity.

In that apex moment in Tanzania, the trigger of a powerful X-Force crossbow released a string, which in turn propelled a heavy, 416-grain, .348-inch arrow carrying a 140-grain broadhead forward toward an unmissable target. All told, the arrow delivered 110 foot-pounds of energy. It was not immediately obvious that "forward" meant into the narrow killing zone, a space of a hand's width at the top of the skin's crease behind the elephant's right foreleg.

That apex moment climaxed unexpectedly with the concussion of the professional's .375 H&H.[3] It was a fast shot, perfectly placed to

[3]Capstick, *The Last Ivory Hunter: The Saga of Wally Johnson,* page 57. Regarding the .375 H&H, Safarilandia's redoubtable PH Wally Johnson once told Peter Capstick, "I still consider and always will consider the .375 Holland & Holland Magnum as 'the only gun.' In fact, I shot many hundreds of buffaloes with the 9.3mm Mauser to save .375 ammo. I had no problems, but I would have preferred the .375 if I could have spared the ammo."

A well-placed broadhead on a heavy, stiff arrow shot from a heavy bow will take down any of the Big Five, including elephant and rhinoceros, by causing a hemorrhage. For such an enormous animal, however, a sharp, deeply penetrating broadhead will not kill as quickly as a heavy bullet from a high-power rifle. The average professional hunter was not accustomed to waiting for an animal's blood pressure to fall before it collapsed.

the charging bull's forehead, the result of years and years of experience. And when the bull fell, showering us with dust and its final nauseating breath, that moment was over forever, and we who participated or simply witnessed it began to sift the bones and blood for truth.

The Evolution of Uncertainty

Tanzania is a far different country today than that which Frederick Courteney Selous explored more than a century ago. The wildlife is the same, though some of it in greater or lesser abundance, but today, the former British Crown Colony known as Tanganyika is free and independent.

To be free in Africa today requires a careful and continuous balancing of accounts. No one knows this better than professional hunter Paulo Shanalingigwa, born into the Iramba people in the Singida district, where five thousand people are so poor they have no public well or electricity, and they are held continually in the clutches of tsetse and malaria.

Bob Eastman took this bull elephant from the Selous Game Reserve in Tanzania in 2006. His weapon was a modern 150-pound crossbow. When the elephant spun and charged, outfitter Paulo Shanalingigwa was forced to whip a .375 to his shoulder and drop it, almost instantly, within yards of the hunting and tracking team.

But it was Paulo who made the perfect shot that saved a life, or maybe two lives, when his Michigan friend and safari client Bob Eastman had apparently—no, obviously—blown a shot at a bull elephant. Missed the gray mountain standing less than twenty yards away, an impossible distance to a wild bull, and yet there it stood, and the bull whirled toward us, and Paulo threw the rifle to his shoulder and pulled the trigger.

Now, a broadhead-tipped arrow does not kill in the conventional manner of gunpowder and lead, which causes blunt-force trauma and

Bob Eastman poses with his 150-pound crossbow and his 2006 trophy elephant from Tanzania. Next to him is government game scout Saidi M'tile, who is armed with an antique .458 Winchester Magnum of German origin, and professional hunter Paulo Shanalingigwa with his .375 H&H.

hydrostatic shock and all manner of smashing physical destruction. Unless it hits bone, a broadhead cuts cleanly, like a scalpel, causing massive hemorrhage. The quarry's blood pressure drops and crashes, even on very large animals such as elephant or Cape buffalo, and the animal collapses.

Depending on the point of impact and the depth of penetration, whether the broadhead and arrow remain inside the animal or pass completely through, sooner or later—and yes, it can be either one—an

When he first hunted in Africa nearly fifty years ago, Bob Eastman took a gross of arrows. After more than thirty safaris and having hunted in most sub-Saharan nations, he takes a dozen set up for broadheads and big game, and a dozen arrows set up for other shooting opportunities.

animal weakens, drops, and expires. Hit the spine and it drops instantly. Cut through the heart or lungs and it may take a few minutes, but a well-placed arrow kills. And it kills an elephant as certainly as a .375, just not as quickly.

It is not a question of pain, either, for there is pain in all dying, and all things die. An elephant falls to a rifleman. An impala falls to a leopard. A pine tree to a wildfire. A carrot to a gardener. Cause pain, accept pain—that is life.

* * *

Paulo was tense. Hell, everyone was tense, even after the five-ton bull collapsed. Six lives had depended on his shot; seven, if you counted the elephant: the lives of the white photographer and Bob Eastman; the government game scout, Saidi M'tile, armed with an antique .458 Winchester Magnum of German origin, which he might have known how to load and fire; Paulo's watchful young tracker, Ramadhani Juma, and his driver and skinner, Abel Shana . . . and Paulo's own life. And each was connected to a dense network of family and friends, tribes, clubs, and churches that would have marked a death and condemned Bob Eastman's failure of nerve or mishandling of the equipment or whatever it was at that apex moment in July 2006 in Tanzania.

Truly, when the dust rose among the weed of the low thicket on that afternoon and the elephant came to rest on its left side, Bob stood silently among us as the accused. Although no one said as much, everyone was a little angry.

Bob had come to the bush for one of the Big Six with a weapon that was untested on African game, untested in this environment. He had difficulty with the red dot sight, which was new to him because he was a recurve shooter; and at sixty-four years old, he used a rope-and-pulley device—or relied on Ramadhani Juma—to cock the 150-pound

There is universal agreement among hunters: Elephants are a very dangerous business. The instant an elephant hears your shot or feels your broadhead penetrate, it whirls and searches for the cause of its calamity, says Michigan bow hunter Bob Eastman, who is an old African hand.

crossbow. It was an unwieldy, one-shot weapon, heavy as a rifle, and it launched a projectile that was five times as heavy as a bullet and only one-tenth as fast. No one had hunted elephant with a crossbow before, at least no one we knew of in modern times—no one without an arrow tipped with poison or succinyl chloride, that is.

So when Paulo allowed us to go forward to the fallen bull that afternoon, the flies immediately beginning to swarm in the intense sunlight only seven degrees below the equator, it was with sadness and respect and perhaps a touch of shame that we patted the rough side and the fine teeth and the lifeless trunk, that sensitive nose now sprawled carelessly in the dirt among the ants.

No one wanted to ask why he had missed, how he could possibly have missed. And Bob, who was normally talkative and upbeat, was silent.

The giant lay on its left side. Instantly dead. Bones split, brains crushed. Victim of the .375. Four to five tons of flesh and guts, eyeballs large as teacups, heart big as a microwave oven, and blood enough for a long, hot shower.

Calling his boss, Paulo, Ramadhani Juma pointed to an odd trickle of blood on the animal's side, about a hand span behind the top of the crease of the right front leg. The two African men—the professional hunter and the chief tracker—were puzzled. They spoke low in Swahili as the sun beat down and the flies and gnats swarmed. The government man nodded, and soon we all wanted to look.

"I don't think you missed, Bob," Paulo sighed, and he placed one of Bob's arrows against the skin. The hole in the elephant's side was the exact size of Bob's two-blade broadhead. "I think your arrow is inside the elephant."

Although he knew his arrow could kill the largest land mammal, even Bob Eastman was skeptical by this time. Thirty-four years before, he had taken one of the largest elephants ever recorded by SCI, by far the largest ever taken with a bow. Even then, his arrow did not achieve complete penetration with a 145-grain Bear Razorhead. In those days he shot a 90-pound recurve, and tracking took two days.

He was now shooting a modern crossbow, 150 pounds of draw weight and short, fiberglass limbs that will shoot through two or three Kevlar vests and the individuals wearing them. It is all about energy delivery.

"That's where I aimed," Bob said. "I want to see if that cut was really made by my arrow."

Paulo thought that was fine, even though it delayed his men's massive skinning and chopping task.

So Bob stepped back ten yards and fired, once again, for the crease, although now, with the elephant on its side, the shot presentation was awkward, and the arrow would have to enter the body off-center. In delivering its 110 foot-pounds of kinetic energy, the broadhead-tipped, 26-inch carbon shaft flies at more than three hundred feet per second—too fast for the human eye to track.

With barely a thud, the arrow hammered home and, astonishingly, bounced off, flung away as if it had hit some irresistibly elastic object. Though it was too late to save them from possible injury, all the men ducked and threw their hands in front of their faces.

The surprisingly elastic object, of course, was one of the elephant's stupendous ribs. Bob's arrow tip achieved barely a half-inch of penetration before being rejected, and even though they spoke different languages, all in the hunting party exchanged knowing looks. Surely the same thing had happened to Bob's first shot, or else he had missed the bull completely, and the strange cuts on its side were an anomaly.

"Once more!" Bob implored.

Everyone wondered why and was annoyed by the man's robust ego. Paulo simply shrugged. Bob handed the bow to Ramadhani Juma, who re-cocked it and handed it back. Bob inserted another twenty-six-inch arrow on the grooved, Teflon-impregnated launching slide and pushed it back against the string. The safety automatically engaged. We backed away, and he shot again.

A shot from a crossbow is startling. Everyone hears the metallic *whack,* but no one sees the arrow disappear. Perfectly aimed, this time it missed the massive ribs and buried full length inside the elephant's

Prior to Bob Eastman's elephant hunt, Pori Trackers' safari camp was visited by the district game manager who said he planned to remove thousands of elephants from the Selous. Balancing the needs of the environment with a growing elephant population is a difficult and often widely misunderstood business.

warm carcass. The arrow's entire length, from the tip of the broadhead to the legs of the nock, was deep inside the great gray beast.

Had it not turned and charged, the sharp, two-blade head would surely have worked the way sharp broadheads, from napped flint to hammered steel, have worked for thousands of years. It would have sliced cleanly, causing the relatively quick and certain death attested to by thousands of years of human survival.

* * *

Bob did not miss, after all. And his shot, at the apex moment, was perfect and would have done its job precisely as designed.

Paulo's shot was also perfect, as was his decision to fire the instant the bull whirled toward our overly large hunting party. And it whirled the instant the arrow disappeared into the soft vitals behind its massive ribs.

At its apex moment, the bull elephant fell to a modern crossbow. As far as we know, it was the very first. Amid the heat and flies, with a continent of black buzzards above and magnificent tusks at our feet.

Two perfect, killing shots. And that is the truth.

Rui on My Mind

2007

Chapter 15

[M]en cooperate after different fashions; even those who find fault with what happens are cooperating abundantly; for the universe has need even of such men as these.

Meditations[1]
Marcus Aurelius

Portuguese food is simply inedible. Americans are accustomed to hamburgers—*hambúrguer* in Portuguese—or, better yet, to a thick, tender Black Angus steak, medium rare, with a side of small red-skinned potatoes, boiled and served in garlic butter with a sprinkling of basil. Begin with a Caesar salad, lightly sprinkled with dressing, end with a crème brûlée, and one has dinner for the ages.

In Lisbon, culinary protocol requires serving food with the least human interference between a substance's original state and the customer's fork. Thus, the goat leg on a spit wheeled to a diner's table—mostly hairy hide and fat, hoof, and bone—will be sliced deli thin and presented with a selection of flavorless cheeses, butters, and hard breads as an appetizer in neighborhood restaurants. Elevate your evening to the Portuguese equivalent of haute cuisine, and you may expect fish sold by the kilo. At first glance your undercooked slab of bony cod would appear to cost one hundred dollars at this writing. Lisbon is an interesting city, but it is not Paris or New York.

[1]Page 64.

It may have been the food that caused retired Mozambican professional hunter Rui Alfonso Barbosa Quadros to lose his composure and begin to grumble. Certainly, the man had been roughly handled by life, and the least he could expect, after coming so far, was a hearty meal. Nevertheless, before day two of his all-expenses-paid vacation in Lisbon had ended, he became increasingly dour and unpleasant.

* * *

At the Safarilandia Mozambique hunting camp on the Save River, Mozambique, Michigan bow hunter Dale Gray (right) met his guide, Rui Alfonso Barbosa Quadros. Born in Mozambique, Bob recalls that Rui knew the game and the country. He was movie-star handsome and drove his clients ruthlessly.

Bob Eastman first met Rui Quadros in Mozambique in 1967. Rui was one of a handful of talented, though idiosyncratic, professional hunters in the employ of Werner von Alvensleben's safari company, Safarilandia Mozambique. Lured by the stories of bowhunting pioneer Fred Bear, who hunted with Safarilandia's Wally Johnson in 1965, Bob gave the

Hunting in Sudan, Bob Eastman took a trophy roan antelope in 1975. All Bob's African trophies fell to a sharp broadhead and well-placed shot. The antelope scored 74 in the Safari Club International bowhunting record book.

redoubtable von Alvensleben a deposit. Bob may also have been lured by the man's exotic scars—said to be the result of fencing duels from his student days in Germany—or by his acceptance of bow hunters.

An African . . . or Not

Rui, it turned out, was Portuguese or Mozambican, both or neither, and therein lies the thorn at the heart of many of the social difficulties in Africa. Rui was born white in a predominantly black nation. Whites have been present in southeastern Africa for five hundred years, but the black Bantu peoples, the majority of the population, have been there in numbers for two thousand years.

You might well ask, "What is fifteen hundred years among friends?" Though black inhabitants gloss over their own migration into lands inhabited "only by bush people," neither the whites nor the blacks entered the land now called Mozambique as liberators, emancipators, educators, or humanitarians. They were not interested in the health and prosperity of the area's earliest Pygmy and Khoe-San inhabitants. Both black and white populations came as invaders—businessmen seeking land, slaves, and ivory. The earliest Bantu migrations overwhelmed the countryside with sheer numbers. The Portuguese relied principally on technology, organization, and force—often brutal, extreme force, like the Belgians in the Congo or the British in Rhodesia.

To the Portuguese people of Lisbon, Rui was a colonial bumpkin. To the black inhabitants of Africa, he was a European and a foreigner. No African nation has yet arrived at a consensus among its people about the broad essence of "being African," certainly not in an inclusive sense. Nor has any African nation accepted its white inhabitants as brothers and neighbors. The colonial scars are still too fresh and too deep.

Rui Quadros was born in 1937 to a minor colonial administrator and his wife on Mozambique Island, a tiny outpost in the Indian Ocean. He was one of nine children, he says, though he first said he had two sisters and later remarked he had three sisters living in Lisbon. He described one as "sort of a sister," but he never explained.

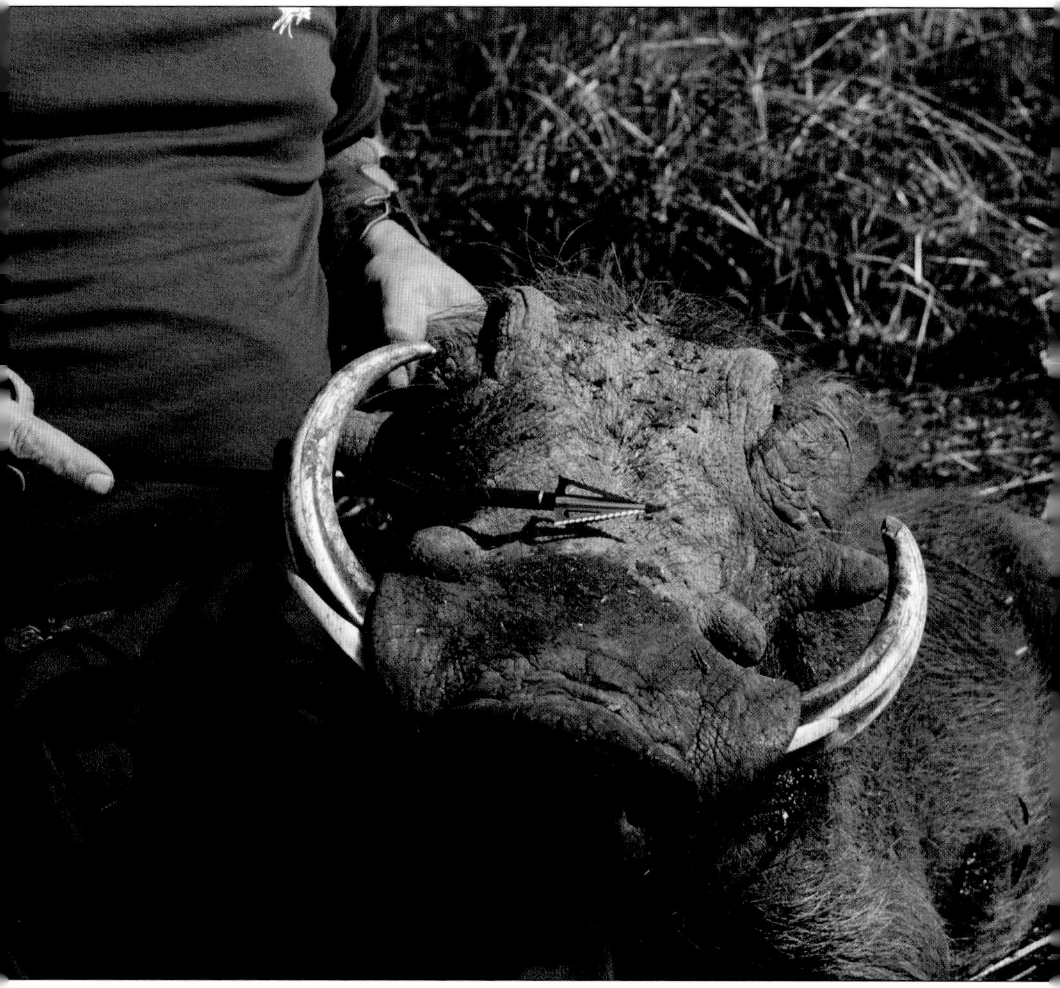

A first trophy for most archers visiting Africa is the warthog; it is plentiful and usually inexpensive. Bob Eastman's Mozambique warthog from 1966 scored 39 12/16 and stood as the largest warthog registered with SCI for thirty-two years.

Rui's father, Alfonso, transferred from post to post, usually in the Mozambique hinterlands. In these rural stations he hunted to feed his family, large families being rather rare among white European colonial officials. The boy tagged along through the bush. He shot his first buffalo at age nine, his first elephant at twelve.

It was a tradition for early safaris—dating before the era of Theodore Roosevelt—to align the skulls of their trophies for a group photo. Like the photos of arrows sticking out of big-game animals, it is a practice that has gradually fallen out of vogue as hunters have increasingly honored their opportunities and the lives of the game taken.

Rui's ordinary exterior disguised a sensitive side as dusty brush thoroughly conceals a wounded leopard. Home schooled until he was ready for secondary education in South Africa, this hard-living man recalled the birds of Mozambique with surprising fondness. Given an opportunity, he talked not about exciting shots at elephant, difficult clients, or the heat and thirst of the bush, but about collecting and preparing bird specimens for the Museum of Natural History in Lourenço Marques, now Maputo, the capital of Mozambique.

At the thought of "what might have been" had he devoted his life to the study of birds, Rui's stubborn face succumbed to gravity, and a wistful demeanor softened the punishment of years in African jungles. There were dapple-throats and green barbets in the trees of the north; grass owls and dwarf bitterns, great spotted cuckoos, and yellow-billed oxpeckers on the plains of the south. And about the fruit bats and hairy bats, the woolly bats and mouse-eared bats of his homeland, the old hunter was practically elegiac.

To become a professor, however, would have required years of study, and that was beyond the resources of his family. When Rui saw the pile of books he would have to read, he said, "I'm not going to spend all my time sitting in a stifling office with a piece of paper in front of me saying doctor of ornithology. No way. I wanted to work outside, where I could be close to the animals. I told my father I wanted to do safaris."

Rui was no more suited to life in an office than was the shaggy wildebeest. When he finished his secondary education, his father said, "OK. Now you can take care of yourself. You're free. Go." Rui left home and, if one were to judge by his wandering life and self-centered outlook, never looked back.

He entered a period of the good life, the young man's life, though he began with humble jobs: hotel receptionist, laborer in a coffee warehouse, pipe jockey at an oil refinery. As an amateur athlete he excelled in the

400-meter (quarter-mile) race, which, at higher levels of competition, is practically a sprint, and in the 800-meter race. It was as a competitive trapshooter and skeet shooter, however, that he truly excelled; and for many years in the '50s and '60s his reputation as the very best in the Portuguese colony opened doors.

The Opening of Doors

The colonial government inexplicably opened one of those doors in the late '50s, when it halted unregulated "meat hunting," especially for buffalo and elephant. Now it was no longer legal to shoot as many elephant as you could find, as Wally Johnson had done for a living, or kill every crocodile for a hundred miles along the Save River, as Rui had done part time. (Later, he would do it full time, selling the crocodile meat for food and the hides for shoes, boots, and handbags.) The government suddenly became aware of the potential revenue from safari bookings for rich foreign clients, and Rui realized that here was an opportunity to capitalize on his love of hunting and the outdoors and to make a good living as well.

Rui applied to become a guide with "the baron" Werner von Alvensleben's Safarilandia Mozambique. The baron said no. Actually, he said, "Yes, on condition you spend a year as an apprentice."

So in 1959 Rui went to work for Wally Johnson and Harry Manners, older hunting guides who were wiser in the practicalities of organizing for the bush and who understood how to manage clients.

Later, Rui recalled that there were three tests to become a full professional with Safarilandia—three tests beyond winning the confidence of his mentors, who, at that time, also included Jorge Alves de Lima, Miguel Guerra, Alfonso Ruiz, George Dedek Prosser, and Manuel de Andrade. This all-star lineup of professionals was arguably the greatest assembly of hunters Africa has ever seen, easily outdistancing such famous companies as Ker & Downey. Rui's close friend Amadeu Peixe, Manuel Figueira, José Saraiva de Carvalho, Manuel Rodrigues, Lobão Tello, and Sérgio Vega also joined Safarilandia. With Britain's colonial interests to the south in South Africa and to the north in Tanganyika, the group was naturally a blend of men of Portuguese and English descent.

The three tests began with learning the tracks of game animals and understanding how to judge trophy quality in the field. This was easy for Rui, who had grown up in the bush.

Rui would easily have understood Brian Marsh, a fellow professional hunter, who wrote, "They walked around the spoor of the water hole, examining the spoor or the game that drank there. The small, round, equine hoof print of zebra, the oval of kudu, and the heart shape of sable antelope were mingled with the heavy ox hoof print of buffalo. The elephant had come in late that night, so the imprint of its tracks had not yet been trampled out. Even when they left the soft sand of the riverbed to start up the bank and went out onto the hard baked earth of the veld, the prints were easy to follow."[2]

The other two tests were no more difficult: to prove he could kill running game animals with a single shot and to stop a charging elephant. The final test separated the men from the boys, the quick from the dead, and Rui very much wanted to be accepted by this group of men.

One lesson he learned right away was that as a professional, his role was to be a guide and bodyguard, not a shooter.

"A new professional has to understand that he is not there to shoot anything, only to help his client find a trophy and to keep him safe and happy. So when a professional says, 'We took such and such an animal,' he means he guided and his client made the shot."

[2]Marsh, Brian, *The Last Trophy,* page 170.

Although he did not say so, becoming a professional Safarilandia guide was often frustrating because, if there was anything the champion trapshooter liked to do, it was pull the trigger of a gun. It was also frustrating because clients were occasionally unable or unwilling to follow his directions.

Thus, Rui Quadros had practically everything required to rise in his profession. He was an athlete, capable of handling the rigors of extended periods of deprivation. Having grown up in multiple provinces of Mozambique, he spoke several native dialects. He was a crack shot with both a shotgun and a rifle; he knew the game species and was enthusiastic about hunting.

In addition, Rui had the good looks and wavy black hair of a movie star. Period photos invariably picture him next to his client, stripped to the waist, his dark eyes peering into the camera without flinching, the perfect image of health and vigor. Indeed, if the Rui of that era and American movie star Orlando Bloom were to change places, only their mothers (or lovers) would detect the fraud. With all this going for him, there was nevertheless one trait that would forever elude him . . . and this would nearly ruin him.

The Closing of Doors

Between trips to Angola and South Africa, Rui worked a dozen years for Safarilandia. He knew hundreds of clients, writer Robert Ruark and bow hunter Fred Bear, corporate multimillionaires and princes from fallen thrones, the obscure and the famous.

"Moçambique Safarilandia are fine outfitters," wrote Fred Bear in his book *Fred Bear's Field Notes,* "operating in a great game area. This part of Africa has a delightful climate at this time of year with an average day temperature of about eighty degrees. The nights can be as cool as forty-five degrees. This is the dry or winter season and there are practically no insects and no rain. Werner von Alvensleben directs activities and manages the operation in a most businesslike way. Seven professional hunters, totaling a great many years in the bush, are at the service of clients."[3]

Rui's run with von Alvensleben's company was so good it just could not last. During the '50s and '60s, an authoritarian, right-wing strongman named António de Oliveira Salazar controlled Portugal, and conditions in the colonies, especially for the native inhabitants, grew ever more difficult. In the bush of central and southern Mozambique between the Save and Limpopo Rivers, hunters and clients were aware of scattered anti-colonial guerrilla activity. Rumors. Conjecture. Imagination. Outdoor life grew dangerous, and tension was a continuing part of the work. Eventually, conjecture became reality.

Now, the personality of their professional hunter is something clients savor and discuss over dinner and cocktails for many years. Was the PH cool and competent in a terrifying situation? Was he inventive when the truck broke down? (Was he romantic when a husband was away?) Was he patient when the client made a poor shot? Rui was none of the above, and his hot-blooded personality was a piece that did not fit. And it was not a small piece.

Rui was extraordinarily sharp with clients. He pushed them to endure thirsty hours of tracking. He berated them when their shots went awry. He cursed savagely if they failed to follow his directions precisely. And on several occasions, he was physical with clients he believed were lazy or were killing without conscience or respect. This aspect of his behavior contrasted with his unparalleled talent for field-judging game and tracking wounded animals, for gun handling and bush lore.

The secret was that Rui cared more for the animals than he did for the clients. He had, after all, thought about becoming a biologist or an

[3]Page 242.

Half a millennium ago, Dutch humanist and theologian Erasmus of Rotterdam wrote, "I doubt if a single individual could be found from the whole of mankind free from some form of insanity. The only difference is one of degree." Bob Eastman discovered, during his early safaris in the '60s and even the '70s, that Africa was a treasure house of unusual and exciting sights.

ornithologist, and he took true delight in studying an area's wildlife. Perhaps the idea of having part-time hunters, sometimes thoughtless tourists masquerading as hunters, marginally competent clients trying to kill the magnificent animals he was passionate about, simply infuriated him. And that all came to a head in his treatment of a man he described as the "big, fat Mexican" who could not shoot straight.

The client wanted "a good buffalo," and Rui's tracker, a Shangaan nicknamed July, spotted one in a riverbed. They crept close, and Rui told the Mexican where to shoot. When the buff lowered its head to drink, the man pulled the trigger. From a distance of barely a dozen yards, the Mexican shot it in the gut.

Frightfully wounded, the buff ran up and over the opposite riverbed. The consummate professional, Rui immediately ran after it. When he scrambled to the top of the steep, sandy bank, the huge buff spun around and was "already coming for me." He shot instinctively from the hip, hitting it in the chest, but the buff was neither down nor out. Without slowing, it hit Rui at top speed. Rui's head snapped forward against the boss of the buffalo's horns, and he felt his teeth loosen. He flew backward into thick brush, an accidental landing that saved his life. In an instant the buff was in the grass, slashing its horns back and forth, trying to hook its tormentor on the vicious inward-pointing tips.

Unable to impale the prostrate Portuguese hunter, the buffalo put its head down on Rui's chest and attempted to mash him.

"Then it tried to bite me," Rui recalls. "All I could think of was to push my finger in its eye and try to gouge its eye out."

Seeing Rui knocked down, July and the Mexican rushed to the top of the embankment, intending to finish off the buff with another shot. When the animal saw them, it lost interest in Rui, who screamed for the men to look out, although that may have been unnecessary. Rui lurched to his knees and found his rifle, but the gun was smashed, trampled by a one-ton buffalo . . . and Rui was not feeling very good, either.

"There was blood everywhere, mine and the buffalo's. July went up a tree, and that fat Mexican bastard was trying to climb after him. The tree was way too small, and I shouted, *'Arriba cabron!'* Higher. Higher!"

Mortally wounded, the buffalo left Rui in the brush and smashed headfirst into the tree. The impact knocked both men out of its branches. Meanwhile, Rui had crawled to the bank and located the Mexican's gun, and now he shot the buffalo again. This time the bull staggered, fell to its knees, and died, frothing blood.

Though he was injured and in great pain, Rui cursed the client. He called him insulting names that would cause any well-bred Latin man to explode in anger. He fouled the man's ancestors, confusing them with pigs and dogs, and if he himself had not been so badly in need of a doctor, Rui would surely have assaulted the client.

Later, he only shook his head and muttered, unapologetically, that it "could have been bad."

* * *

Whatever was festering inside him, Rui's self-willed obstinacy, his butt-headed approach to clients in the field, and to the management of Safarilandia, eventually caused von Alvensleben to fire him in 1969. On the spot. Without waiting until the client was finished hunting or the hunting season ended.

"You're finished," he said.

That year, a government ministry had declared a portion of the Safarilandia concession along the Save temporarily "off limits" to hunting. Rui thought that was stupid, and he said so. He also thought it was stupid that his bosses agreed to this rule and abided by it, and he let them know that as well. (Nearly forty years later, he still thought it was stupid.)

On the way back to camp late one afternoon, his client, who had expressed a high interest in shooting an elephant, saw one lumbering through the concession . . . and straight into the off-limits area. Rui explained that the area was temporarily out of bounds, but his explanation caused the client to "throw a fit." The man argued "most forcefully," Rui said, although, in truth, it may not have taken a great argument to win Rui over. At heart, Rui resented and rebelled against all authority, except his own.

"I've paid for my safari and I want an elephant. I want that elephant!"

Rui gave in, his personality overwhelming his better judgment and his professionalism. While he pleased his client, he undermined his employer.

Rather matter-of-factly, Rui recalled they tracked the elephant into the off-limits area and killed it. When von Alvensleben found out, he had no choice but to thump his finger on Rui's chest and tell him to pack up; he was done with Safarilandia Mozambique.

Crocodile Pools of the Save

It is in the nature of all things Rui that the stubborn Portuguese-Mozambican wanted to have the last word, and he applied for a permit to hunt crocodiles. Crocodile skins were worth a great deal in those days, and are still in demand for women's shoes and handbags, men's boots, motorcycle seats, and wallets.[4]

License in hand, Rui motored into the middle of the Safarilandia concession and began to bang away with his rifles at the plentiful reptiles on the Save River. Day and night, pushing himself to work extraordinary hours, he quickly became a nuisance to his former employers and companions not far away at Camp Ruark.

[4]The 2007 price for a salted, cured crocodile skin with CITES permit (or from a registered farm) was about $170, plus another $15 for shipping and insurance.

Rui's stubborn impertinence angered von Alvensleben, who drove a Land Rover to the river to confront him. The confrontation was heated, as one might expect between two headstrong men, but Rui maintained that as long as he was hunting on the water rather than on the land, there was nothing they could do about it—not even the baron, who was something of a big shot in East Africa's hunting and wildlife community.

Ultimately, Rui shot nearly five thousand crocodiles, and for several years he made a fine living selling their hides. (Although that was a large number, he said he knew people who had shot five times that many.)

Although he found a way to poke his finger in Safarilandia's eye, wider events would soon crush Rui's bush world and von Alvensleben's as well.

A Place in History

2007

Chapter 16

Actually the second bullet was unnecessary, but Brian Dermott, as a former game warden and a seasoned professional hunter, made an inviolable practice of always killing the big, dangerous stuff twice. He had been a professional hunter of animal and man for much too many years.

Uhuru[1]
Robert Ruark

When Bob Eastman first hunted with him, Rui Quadros was every inch the Hollywood professional hunter. He was also very good at his job. Rui knew the game, the people, and the territory. He was tough and determined, and his clients were successful, although many of them ultimately wanted to shoot him practically as much as they wanted to shoot a kudu or a lion.

Rui possessed most of the ingredients that made for the classic PH, the unforgettable PH. As he approached the peak of his abilities, however, the African continent began to change in dramatic ways that were disturbing to Rui.

Perhaps humans are naturally restless and quarrelsome, but, whether or not this is so, one could date Rui's ultimate downfall to the end of the Second World War, when he was only a child. The cessation of that conflict marked the intensification of competition between the Soviet Union and its satellite states and the United States, which was at the head

[1]Page 19. This novel was set during the early years of the Mau Mau Rebellion in Kenya and highlights the horror of that guerrilla struggle.

of a hodgepodge of democracies. Meddling in Africa, Asia, and Latin America left both sides, the autocracies and the democracies, with hands dripping in gore, but it was rarely the gore of Russians or Americans.

In America during those days of confrontation, fathers who had crawled on their bellies through Iwo Jima's volcanic dust, who had lost fingers or toes to frostbite during their bitter march on the Rhine, studied diagrams of family bomb shelters. Their children practiced ducking under school desks to avoid becoming atomic shadows, even though the lingering horror of radiation poisoning was perhaps a more terrible fate.

Though the great days of the six-month bush safari were long past, and the pressure of twentieth-century business sent more men to the field in gray flannel suits than in khaki safari gear, those who could afford to do so reveled in Africa's lingering magnificence.

Superpower competition was especially intense on the African continent. Despite hundreds of years of plundering, it yet possessed enormous natural resources. There, the long-simmering restlessness of natives yearning for freedom was brought to a boil by foreign advisors and handled clumsily, often brutally, by colonial regimes. The influence of the Axis powers, Germany and Italy, had ended in 1919 and 1945, respectively.

Uhuru!

The idea of *uhuru*, Swahili for freedom, spread like an irrepressible wave following the Mau Mau Rebellion in Kenya from 1952 to 1960.

"*Uhuru* is a Semitic word used commonly in both Arabic and Hebraic," wrote Robert Ruark in the foreword of his 1962 book of that name, "and it sneaked into Swahili, which is the lingua franca of East and Central Africa, via the slave trade. *Uhuru* is synonymous to *l'indépendence* in the Congo, or freedom in West Africa."

Hernani Espinha of Angola Safaris was one of the old-time guides who struggled to understand archery as a viable hunting tool for Africa. Nevertheless, Bob Eastman remembers him as a quiet, competent professional.

The red pulse of *uhuru* appeared in northern areas of Mozambique around the time Rui Quadros became a licensed professional. Calling itself FRELIMO, the Front for the Liberation of Mozambique, a rebel army insinuated itself into areas Rui and his clients hunted along the Save River. The fighting spread like a slow tsunami, aided by internal difficulties in Portugal, where the dictatorship of António de Oliveira Salazar was collapsing, eventually to be replaced by a modern democracy.

As fighting intensified between FRELIMO guerrillas—trained by Eastern Bloc nations—and the Portuguese and Mozambican armies, Rui convinced his friend and fellow PH at Safarilandia Mozambique, Amadeu Peixe, to join him and begin their own safari business at a camp in the south. From 1972 to 1974 they operated Nyalaland Safaris along the Limpopo River bordering South Africa.

Rui recalled that after the former owner of the camp died, the game department unexpectedly awarded the business and its concession to him and Peixe. Thus, Rui became his own boss. He could not have been happier or better positioned to fulfill his dream of a life free of traffic and offices, politics and civilized niceties. Then, almost immediately, the government began to collapse, and the nation disintegrated into chaos.

Chaos Theory

"Our last clients were from Chicago," Rui recalled, matter-of-factly. "Then, in September 1974 we left Mozambique."

Unadorned, "We left Mozambique" left so much unsaid, so much unaccounted for, but, nearly forty years later, Rui was still cautious about his politics. After all, he was born in Mozambique and he still lived there, a member of the tiny white minority. Not African, but "white," as if that were a permanent division on the continent credited as the cradle of mankind.

When the Portuguese army pulled out of southeast Africa, FRELIMO's ragtag forces steamrolled into Lourenço Marques. There, following an extended, though poorly publicized, period of murder, rape, and looting, FRELIMO began the political reconstruction of the nation's people from the muzzles of its AK-47 rifles, rocket-propelled grenades, and "reeducation centers" (prisons).

Rui, Peixe, and thousands of other "white Europeans," whether born in Mozambique or elsewhere, were "sent away," marched to the borders of the country at gunpoint. There they were told simply, but with the unwavering forcefulness of an armed man who knows he is confronting helpless people, that if they returned, they would be shot. Immediately and without trial.

Most refugees fled with nothing at all; a few had friends elsewhere who could help them, but FRELIMO soldiers seized passports and wallets, confiscated watches and rings, even tried on shoes and clothes. A refugee with gold fillings dared not open his mouth too wide. The refugees were relieved of everything of value except their lives, and to protest such treatment, even for a moment, meant a savage beating or death.

The size of the game does not always indicate the difficulty of the day's hunt. "The pygmy antelopes of Africa—the klipspringer, oribi, dik-dik, grysbok, and others—are numerous and very difficult to hunt by bow," Bob Eastman says. "Unless you hunt from a fixed blind, they blend perfectly with the underbrush and are exceedingly fast and wary."

Rui's former boss at Safarilandia Mozambique, Wally Johnson, who had been purchasing business supplies in the former Rhodesia, wrote that he was halted at the border by a ragtag, heavily armed gang. The weapon-toting soldiers seemed no older than ten or twelve, but Wally understood that these children would kill without mercy or remorse, would in fact revel in the hacking and dismembering while singing nursery rhymes and drinking milk. Wally eventually survived a year under miserable conditions in a Mozambican jail.

Peixe's Path

If opposites attract, it was natural for Rui Quadros and Amadeu Peixe to become friends while in the employ of Safarilandia. Both were talented hunters, but Rui offered a gruff, no-nonsense, "do it my way," hard-trekking safari, whereas Peixe was less demanding, a guide in the "Let's try it this way" school.

"Moçambique is a paradise for game," Fred Bear wrote on 3 June 1964. "We have seen almost everything except elephant and buffalo in the short time we have been here. Yesterday, in a little pre-hunt sortie, Bob and I and our Portuguese hunter, whom we call 'Fish' (because his name, Amadeu Peixe, means just that), saw hundreds of impala and warthogs and many, many other species—eland, nyala, wildebeest, oribi, reedbuck, dik-dik, and baboons. . . ."

Four days later, while hunting elephant, Bear continued, "Fish had his gun at ready as we also took off. Fish had never seen so many elephants at one time, he told us. He is a young fellow with limited experience, although very reliable and a good shot. He is the present champion of trapshooters in Moçambique."[2]

[2]Bear, *Fred Bear's Field Notes,* pages 184, 187.

Consequently, when it came to squiring high-profile clients into the bush, Peixe was the natural choice. He assisted with Fred Bear's elephant safari, and his friendly, helpful manner went a long way toward ingratiating Safarilandia with the extraordinarily popular, outwardly mild-mannered U.S. radio personality Arthur Godfrey, who also tried his hand at archery during the safari. Peixe worked alongside the boss, Werner von Alvensleben, to guide Juan Carlos I of Spain and Count Alberto Marone Cinzano, the Italian business impresario of popular wines. Peixe is consequently mentioned and pictured in Brian Marsh's book about von Alvensleben, *Baron in Africa*. In contrast, Rui is ignored in Wally Johnson's books and merits only a small notation in Fred Bear's books.

When FRELIMO swept to power in 1974, Peixe borrowed enough money to escape to Brazil. It was a natural choice for an engaging young man who had just turned thirty. He was fluent in Portuguese, the lingua franca of that largest nation in South America. Brazil was not a state that promoted big-game hunting—it had no big game to hunt, except stray water buffalo and the highly elusive and dangerous jaguar, sometimes spotted and sometimes black. Nevertheless, the country had a wild and unsettled frontier. In Brazil it was possible for a man to begin life again.

In Brazil, Peixe lived well under the radar. He chose not to resurface in the world hunting community. His options were limited by lack of funds, and although Rui heard occasional news about his old friend, little is known about the remaining thirty-three years of Peixe's life in Brazil.

He began with nothing more than his bare hands, a friendly smile, and an appetite. This meant that Peixe looked forward to years of hard work, which led him through cycles of wealth and poverty. Soon after arriving in Brazil, Peixe opened a business making elephant-hair jewelry, a popular pastime for out-of-work professional hunters. He worked his

Bob Eastman's first leopard fell on a hunt with Safarilandia Mozambique in the '60s. His guide that day was the competent and affable Amadeu Peixe (literally translated "Lance Fish") who had also guided Fred Bear.

way from elephant hair to gold wire and was building his clientele when thieves broke into his shop and stole everything. For the second time in his life, he was ruined.

Rui heard reports that Peixe then got involved in a catering and bakery business in São Paulo. Fashioning small cookies and pastries in the shapes of African game animals, he "sold them to rich people." This enterprise did not draw heavily on his African bush experience because apparently none of the cookies were shaped like biltong or natives washing clothing in a crocodile-infested river.

Peixe's final downfall began when he got married. ("Married again," Rui noted distastefully, since Peixe's first wife had remained in Mozambique, abandoning her husband when he was forced to emigrate.) His second wife was alcoholic, and she drank the profits from the bakery. She convinced Peixe that if they could only move north, near her family on the Amazon River, with their help she would soon recover from her addiction. They moved, but her passion for alcohol continued, even increased. With no money and an unrepentantly alcoholic wife in a Roman Catholic country that frowned on divorce, Peixe's health began to decline.

The sad story would not be so unusual had it ended there. But Peixe, like all the penniless of the world, had great hope for an earthly salvation. So he played the lottery, the *Loteria,* and in early 2007 he struck it rich. In the midst of the celebration, however, the former professional hunter discovered he had cancer. Two months later, he was dead. His alcoholic spouse inherited and presumably soon remarried.

On the Road with Rui

On 10 September 1974, Rui escaped from Mozambique, not far behind his friend. "I left everything," he says, "two cars, two apartments, a home. They seized my clothes, my bank accounts, and my mother's boutique business."

Rui slipped across the border into South Africa, where he remained for the next ten years. "If I had stayed, made nice with the Communists, I'd be a millionaire today. But I didn't like those f@#&ers. They'd shoot their children for a banana."

In South Africa "a friend brought me a bag of elephant hair, and I made bracelets. Hell, I probably made ten thousand rand." (South African currency).

With his little bag of cash and help from a bank, Rui developed a game farm close to the Mozambique border in Zululand. Although he would not talk about it in detail, his farm was used not only to grow trophy nyala and sable but as a government staging area for fighters of the Mozambican National Resistance, or RENAMO. Otherwise, the leap from elephant-hair bracelets to owning a substantial game farm is difficult to understand.

The United States and the white Ian Smith government in Rhodesia supported this "resistance movement," hoping it would destabilize what those states viewed as a Soviet or Chinese satellite in southeast Africa. Both the United States and Rhodesia were concerned that Mozambique's new rulers would export guerrilla war into white-ruled Rhodesia and apartheid-dominated South Africa. In spite of the continuing vicious but low-level conflict with RENAMO, Mozambique's *uhuru*-besotted battalions soon accomplished that very thing.

Finally, in 1983, Rui sold his South African game farm and moved to Portugal. The tedious but deadly guerrilla conflict in Mozambique (which did not officially end until 1992), the loss of minority white rule in Rhodesia (Zimbabwe), and perhaps the spreading violence in South Africa

Bob Eastman hunted in Sudan with Carlos Fortunato before that country was torn apart by a seemingly insoluble conflict. Near Juba in 1975 he took an East African eland with a broken left horn. Had that horn not been broken, it would rank among the largest eland ever taken with a bow and is still, by date and location, a remarkable trophy.

were a terrible strain, even on a tough character like Rui. Thus, when a consortium of Europeans put together an offer he could not refuse, Rui gladly sold out. He thought the arrangement would last forever.

Rui intended to establish a game farm and safari park in Spain or Portugal. His plans proceeded well until the first check arrived from his erstwhile partners. It was worthless. Rui said he was "broke and screwed . . . again."

Eventually, he found a job as a hunting guide in Europe, a lucky find indeed because not that many hunting guides are needed in Europe. Rui learned the various national laws and temperate zone animals, and his hard work earned him the trust of several wealthy clients, who employed him as personal guides on trips to Asia and North America. Rui said he even guided clients to a Grand Slam of North American wild sheep.

"I was always moving, always moving from one side of the world to another."

Rui became a bushman, although of a different sort than the San peoples scattered in the south of Africa. He, too, was itinerant. Living from hand to mouth, but usually among well-heeled clients, he hunted in Alaska's Brooks Range for bear, Dall sheep, and mountain goat, in Canada for Stone sheep, poaching in Brazil for black jaguar and water buffalo, in Australia for water buffalo, in Mexico for desert bighorn sheep, in Europe (Portugal, Spain, England, and France) for Barbary sheep, pig, ibex, and red deer, and even back to Africa (Angola, Cameroon, Zambia, Gabon, C.A.R., Sudan, Zimbabwe, and ultimately Mozambique).

By 1999, Rui had saved just enough to return permanently to Mozambique. He was sixty-two, worn and tired. He had survived attacks by spitting cobras, elephants, and Cape buffaloes. He lived on when airplane engines sputtered and died; when clients abandoned him; when children without conscience, armed with machetes and automatic weapons, would have preferred to cut his head off or simply shoot him in the belly and leave him to die. Rui had survived the feast and the famine. The economic cycles left him willing but mistrustful, hopeful but doubtful. And a lifetime readiness to tear into the bush after big game contributed its own portion of personality overload, leaving him breathless, limping, disgruntled, and easily irritated. Except for his memories and the depressing sweat and shake of malaria, he would certainly die with very little to show for a hardnosed life that was always full steam ahead.

"Unfortunately, things went wrong in my life, and I lost everything."

Everything except his life or a client's life, and that is no small accomplishment during forty-two years of bush hunting.

Rui Today, Rui Forever

Rui settled in Maputo, the seaport capital of Mozambique, just north of the South African border. When he returned in 1999, he discovered that resident white people were still looked upon with suspicion, often with outright hostility, and his meager savings were quickly exhausted.

Nearly seventy-one years old, the professional hunter earned a living free-diving to spear fish, which he sold to tourist hotels in Maputo.

"I used to dive to fifteen meters and even beyond," he bragged, leaning forward and tapping the table with his finger, giving the direct stare of unimpeachable honesty. It was a glimpse of the old Rui, the buffalo coming despite being hit and hit again, hit on the nose and knowing it is going to die and not caring a whit, that old Rui. "But since the automobile accident, I can't go beyond five meters."

It was the unrelenting necessity to earn a living that resulted in Rui's final train wreck. He rolled his trousers up, exposing his right knee and leg; they were heavily scarred from being hooked by a buffalo. The leg was bent at a slight angle, which prevented running. He pulled up his polyester shirt to show how another buffalo, the one that broke his ribs and caused him to lose four teeth. ("The problem with buffalo is that the client often makes a shot that is not perfect, and then I have to go find it and finish it.") He pointed to his drooping eyelid, the one with the scars caused by venom from a spitting cobra. He held out his hands, knotted and mean looking—a working man's hands. It was impossible to imagine them turning the pages of books or delicately examining the plumage of the birds he so loved.

All these things and more were the daily bread of a professional hunter in the African bush.

"My boy saved my life twice," Rui said, patting his chest, "once from an elephant and once from buffalo." He was referring to his unforgettable Shangaan gunbearer and principal tracker, July.

Rui laughed about his injuries the way he might have laughed about the scratches and humiliation one of his clients endured when he disobeyed or simply misinterpreted Rui's instructions and was run up a thorn tree by a grumpy buffalo.

"A friend of mine is going to Tanzania, and this year he has already been caught by three of the Big Five. He got caught by a buffalo in the leg; didn't break it by luck. A leopard jumped on top of him; and two weeks ago an elephant grabbed him and threw him up in the air. He says, 'This year I got three of the Big Five!' He only needs the rhino and lion to complete his African Slam!"

A mundane vehicular accident, not the daily bread of a professional hunter, nearly killed him in July 2007 (winter in Mozambique). Returning to Maputo at night with fish to sell to the hotels, Rui slept in the cab of the truck while his assistant drove. Rui recalled that the truck suddenly lurched sideways and began to slide. Perhaps it was top-heavy with their catch, but it soon began to tumble, and both Rui and his assistant were "smashed up pretty badly." The truck and its contents were a total loss.

"In Mozambique, there is insurance only for the rich," he grumbled, "and outside Maputo there are no streetlights. The roads are littered with junk and are not marked, either, so there is only the black of night. We were lucky a car came along within a few hours and stopped to help us. Usually, it would have kept going because people are afraid of bandits."

The first doctor sent Rui home, explaining that he had nothing more than a few broken ribs, and it would simply take time for them to mend. When Rui began coughing up blood, he sought a second opinion. That cost money he didn't have, he complained, but what choice did he have. This time the diagnosis was broken ribs . . . and a punctured lung. There is no such thing as a malpractice suit in Mozambique—at least, not for a poor and beat-up old bush hunter.

* * *

Bob Eastman had invited Rui to meet him in Lisbon. Paid his way from Mozambique. Double-check the memories. See what the old man recalled. Maybe renew a friendship. By day two, however, Rui had begun to complain. At first Bob thought it was the food. Palatable and about as delicious as kidney pie in England or tripe in France, if one has been brought up to believe it is tasty and nutritious. But in Maputo, Rui would surely have eaten similar dishes, even similarly prepared.

By the end of day two, nothing was right. Rui did not feel well. His stomach, he said. After Bob left, he would have another five days to spend in Lisbon, and Lisbon was an expensive place. Where would he stay? How would he eat? His sisters could not or would not take him in; they were busy with their own lives and families. Why had Bob really brought him all the way from Mozambique? Rui asked. Bob gave him more money, paid for a doctor to see him in the hotel. It was not enough. Rui wanted more; he deserved more. . . .

What would he do when he returned to Maputo? Rui asked. He had no money and no job. He didn't feel well. His seventeen-year-old daughter was pregnant. No one would hire him. He was old, sick. Slumping, shoulders bent, he shuffled off to his room at the Sheraton.

The next day, though, Rui began talking about hunting opportunities in southeastern Africa. Special places he knew on the Limpopo, even on the Save, places not far from Safarilandia's old Camp Ruark, places he could guarantee a hunter a leopard or a lion. Guarantee. The bush is full of leopard and sable and lion now, he said. He could guarantee a trophy. Within an hour, he argued.

Or how about a hunting preserve just for bow hunters? Rui knew how to set one up. He had contacts. He knew people. It would only take an up-front investment of maybe half a million, and he could guarantee a return of two hundred and fifty thousand a year. Guarantee.

As Bob watched and listened, he thought of the boxer, the beat-up prizefighter in *Requiem for a Heavyweight.*[3] How nothing except taking a punch and continuing to shuffle forward had meaning for him any longer; only the pain and the movement mattered. Rui's face began to melt into the face of Mexican-born actor Anthony Quinn, who portrayed Louis "Mountain" Rivera in the movie. Rivera talks about how to throw a punch and how to take one. How in the end the people closest to him betray him: "You're not a winner any more, Mountain, and that means there's only one thing left—make a little on the losing."

Bob realized that throughout Rui's life the spotlight had always sought out men with a more ingratiating smile, easier men, softer men, men like Rui's friend Peixe. In spite of the old hunter's disagreeable

[3] Serling, *Requiem for a Heavyweight,* Act II, Scene 5. Written in 1956, this American teleplay was first produced for the live television show Playhouse 90 in 1957. Jack Palance starred as boxer Louis "Mountain" Rivera. Five years later, the teleplay was made into a movie with Anthony Quinn as Rivera.

grumbling, it was hard not to admire him. How he was cheated and knew it, and lost a fortune but did not quit. How he lost his home and started over. How he kept on keeping on. And how he was like a character from a Carl Sandburg poem.[4]

And man the stumbler and finder, goes on,
man the dreamer of deep dreams, man the shaper and maker,
man the answer. . . .
The people will live on.
The learning and blundering people will live on.
They will be tricked and sold and again sold
And go back to the nourishing earth for rootholds,
The people so peculiar in renewal and comeback,
You can't laugh off their capacity to take it.

Rui Alfonso Barbosa Quadros died alone and broke in Maputo, Mozambique, in 2010.

[4] Sandburg, "The People, Yes," in *Harvest Poems,* pages 102–103.

The Jims: A Jim Named George

2007

Chapter 17

In Africa a thing is true at first light and a lie by noon and you have no more respect for it than for the lovely, perfect weed-fringed lake you see across the sun-baked salt plain. You have walked across that plain in the morning and you know that no such lake is there. But now it is there absolutely true, beautiful and believable.

True at First Light[1]
Ernest Hemingway

For hunters who have never been to Africa, every sight and sound upon landing can be as delicious and disconcerting as a new flavor of ice cream. One hears Swahili and Arabic, Shambala, and Makonde, languages not routinely spoken in America's trimmed and mowed neighborhoods. Naked children play tag in waiting rooms, and when planes are late, families start fires and cook chickens on the terminal grounds.

East African airports especially are ramshackle has-beens. Julius Nyerere International in Dar es Salaam and Jomo Kenyatta International in Nairobi, both named for revolutionary leaders, are giddy, patched-up leftovers from some long-ago Independence Day when all things still seemed possible. Even at Bole International Airport, an expensive new edifice outside Addis Ababa, one could already detect fatigue and dementia prior to its completion. Compared to airports from which travelers departed in the United States, or

[1]Epigraph.

through which they transited in Europe, even compared to Tambo International in Johannesburg, these African airfields dispense with the crisp and sanitary to exude the soft, though not unpleasant, body odor of meals wrapped hours before in a downtown shanty, the smell of casually maintained toilets and air-conditioning systems designed for a country with energy and cash.

And then, there are the crowds of black and brown people waiting to board planes. Colorful and unusual garments, magnificent hairdos. Shining black faces and arms ritually scarified. Crowd control, security, even ticket taking are haphazard, and usually a small *pot-de-vin* or bribe is required for something as routine as checking a gun or bow through customs. Even seasoned travelers can feel overwhelmed.

Thus, accompanying "newbies" to Africa is a way to experience hunting there afresh. Such was Bob Eastman's experience in 2007 when he once again hunted in Tanzania with professional hunter Paulo Shanalingigwa and "the Jims," Michigan Safari Club friends Jim George and Jim Barcia. Barcia was an experienced African hand, but George, eager to do good, be good, look good, exhibited signs of wide-eyed amazement.

Everything, Jim George recalled, seemed very strange and yet oddly similar to the way he had expected to find it.

On Hitting Hair

In many ways, Jim George had developed (or inherited) the best qualities of a top competitive archer. Observant, persistent, and aggressive, the five-foot, ten-inch, two-hundred-pound American of Indian heritage was a fine shooter, excellent at placing his arrow inside a two-inch circle at twenty to thirty yards.

The George family crossed the divide of generations and culture. Jim took up archery fairly late, searching for an outlet for energies that

Railroad entrepreneur Jim George with his Tanzania buffalo. In Michigan, Jim was a capable bow hunter, having taken several whitetails with the bow and arrow. In Africa, however, the sights and sounds were startling, perhaps even a bit overwhelming, and he borrowed the outfitter's rifle to complete his hunt.

his business—operating two railroads—and being part of an extended family somehow did not exhaust. American families are under pressure from popular culture, a pressure that intensifies in cross-cultural families, and when railroads are thought of—if they are thought of at all—they are like part of an old-fashioned board game or a hindrance to driving; in other words, railroads are "so nineteenth century."

In his dozen or so years of shooting the bow, Jim George had become a competent Michigan deer hunter and had taken several fine bucks. So, for his Tanzania expedition, he was confident shooting a Mathews compound bow, although it was set at only fifty-eight pounds draw weight, and matching Eastman Carbon Express arrows.

"I met Paulo Shanalingigwa, head of Pori Trackers, at the Safari Club convention in Reno a few years ago," Jim says. "When Bob Eastman recommended him, and said he would go along as both a friend and a friendly guide, it ignited my interest in going to Africa. Some people might view an African safari as an expensive indulgence, but I have worked very hard for many years making my business successful. So now I have the time and the money and would like to do something fun, something just for me. I want to enjoy some of the benefits of all that work."

Jim set his sights on taking a Cape buffalo and a leopard in Paulo's Selous Game Reserve concession in Tanzania in 2007. It was an ambitious goal for an African newbie. Most first-timers stick to thin-skinned plains game, a few antelope species, and maybe a warthog, and are otherwise content to observe and learn.

Jim's goal—to take both a buffalo and a big cat on one expedition—was ambitious, but it was doable. The big-game animals were each hunted in a very different manner—the buff by stalking across the open veld and the leopard from a ground blind over bait. Jim would have to exercise the full range of his competitive energies and all his bowhunting skill to take them both. A little luck would help as well.

Leopard: The Essential Cat

Although lions can climb, it is leopards who are tree feeders. If possible, they pull their prey into a tree to eat it because although they are fast, efficient killers, they are half the size of their number one competitor, the lion. And leopards are solitary cats, while if one detects a single lion, one can be reasonably certain that a dozen others are not far away. For a leopard, those are impossible odds, and while lions do climb trees on occasion, such a height—even six to ten feet—normally gives the leopard time to take a meal undisturbed.

Hauling an impala into a tree may provide some protection from lazy lions, but it certainly puts the leopard and its dinner out of reach of hyenas. Although we may disdain hyenas for their seemingly comical, slovenly appearance, cackling barks, and irregular, loping gait, a few determined hyenas will steal a leopard's kill if it is on the ground. And, as is the case with lions, where there is one hyena, there are often many others.

Leopard hunting proper begins with finding fresh leopard tracks; shooting a bait animal, such as a zebra or an impala; and finding a suitable tree in the leopard's range in which to hang the bait (or part of it, as either an entire impala or a rear quarter of zebra or wildebeest will do). The odor of blood and decay is apparently irresistible to hunting felines. If a hungry cat is in the area, says Paulo Shanalingigwa, it will find the bait. Whether it then commits to taking the offering may depend on the precautions the hunters have taken in setup or the presence of the leopard's own kill nearby.

The animal's individual history plays a role as well. If just once it has been hunted or shot at, or if perhaps it has been injured in a native snare, it may become too shy to ever be successfully baited. In such a case, although life in the wild presents constant challenges, a leopard will probably live the balance of its life in good health. Leopards may live more than twenty years and never be seen by a human being.

Bob Eastman's friend Jim George made one trip to Africa and took a magnificent leopard with a rifle after missing with the bow and arrow on several occasions. Tracking the big cat into a gully, the professional hunter's team quickly realized that the wounded cat was stalking them.

After locating leopard tracks, Paulo's game scouts hung three baits in trees they judged would give leopards inviting access, hold the baits securely, and allow for the setup of a ground blind within effective bow distance. A difficulty in bait placement is that the leopard must feel safe, and yet the hunting client must be within comfortable shooting range. Leopards are so stealthy that many hunters swear they never knew a leopard was in the area until they saw it on the branch chewing on the bait.

On the other hand, no less an authority than Jim Corbett, the early twentieth-century slayer of man-eating leopards and tigers of India, allowed hunters one significant advantage. It is especially significant to American bow hunters who rarely shoot at big game beyond forty yards and are thus obsessively observant of changing wind patterns: "Leopards—other than man-eaters—are the most easily killed of all animals in our jungles, for they have no sense of smell."[2]

* * *

Jim George was certainly excited, but, from the professional hunter's point of view, excitement can be a troubling and unknowable contribution to the hunting equation. It is good to have an eager client, but will he overcome his anxiety and make a quick killing shot; will he freeze when he ought to pull the trigger of his release; will she collapse when the moment comes to lift and draw her bow, sight on a snarling carnivore, and take a cleansing breath before letting the string go forward? Experienced professionals have seen a multitude of client reactions, and that is one reason they carry a loaded gun.

Now, Jim admitted that the preparations for hunting his leopard were exciting. This was, after all, his first exotic hunt, his first trip to Africa. The closest he had ever been to a live leopard was in a zoo. A

[2] Corbett, *The Man-eating Leopard of Rudraprayag,* page 458.

leopard hunt ought to be exciting, though, for a leopard can quickly become a deadly foe if it chooses to do so.

The adrenaline-induced excitement of hunting an animal that could hunt him in return was an attraction for a man who spent his time with inexplicable spreadsheets, on conference calls with million-dollar results, and in jawboning sessions with squads of briefcase-wielding lawyers. The tension was also an encumbrance—the devil was thrilling from a distance, but one did not especially want to dance with him . . . or her.

Bob Eastman's company, Eastman Outdoors, sent Paulo several lightweight pop-up blinds for use with his leopard-hunting clients. Paulo had become a friend, and Bob also sent the blinds because they set up silently and rapidly and are appropriate to the leopard equation. With the narrow window slits facing a bait tree, a leopard would be silhouetted the moment it began to gnaw on a carcass. Inside an enclosed, camouflaged, and black-lined blind, a hunter can make slow, quiet movements to adjust a stool or to pick up a bow or rifle without being seen by Africa's cautious cats.

After hanging baits, it was only a matter of waiting, and waiting was hard for Jim George, as it is for any novice hunter. The fretting. The questions. Would a leopard come to his bait during daylight? If it came at night, would it remain nearby? Would checking the baits disturb it, cause it to stay away? Jim harbored not a single doubt, though, that he could place a broadhead-tipped arrow from his fifty-eight-pound compound bow into a leopard's vitals at any reasonable distance, perhaps to thirty yards.

The questions were answered swiftly. Two of the baits were chewed on the first night they hung. It seemed only a matter of throwing up the blind and sneaking inside undetected. At this point, however, Paulo and Bob Eastman disagreed about the setup.

It is the standard professional hunter's argument with archers: How far is too far, how far is far enough? At what point does the archer reach—and recognize—his level of incompetence? Realizing that Jim was excited, Bob wanted to give him the best possible opportunity. It was not a matter of skill; he knew his friend was skillful enough. It was not a matter of courage because he knew Jim George was tough; one has to be tough to make it in the railroad world. It was simply a matter of learning to cope with the adrenaline.

Bob asked Paulo to set up the blind for a twelve- to fifteen-yard shot. Although he was no less interested in his client's success, Paulo argued for twice that distance, at least twenty yards, "for safety." This was a very dangerous animal, he argued. If Jim did not deliver a killing shot and only wounded it, Paulo would be responsible for finding and killing it, based on the two-hundred-year-tradition of professional hunters. The following story from Brian Marsh's *Baron in Africa* illustrates. Known as "Zecas," José Saravia Carvalo was a Portuguese professional hunter employed by Werner von Alvensleben's Safarilandia Mozambique in the 1960s.

Zecas was hunting with two Swiss clients out of Alves Lima Camp on the Save River. Not long into the safari, a leopard commenced feeding on a bait he had put up not far from the camp. He took his clients to the blind one afternoon to sit for it. The leopard, which by then had been feeding for some days and had become comfortable there, came in early. The client fired but only wounded it, and it ran off into a thicket of ilala palms. Zecas immediately followed. The leopard was well concealed, and it took Zecas by surprise, charging from a very close range. The animal was on Zecas before he could bring up his rifle to shoot, and it proceeded to give him a severe mauling. Fortunately, the client's bullet inflicted a mortal wound. While holding the hunter down, it gave a sudden gasp and fell dead on top of him. Zecas spent some weeks recovering in hospital but was able to return to running safaris again before the season ended.[3]

[3]Marsh, *Baron in Africa: The Remarkable Adventures of Werner von Alvensleben,* page 114.

In 2009, just two years after what he described as the greatest adventure of his life, Jim George died suddenly at his home in Michigan. Here he poses with his 2007 Cookson wildebeest.

About Missing and Making Decisions

A leopard came to bait on Jim's first night. The bow hunter knelt in the blind, drew the compound bow and held, sighting on the hardball-size kill zone of the cat's chest. At last he shot through the blind's narrow window, slightly upward at a little less than twenty yards, his mentor's compromise distance. The arrow flew high and landed somewhere in the drying grass of the veld, possibly a half-mile from the blind. There it would lie until the stainless blades of the broadhead rusted away, for, given enough time, even the hard steel would deteriorate, as would the plastic vanes and nock, and ultimately the fiberglass arrow shaft.

Jim George was upset. He knew, however, that every hunter will eventually miss or make a poorly placed shot, draw blood on an animal that subsequently escapes and cannot be found. A hunter who says he has never missed a big-game animal is either being untruthful or has conveniently forgotten.

The same is true of shots that wound rather than kill. Such things happen. One works hard for the quick, clean kill, practices to prevent a miss or a wounding shot, and then spends hours—sometimes days, as in the case of an elephant—tracking, blood-spooring. One shoots and tunes the nock and the head, double-checks the spine of the arrows, anticipates difficulties and practices some more, and still, it happens. Not often, but it is an undeniable fact. No lawyer wins every case; no doctor cures every patient; no evangelist saves every soul.

Jim's leopard, or possibly another leopard, returned the next evening. Again, Jim and Paulo waited silently, patiently, unmoving in the blind. They had agreed upon a strategy. Don't draw the bow too quickly; give the cat time to feel comfortable, but not too much time. Apparently, the sibilant swish of the razor-tipped shaft had startled the cat the evening before, but not so much that it would pass up a free meal.

This time the men heard the leopard before they saw it because it came from behind them and sniffed at the blind. The hunters froze, their hands tightening on the aught-loaded shotgun and the bow, respectively. Sweat materialized instantly on their foreheads. They could not even wipe their hands on their trousers; the carnivore was too close. It may have been only hunger, its subtle feline shortsightedness overruling the wisdom of bypassing this strange human contraption. Perhaps the blind successfully disguised the hunters' odor, even their breath, for it was warm and close inside. Paulo says the leopard stood for a moment outside the zipped entrance before it walked past, disappearing momentarily in the grass before leaping upward into the tree. And even then, from the tree branch where it was silhouetted darkly against a still-bright sky, it paused to glare at the blind.

The evening before, Jim George's arrow had flown slightly over the feline's back; this second arrow missed low, below the thick limb. And although Jim could not follow its flight—his gaze, in the best tradition of baseball pitchers, field goal kickers, and bow hunters, was fixed on his target, the quarter-sized spot of chest he willed his bright blades into—Paulo, sitting to his left, could see the speeding shaft and knew the miss was as clean as the miss the prior evening.

The third day, a leopard came to George's bait just at dusk. Once in the tree, it too turned its head and stared at the blind.

On video the stare of a leopard is chilling. Its ears flatten; the slits of its eyes narrow, and one is sure that the vertical pupils have a penetrating sense beyond vision, as if the spotted cat could look inside a man's conscience. In the slow-motion frames of a movie, the animal's nostrils flare, and the long guard hairs around its nose puff outward. But it is the mouth, the insolent, grinning lips and beautiful incisors, that draw the watcher's eye. Long yellow teeth perfectly adapted for seizing and ripping flesh.

It is the leopard's teeth that bite the throat and crush the windpipe, but it is the claws that do the evil work of shredding and gutting. The claws and those delicate but powerful legs become a disemboweling machine that no medical team, no matter how well equipped or how quick to arrive, could save one from.

The leopard pants, and in the stillness Jim hears it and either imagines or recalls, by some persistence of racial memory, its final stalk. The ancestors hauling themselves upward into trees on the edge of the veld like so many frightened monkeys, screaming and straining to climb, staring at every breeze-whipped blade of grass, knowing that the predator is coming to kill and eat someone, knowing that when it finally shows itself, it is already intent on a particular tree, a particular member of the band. And all break out shouting and gesturing, as if the noise will distract the cat, but it has someone in mind and leaps gracefully onto the trunk and upward to the first branch. The victim knows he is going to die, but the horror will, mercifully, be short. Half a minute of futile struggle to end a lifetime.

All of this may flash through Jim George's mind, consciously or otherwise. He takes a deep, calming breath, brings the bow to vertical, and shoots. And misses. Again. Unaware of its peril, this leopard turns and stares into the blind and snarls, but remains in the tree, for hunting blinds and carbon arrow shafts are not a part of its ancestral memories. The leopard is disturbed, interested in the way of a cat, but it is not anxious because the source and intent of that disturbance is a mystery, and it is not afraid.

Cautiously, Jim reaches for another arrow. Instead of pulling a shaft out of the quiver, though, he pauses to take a deep breath. It is a ragged intake, and the professional hunter realizes that leopard—panting, stalking, silent, man-killing leopard—is now inside the American railroad man's head.

Jim hesitates. As he does, Paulo detects movement not far from the bait tree. It could be a lion or an entire pride of lions. Sunset will not be long in coming, and the king of beasts will also be shopping for dinner. Unless it quickly abandons the bait and flees, the leopard might become that meal. The movement could also be hyenas, which might not bother the leopard, safe with its dinner a dozen feet above the ground. Hyenas could mean trouble for the hunters, though, for all that hides them is the thin, camouflaged cloth of the blind.

But the movement is a second leopard, a huge animal that springs effortlessly upward and into the tree. Paulo feels the hair on his arms stand and shiver in amazement, for here is a world-class feline. It is certainly a male, the alpha male in this territory, and now two leopards maneuver around the impala carcass.

Oddly, even though he is at last ready, the bow hunter does not have a clear shot at the largest leopard, for it has positioned itself on the one limb that is obscured by branches. And so the smaller one, probably a female, Paulo thinks, feeds on the maggoty mass of impala. The large cat seems content for the time being to lick and nibble, almost daintily, at the opposite side. The PH has never seen anything quite like it.

Night falls, and another problem arises. How do they sneak out of the blind without advertising their presence, without so alarming the cats that they will not return? Paulo keys the hand-held radio, which crackles, alerting but perhaps momentarily confusing the leopards, for they tense and raise their heads but do not leap immediately out of the tree. At some distance Paulo's tracker and the government game scout hear the radio static and pile into the truck. It rumbles over the veld toward the blind, and the leopards vanish.

Hippos and Final Acts

It is Paulo who suggests they take a few days off. "To break the spell," he says, leaving "of bad luck" unsaid. So he takes Jim hippo hunting, which is fundamentally different from anything Jim George has ever done or imagined. Again and again the hippos melt away, if a hippo can be said to melt. They vanish. They splash away into the water or simply submerge. Jim's shot will have to be good; the hippo must fall on dry land, on a sandbar, or in shallow water, for dropping—sinking into a deep river pool—means very hard work for Paulo's men. Deep water also means contending with crocodiles or other hippos, and no one wants that.

Selous hippos are hunted in the same manner as crocodiles, which is to say, carefully. One patiently and quietly stalks through the wood toward the river because the massive mammals are keenly aware of activity on the banks around their swimming holes in the Greater Ruaha. At night they come out of the river to feed in nearby meadows or farm fields, and with stealth and luck they can be ambushed as they return to the water in the morning.

Hippos, it is widely reported, long ago replaced lions and leopards as the number one man-killer in Africa, dashing to pieces residents and tourists, bathers, canoes and small boats equally. These vegans do not eat humans, and that is certainly a good thing, but the adults, both male and female, are fiercely territorial and unbelievably agile, both in and out of the water, for such a ponderous animal. (It is no wonder Disney dressed them in tutus for his feature-length cartoon Fantasia.) And a hippo, thundering in one's direction, slack jawed, with its massive yellow teeth flashing, is terrifying at any range.

Ultimately, Jim shoots an enormous bull hippo. Six members of Paulo's crew work half a day just to haul it out of the river, and Jim gives the carcass to his hunting partner, Jim Barcia, who has run short of lion bait. It is a generous gesture, although the meat would otherwise probably go to waste; one would have to be very hungry indeed to toss a hippo on the barbie. Lions, on the other hand, are not known to be picky eaters; indeed, they prefer the taste of road kill to the danger of fresh buffalo, for hunting is not about trophies so much as sheer survival. When it comes to hippo guts, however, the king of beasts is hooked.

Until one stands beside a downed hippo, its size is merely hypothetical. In the water it is as nimble as a ballerina, as fast as a racehorse, and as ferocious as a cobra. A hippo's bite force is about 2,000 LBF; an adult Rottweiler has a bite force of about 325 LBF.

When they return to leopard hunting on the tenth day, Jim takes the professional hunter's .375 H&H rifle and, just at nightfall, nails his leopard.

It was never quite that cut-and-dried on this hunt, however. It rarely is anywhere in Africa, north of the blind-and-water-hole shooting in the Republic down south. And so there is a little more to Jim's story.

Kena Laheri (Good Luck)

Jim has "nailed" but not recovered his leopard. Thus, in the morning the hunters are up and away early, for there is either a dead or a wounded leopard to deal with. Dead is one thing; wounded, quite another.

No blood is pooled near the bait, and very little is sprinkled in the narrow streambed nearby, which is only yards wide. The bottom is sandy, and, with thick brush overhanging the sides, much of it cascading onto the streambed itself, the few drops of blood show up as tiny dark spots. The tracking party strings out for a dozen yards, the tracker ahead of the professional hunter, who is followed by his driver, the client, and finally the government game scout. They search carefully but thoroughly, disturbing evidence of the leopard's earlier passage. In the slanting rays filtering through the brush, glimmering golden with dust, the streambed feels close, clingy. The men stoop or crawl beneath overhanging trees, edge sideways between the bank and thorny tangles of vine. Soon everyone is uncomfortable, on edge.

Jim George is perspiring heavily, and so is his professional hunter, who unexpectedly halts the small parade and signals for them to return the way they came, back through the ravine.

"It's just too dangerous," he says, indicating the thick scruff at shoulder height along the sides of the gully. "If the leopard is wounded, it could be on your head before you could react."

Everyone turns around, but after a little more than twenty yards, the government game scout—who originally brought up the rear of the procession but now finds himself in the lead—stops and whispers for Paulo to move past the others and come forward. His voice is unusually soft but urgent. The game scout kneels and points down at the sand. Instead of looking down with the PH, however, he stares into the brush and thumbs the safety off his old bolt-action rifle. There is a fresh spot of blood, a glimmering red droplet in the soft sand impression of a boot print. Suddenly, everyone wants out of the confining gully, which now feels like an ambush.

So the leopard is not dead. They assume it is the leopard's blood and that Jim's ill luck has persisted. Now the big cat, wounded and in pain, is stalking the hunters. It could be anywhere, but it is certainly close. It knows exactly where they are and how many. It hears them shuffle along, speak, breathe. It hears hearts beat, faster now, and blood coursing in gurgling spurts through their veins.

Paulo lifts his shotgun to the ready position. He, too, eases the safety off. It is no longer a casual morning, no longer business as usual. This cat understands; it has made the connection. It has become the hunter. A wounded leopard thinks like a wife who has been humiliated in public or like the skinny kid with thick glasses who is alone in the locker room and spots his tormentor's wallet on the floor.

For revenge, this leopard will do anything, even commit an act of certain self-destruction. And who says that revenge is solely a human emotion, that we should not ascribe human feelings to "mere animals"? Such people know nothing about leopard.

This feline could be in front of them or behind them or a few feet away on either side. Even now, this very instant, it might be tensing its powerful, stringy muscles to spring. Five men in a narrow, twisting gully overhung with brush. So many tempting targets. Paulo checks the double-aught shell in his 12-gauge. What was he thinking, allowing all these men to follow him into this death trap? Now it is his responsibility to see that they all make it out in one piece—or at least alive.

Then there is a slight rustling. The leopard's perfectly camouflaged head takes shape in the leaves as it balances to begin its rush, and Paulo throws the shotgun toward his shoulder and fires. The cat leaps, and the buckshot hits squarely in its head and chest. It falls into the sand, writhing for a moment; then it lies perfectly still.

And so it is over, at last.

The cat is old; its teeth are worn from years of killing and eating. It has fed off many lives, and although it is dead, some part of it may still live inside Jim's head.

* * *

Jim George died suddenly on 16 December 2009. He was fifty-eight. The story of Jim's leopard hunt had recently been published in the September/October 2009 issue of *SAFARI* magazine. Bob Eastman says the grieving family enlarged the magazine pages and displayed the story on an easel beside Jim's casket at the funeral.

Jim attacked his work with vigor, intensity, and intelligence. He was born in Madras, India, but his story is nevertheless all-American. He began his lifelong love affair with railroads as a mail clerk and, at his untimely death, was president and chief executive officer of Michigan's Lake State Railway and Saginaw Bay Southern Railway.

"Jim had a drive that was unreal," said Judy George, his wife of twenty-eight years and mother of his three daughters. "He was charismatic, larger than life, and yet very humble at the same time. He loved nature and lived and breathed being outdoors."

The Jims: A Jim Named Barcia

2007

Chapter 18

. . . the most appreciated, enjoyable occupation for the normal man has always been hunting. This is what kings and nobles have preferred to do: They have hunted.

Meditations on Hunting[1]
José Ortega y Gasset

One could not realistically call Jim Barcia an "old African hand." Nevertheless, he has hunted big game on that continent three times: the Moyowosi region of Tanzania in 1991, a South African ranch in 1997, and the Selous Game Preserve in Tanzania in 2007.

If Barcia was not exactly certified in the subtleties of the bush, neither was he a newbie. He had hunted with Bob Eastman across North America, but, unlike Eastman, who is one hundred percent bow hunter, Barcia remained neutral to positive about pulling the trigger of a firearm on occasion. At times, he says, guns are a practical solution to hunting problems; in other words, sometimes they just make sense. Thus, while he has taken numerous species of African game by bow—for example, greater kudu, gemsbok, and impala—and several with a gun, he had, as of 2007, failed to connect with the one species that truly ignited his imagination, a lion.

Nevertheless, when the new 2007 calendars appeared, Jim Barcia had not given up hope of scoring a big cat—somehow. And the more he thought about lions . . . well, the more he thought about them. In

[1]Page 27.

truth, he was a little obsessed. Then, at the January 2007 Safari Club convention in Reno, his Michigan friend Bob Eastman proposed another Tanzanian safari. They could book ten days in a concession in the Selous Game Reserve with outfitter Paulo Shanalingigwa of Pori Trackers at their old friend's best possible rates. So Barcia manipulated his retirement strategy and began to spend time at the archery range.

Tanzania, however, was in the midst of developing a hunting crisis in 2006 and 2007. Spurred by myopic antihunting organizations, typically European and American, half of that desperately poor country's

At Bob Eastman's elaborate hunting lodge in northern Michigan, hunting guide Mike Bergeron explains the relationship between the ridgelines and the oak trees to bow hunter and state senator Jim Barcia.

outdoor community was promoting a plan to dramatically increase hunting concession and trophy fees for archers. Bowhunting fees were already twice those of gun fees, as if the government of Tanzania preferred the growing legion of world archers to schedule hunts in Mozambique or South Africa or Namibia, as if they preferred riflemen who take half-a-dozen game animals for each one taken by a bow hunter. Despite this, the party of three—Bob Eastman, Jim George, and Jim Barcia—optimistically booked a hunt with Paulo's company. This great adventure—planned in detail, celebrated and saved for—was nearly Jim Barcia's undoing.

A Politician, with Standards

Jim Barcia is a politician, a very good one. He has served Michigan in the United States Congress and, after having his seat gerrymandered into something altogether unrecognizable as a coherent political or social community, is now a state senator for the people of east central Michigan. He wrestles with issues as dissimilar as the multi-billion-dollar automobile industry bailout and negotiating the sale of bonds for sanitation projects. To serve the people as a politician, one ought to be versatile and yet maintain standards of conduct and an open mind. Jim Barcia has standards.

When the hunting party landed in Dar es Salaam, he said his standard for lion was a mature male. He wanted to stick an arrow through the heart of a muscular, yellow-fanged bruiser with a big harem, a black-maned male that could dismember a Cape buffalo while polishing its toenails with crocodile teeth.

Such standards are high, indeed. Lions of that caliber are rare today. Perhaps they were always rare. For most of human prehistory we hairless, two-legged scroungers would have considered that a good thing. And now, opportunities for bow hunters are expensive as well as dangerous. A bow hunter must, after all, be close to his quarry—literally a heartbeat separating predator and prey, and a lion's heart beats faster than that of a human.

Although four lion tags were awarded each year in Paulo Shanalingigwa's East African concession, he cautioned Barcia prior to booking that lions were difficult in his section of the Selous. There were several reasons why, he said. They were difficult because they were rare and because the grass would probably be high, wet, and unburned in July. Normally, in fact, hunters—riflemen—filled only one or two of Paulo's lion tags. Almost everything else was plentiful, from pounding black Cape buffaloes to delicate impalas, with the exception of cheetahs and rhinoceroses.

Unfortunately, no government bureaucrat or NGO official had yet convinced the various prides in Paulo's eight-hundred-square-mile concession to sit for a census. Located on the northwestern bank of the Greater Ruaha River a hundred miles or so as the crow flies southwest of Dar es Salaam (locals refer to it simply as "Dar") and the Indian Ocean, the high-grass prairies were believed to conceal plenty of lions. But no one truly knew.

The trouble, Paulo said, was that the rains had become unpredictable, irregular. No native villages existed inside his concession, and in years past, beginning as early as mid-June, his men would burn enormous areas of high grass, which by that time of year should be withered and dry. After the first rainfall, one could watch the fresh grass pushing up through the thin tropical soil. These days, though, puddles lingered in the dirt tracks, and the hippo pools beside the Chinese-built railroad-to-nowhere overflowed as late as August. Lions were thus difficult to locate and, once hit, difficult and dangerous, frightening, to track.

But could they find a lion? Barcia asked, his voice betraying a foundering hope and perhaps a sense that money for African safaris was not unlimited, even for a popular politician.

"It depends on many things," Paulo replied honestly. "I can't give you a guarantee, but we will try very hard."

So Jim Barcia knew the odds were not in his favor. The odds were even worse, perhaps, because he had his standards. But he was among friends and had hunted with Paulo in the Moyowosi. He knew that whatever the circumstances, his outfitter would do the best that could be done, legally and ethically. And if he succeeded in shooting a lion, the animal would be a credit to the hunter and to the guide, which is all a good hunter can ask.

In the Days to Come

Hunting *Panthera leo* may cease entirely in the near future; the cost may become prohibitive, except for the ultrarich. Hunters around the world, from conservationists to subsistence hunters, work to ensure that big-game populations are stable to increasing throughout their range. But African lions are only one small piece of a vast and seemingly insoluble puzzle.

The problem is, the world has become a very crowded place, and every human inhabitant chafes when his or her lifestyle does not match that of the movie stars or when some fool has the temerity to express faith in an alternative expression of godhead. With cellular phones and the Internet, perceptions, communications, and even diseases are now shared globally. It is unfortunate, if understandable.

Additionally, Africa suffers from persistent tribalism and extractive economic policies that are, at this writing, causing the violent death of thousands in Kenya, Ivory Coast, Angola, Nigeria, Chad, Eritrea, Zimbabwe, and Sudan. In a period of unaccountable though common savagery less than a generation ago, tribalism resulted in genocide in Rwanda, and one million people were burned and hacked to death. On a lesser though no less miserable scale, the savagery is now loose in the Congo and C.A.R., in Ethiopia and Ghana. . . .

The continent is choked with poverty, insoluble health issues, corruption, and an intolerant Muslim militancy. It is almost enough to cause one to turn one's back and let the chips fall, but if there is to be any hope of saving Africa's magnificent wildlife, including the lion,[2] the developed nations and the Africans, themselves, must find a way.

Still, Bob Eastman's group of Michigan hunters did not fly to Tanzania to solve Africa's problems or to exploit them. They accepted the economic value that nation placed on what may be its most valuable renewable resource, its wildlife. Neither did they begrudge the hundred thousand dollars or so they spent for food and travel, for the services of a professional outfitter and his crew, for the trophy fees and tips that bought them a couple weeks of guided hunting in the deep bush. It

[2]Creel, "Lion Density and Population Structure in the Selous Game Reserve: Evaluation of Hunting Quotas and Offtake," in *African Journal of Ecology,* 1997. In 1992 tourist hunting in the Selous Game Reserve generated $1.28 million for Tanzania, of which $.96 million was returned to wildlife conservation. Lions are one of three critical species for tourist hunting, consistently generating 12 to 13 percent of hunting revenue from 1988 to 1992. Because of their ecological and economic importance (and intrinsic value), it is important that lion quotas be set so that off-take is sustainable.

- The population density of lions in Selous ranges from 0.08 to 0.13 adults per square kilometer and is thus comparable to un-hunted ecosystems.
- The adult sex ratio (36 to 41 percent male) and the ratio of cubs to adults (29 percent cubs) are similar to those of un-hunted populations.
- The ratio of lions to hyenas is lower in heavily hunted areas (0.17 lions/hyena) than in un-hunted areas (0.43 lions/hyena).
- Hunting levels between 1989 and 1994 took 2.7 to 4.3 percent of adult males annually, which is sustainable.
- The current quota is 10 to 16 percent of the adult male population, which exceeds natural mortality rates for male lions.

To remain stable if the quota was filled, the population would have to compensate via increased fecundity, increased juvenile survival, or an altered sex ratio. Compensation occurs in the Selous by producing (or raising) more male than female cubs (66 to 81 percent of juveniles are male). Only 28 percent of the Selous quota was filled in 1992. The percentage of quota filled (both in Selous and nationwide) has dropped since 1988, even as quotas have increased. The current intensity of lion hunting in the Selous is sustainable, but the quota cannot be filled indefinitely [cannot be filled 100 percent and remain a sustainable yield].

was a fair and open-handed economic exchange in the way this world of give-and-take exchange operates. It was the one way they could make a positive and personal contribution to Africa's future.

Jim Barcia went to Tanzania dreaming of a lion. He went with all the enthusiasm a political pro can muster, which must have been a great deal in his case, considering he stands for reelection every two years.

Grey Poupon for My Hippo, Please

On Jim Barcia's first day in the country, the Bantu guide assigned to help him ferret a lion out of the bush and the PH, a tall, earnest, and experienced man named Webster, talked strategy. Because a lion was the only animal the American bow hunter wanted, their first task was to locate likely areas to bait. That meant scouting for a pride with a mature black-mane male.

The second step was to shoot a bait animal or two. A lion can eat eighty pounds at one sitting, so just any one-hundred-and-forty-pound impala would not do, as it might for a leopard. For obvious reasons and because it is widely believed that lions favor the meat, hunters prefer a hippopotamus. Shoot a hippo; haul it out of the crocodile-infested water; save the head for a trophy, but cut the carcass into manageable quarters; drag each section behind the Toyota Land Cruiser through areas where lion spoor has been found to create an inviting scent trail; and chain the quarters to trees to prevent their being dragged away. Finally, set up a ground blind for the hunter and the guide. It seems straightforward enough, but this procedure involves a great deal of grunting and sweating, even in Tanzania's winter.

At the time this chapter was written, the trophy fee for hippopotamus was about twenty-three hundred dollars. So before a lion is ever spotted, a hunter is going to deposit twenty-three hundred-dollar U.S. greenbacks into the hands of his PH. It is intimidating even before one has to write

A hippo shot for lion bait is chopped apart in the river and hauled out in quarters. It is an article of faith in East Africa—though whether it is literally true no one can truthfully claim to know—that lions prefer the taste of hippo to practically any other meat.

the actual check . . . and there are no ATMs in the Selous. Additionally, the lion carries a trophy tag of around eight thousand dollars—double that for a bow hunter in Tanzania. Therefore, perhaps coming to terms with the expense is step one; and that usually must be done in consultation with one's significant other—in Jim Barcia's case, his wife, Vicki—prior to booking a hunt.

* * *

Fortunately, Paulo's camp was staffed with men who were prepared to haul Barcia's hippo out of the Ruaha River. Once the senator made the shot (borrowing the outfitter's rifle), the hippo's corpse tumbled slowly downstream until it lodged against a sandbar. It was imperative to rope it and winch it out of the water before the crocs became too excited by the blood.

Paulo's men knew exactly what to do; this was not the first hippo they had wrestled to shore. As the men from Michigan stood helplessly by, the Africans stripped to their shorts and waded into the muddy water with ropes. Inside of an hour, inch by inch, several tons of guts encased in a leathery, brownish-gray bag emerged onto the shore. Overhead, white-headed vultures noticed the activity and began to circle.

One could drown in a hippo's guts. Even after the animal is quartered and the head removed, and each quarter is dragged out of the river bottom and up the sandy bank by the straining Land Cruiser, the amount of offal left behind is stunning.

Even more stunning is the immediate appearance of scavenger birds. White-headed vultures spun down, followed by larger griffon vultures, gulls, and ravens. Then came majestic and eerily imposing marabou storks, tall and stiffly formal, the Addams family's Lurch dressed for dinner. Dozens, then hundreds and ultimately thousands of birds, large and small, all fighting and screeching and tearing for their share of dead hippo.

The Waiting Game

To this point in the 2007 safari, none of the guides or trackers had seen a live lion. Based on fresh tracks in likely spots, Webster selected five locations for lion baits and chained chunks of hippo carcass to various trees. First he gave each chunk a scenic, if bumpy, ride around the Pori Trackers' concession. The huge hunk of meat slogged along behind the slow-moving Toyota, laying down complex trails of odor and fat.

"African lions have excellent eyesight, good hearing and sense of smell. They also have very quick reflexes, which allows them to keep up with the agile antelope." So says The Big Zoo at www.TheBigZoo.com, a "virtual zoo" that is, in reality, an online retail store. The Big Zoo's shtick is enticing children and their parents—people who have never imagined a lion except as a Disney cartoon character—to purchase cute T-shirts, rubber snakes, stuffed animals, saccharine posters, and infantile books. Perhaps the assumption is that wearing a T-shirt showing a lion cub licking its mother's snout will save it from the dominant male, which will, within a few days, kill and eat it; that by donning the T-shirt, the wearer becomes somehow closer to nature, a part of "the solution." This Internet site also prints insightful wildlife and survival data, stating that lions have "good hearing and sense of smell" and that antelope are "agile."

The lion's senses are, in fact, the finest in the world. Whereas a human could not smell a freshly cut haunch of hippo unless his nose was rubbed in it, a lion's senses are keenly adapted to the slightest alteration in its life zone. Those tiny adjustments—a baboon troop humping through its territory, rains beginning early in the year, the cry of a field mouse impaled on a thorn—are the difference between living and dying on the treacherous plains of the Selous.

Lions kill because they must kill. For a lion, killing is not a game; it does not result in a trophy or a T-shirt or a line in a record book. A lion is not making a policy statement or participating in some cruel ritual when it breaks a zebra's back or sinks its fangs into a buffalo's throat. Killing is what the universe has programmed a lion to do. It is

A baboon makes an ugly trophy and even Jim Barcia admits that it is not the preferred mount for his state senate office in Lansing, Michigan. Still, when he took one with a crossbow in Tanzania in 2007, the men of Pori Trackers applauded.

an absolute imperative, and regardless of the dream that "the lion shall lie down with the lamb" and similar fantasies, killing is the reason God Almighty put lions on earth.

Thus, to sense that a fresh hippo carcass is nearby—whether lions realize this by smell, by sight, by hearing, or by some sleight of hand that verges on a Vegas card trick—is everyday stuff for the king of beasts. A lion's senses are keen and hard-edged. It is merciless because at some ancient birth, the godhead said, "Go. Kill. Enrich the lands." And so it does.

Five baits were positioned near fresh lion tracks, but only one was consistently hit. How exactly to interpret that message was irrelevant to Webster and to Barcia. They set up on the active bait and waited.

Now, lions tend to hunt and eat at night, then lie around in the shade all day, posing for nature documentaries. This day-night role reversal may violate our human sense of order, but lions are not mechanical windup animals from thebigzoo.com. They have fleas and get upset stomachs; they can break a tooth and become irritable; they occasionally are disemboweled on the horns of a buffalo. In short, they have lion personalities, which means that one size does not precisely fit every animal, and one can never precisely predict how they will behave. On occasion they are known to hunt and eat in broad daylight, or at least in the margins between day and night, and it was in those margins that Webster and Barcia expected to have their best chance.

Eventually, lions came to the bait. Female—female—female—maneless male. Because Jim Barcia had his standards, however, none

Peter Dafner is originally from South Africa, but now lives in Namibia. As a freelance professional hunter, he finds employment wherever he is licensed. His ability to converse in German made him especially useful to Pori Trackers in Tanzania when rifleman Torsten Rademacher visited in 2006. Here Dafner inspects the head of a hippo shot for lion bait.

of the above were suitable. He was simply not going to hang a maneless king of beasts (much less a female) on the wall of his Senate office. So he waited . . . and waited.

They shifted hippo meat to the "hot bait." The meat was rancid now, even though they had covered it with palm thatch to keep the buzzards and carrion eagles away and to shade it from the intense rays of the equatorial sun. When the breeze shifted, wafting the odor into their blind, Barcia came within a hair's breadth of gagging, but to retch inside a small, warm, and enclosed space and have to stay inside it would have been terrible. Even the Eastman blind's scent-absorbing properties would not have withstood such an assault.

For two weeks they sat and waited. Not all day, of course, but part of each day: forty-five minutes to an hour at first light, longer in the evening. Webster and Barcia, and the trackers waiting in the truck half a mile away, agreed that the lions knew they were present and simply did not care, did not believe the hunters were any more of a threat than flies and fleas or the occasional outbreak of veld mange. A nuisance, but not deadly.

When Barcia began to worry that time was slipping away, Webster would reply, "Be patient. Wait for a good lion." Then he would take Barcia to shoot a warthog or to scout for buffalo, and, for that day, his client would be appeased.

Barcia freshened the bait with a few smaller antelope and his warthog, offal from other kills, anything that came readily to hand. And suddenly, incrementally, the bait began to cost as much as the lion.

With only three days remaining, Barcia's friend Jim George pitched in and shot a hippo. Although a hippo was not on George's "animals of interest" list, his dilemma prompted the generous gesture of his friend.

By 10:30 that night, fresh meat was chained to the hot bait tree, and, as if it were a sign, they heard a male lion roaring and growling.

Surrounded by men working to chain the meat and shelter it from the vultures, in the glare of the Toyota's bright headlamps and beneath the cold, blinking canopy of southern constellations, Barcia felt exotic and blessed, and he shivered when the lion roared again.

Webster turned toward the sound and stepped forward, as if putting an extra few yards between himself and the straining, sweating men would sharpen his senses. He lifted his sharp face toward the dark.

"It smells the blood," he said. "It's coming."

"It's Coming"

"We're going to hunt a different place this morning," Webster said. "Give the hot bait a rest."

"But after today, I've only got two more days."

"Tonight we'll go back to the hot bait . . . and we'll see."

Webster had spoken, prophesied even. Tall and thin, austere as the marabou, the black Muslim hunter was a man of few words, carefully chosen. He was not a drinker. Nor was he of any special comfort as Jim Barcia's anxiety mounted toward his final, expensive hours in Tanzania.

"We'll see what happens," said Webster.

And that was all he said. Not impolite or mean or lazy. Just quiet. He cupped his hands and massaged his bony, hairless face, drawing his hands downward and together at the tip of his chin, as if whispering a prayer. A prayer to the lion god, perhaps, although his Muslim mind would have recoiled, denied the thought as blasphemous.

"We'll see what happens."

Of course, they saw nothing at the alternative bait. Sand, shrubs without leaves, and drying grass. Barcia was perspiring, nervous, and Webster was silent. Distant. The men were ready and unready, in the same breath. The new bait, however, the dripping hippo quarter, had drawn a crowd of females. And they barely looked up when the hunters motored past.

Three friends pose with a trophy warthog on their "Three Amigos" hunt with Paulo Shanalingigwa's Pori Trackers in 2007: (left to right) Jim George, Jim Barcia, and Bob Eastman.[3]

One day left and Jim Barcia wanted to talk, had to talk. Webster listened, but only shrugged. Barcia, the politician with standards, kept talking. Webster kept shrugging. It was as if some invisible neurochemical bond connected the two men, drawing the American toward the African while that man remained, elusively, just at arm's length. Jim Barcia's internal pressure gauge, however, indicated an approaching red line.

"We'll go out a little early this evening," Webster said, his English practically flawless.

Midafternoon and hot. The little blind feels too close, breathless and steamy. And suddenly, it feels wrong. Without consulting his American client, Webster presses the "come now" signal on his radio. The men tumble out of the blind and walk toward the rumbling Toyota.

"We'll go to the new bait," Webster says, before falling silent.

Jim Barcia groans, but does not protest or ask questions.

"What was the point?" he later says, shrugging, as if negotiating with the guide is beyond even his considerable political skills.

By 4:30 PM they have cleared a shooting lane and set up inside the camouflaged, pop-up blind forty yards from the new bait. Plenty early for something to happen . . . or for something to become screwed up beyond all hope of salvation. FUBAR as they say in the army.

"If you get a good shot at the right lion," Webster says, unnecessarily, "take it."

[3]According to Senator Jim Barcia, some of the hunts we enjoy today may soon become unobtainable at any price. The problems are familiar: loss of habitat and increased human population. Still, Barcia believes that outdoors people will enjoy reading about the pioneers of bowhunting, and Bob Eastman is in that league with Fred Bear. "I cherish my friendship with Bob and Ann (Bob's wife)," he says. "Bob is a phenomenally talented individual in many respects. It takes a lot of talent to start and run successful companies like he has done—and to have success hunting dangerous game with a bow. As a bow hunter, Bob is a purist. Very ethical. He wouldn't touch a firearm. He's a unique individual. Nothing fazes him and he never looks back. He is always focused on the next hunt, the next challenge."

Now, both men are silent, perspiring inside the warm blind. Waiting. Barcia rolls up his sleeves, and as he does so, the head of a lioness, a very big lioness, emerges from the brush to their front and right. Watching through the blackened screen that covers the blind's window openings, Barcia and Webster freeze.

Surely the lion perceives that the blind was not there the day before. Lions are animals, but they are not stupid. In fact, they are clever, smart in the way of cats. This female turns and walks directly, purposefully, toward the blind. Webster must decide quickly. Here is a lioness weighing three hundred and fifty pounds and as tough as an animal can get. She is a killing machine, now only thirty yards, now twenty-five and ten . . . and finally, barely a foot from the flimsy polyester, which is all that separates them.

Webster might have shot her, and no one would have second-guessed his decision. He does not, however. He only motions for Barcia to be cool, be silent, and be still. It is a slight movement of his right hand—the raised fingertips of his right hand—as if he is patting a child on the head. The brown hand, dark on top and light as a white man on the palm. But Barcia understands, and both men shrink into themselves, becoming smaller, inconsequential, insignificant, as if they had caught their breath and now choose to slide softly beneath the surface of a still and reflective pond without creating so much as a ripple.

The lioness breathes heavily. She pants. If she springs forward, as much from curiosity as aggressiveness, she will pin the men helplessly beneath the cloth, as effectively as if she has caught them in a net. They could not even lift their arms to shield their faces. Then she would bite, and bite again, while the men struggled and screamed, and, swinging her massive head and neck from side to side, she would shred the cloth and the men beneath it, their agonies exciting her, urging her to greater efforts, attracting other members of her pride.

Whether she crushes their skulls or only bites through their shoulders or abdomens, it will be terrible, and almost certainly deadly.

For a while, she does not move. Only stands before them, the hunters, crouched inside their blind, daring not even to tremble. She cannot see them or perhaps even hear them, but she can smell them. She has smelled men before, this lioness, although how she interprets the signals may never be understood. Are they simply more meat, one fat, one lean; light meat, dark meat? Or are they a threat, they and their oily machines and acrid-smelling weapons? Only another cat could understand.

With his sleeves rolled, Barcia slowly rotates his wrist and stares down at his watch. Perhaps he wonders how long he has to live, mentally bidding goodbye to a man's toys, joys, and measures. Like some innocent victim of a drive-by shooting, worrying that the blood will stain his clean shirt.

A whole minute she stares into the blind. Then two minutes. Three. Four minutes! She steps to her right, slowly circling, her powerful bulk looming over the men as she slides by; then she steps to the back of the blind, where the hunters cannot monitor her vague image through the cloth, and she pauses.

The lioness exhales loudly, almost huffs like a bear. Jim Barcia says that at that moment, he almost lost it, even knowing that if he turned to face her or tried to grab Webster's rifle and shoot, the lion would pounce on the blind, pinning the men inside.

With time dwindling before the bush plane returns the Americans to Dar, Barcia elects to use one of the outfitter's rifles. He has not lost confidence in the bow so much as chosen the immediacy of the 7mm magnum's knock-down power.

Circling, one cautious step at a time, the lioness again stares into the window at the front of the blind . . . and, as suddenly and unexpectedly as she has turned toward them, she turns away. She tugs languidly at the raw hippo quarter, ripping off two bites, three at most, and then disappears into the bush, her scruffy tan melding with the withered scrub as impossibly as a dark star shining through the Southern Cross.

Barcia shivers. His shirt is soaked with sweat, and it must smell strongly, he realizes. Fortunately, the scent-absorbing properties of the blind have contained his stink—and that of Webster also. Although Webster is experienced with dangerous game, he is human and must feel overwhelming relief that the lioness is no longer within arm's length, her long tail twitching in indecision.

Ten minutes pass before the men hear a deep, guttural rattle, unmistakable and provocative.

"That's a male," Webster whispers.

Somewhere in the bush a baboon chatters nervously.

"Get ready," Webster says. "He's coming."

Barcia picks up the rifle, which now feels as if it is made of cement. How can he possibly lift it to his eye, sight through the low-power scope, and pull the trigger? He might need Webster to help him steady it, he thinks, and, turning toward his guide at this moment of utmost opportunity, begins to speak, although he does not recall whether any words actually came out of his dry mouth. Webster shakes his head and refuses to look at him.

The sun seems not to move, and yet shadows creep deeper into the shooting lane. Even as day loosens its grip, the blind feels like a prison. Then, at 6:45 PM on the twentieth day of his twenty-one-day hunt, the alpha male appears.

"Take it," Webster whispers.

Barcia hefts the rifle, sighting through the dark mesh of the shoot-through window screen of lightweight, black cloth. Forgetting how heavy the gun seemed just minutes earlier, he places the scope cross hair on the lion's shoulder and pulls the trigger.

Neither the American hunter nor the Tanzanian guide are wearing earplugs. Because a human's delicate circuitry is fundamentally electrochemical and is easily disrupted under pressure, the concussion from the magnum round causes a temporary short-circuit in Jim Barcia's vision, not to mention a painful roaring in his ears. For a few moments, he is utterly speechless. Webster's lean, intelligent face contorts in shock.

The pride lion leaps into the air, roaring. When he comes down, he slumps and lies twitching on the ground.

A female, however, presumably the same female that had circled the blind earlier, lunges forward into the shooting lane, growling and snapping. The hair on her neck and back rise stiffly. Caught off guard, she is ready to attack the source of the loud noise, the source of her pride-partner's sudden immobility.

Webster clenches his fist and moves his hand forward and back, indicating that Barcia should jack a fresh shell into the rifle's chamber.

"Watch her tail," he whispers. "If it begins to twitch, she's going to charge. Be ready to shoot."

Webster picks up his own double rifle, checks that the safety is off, and holds it in both hands.

For a few moments, the female stares directly at the blind.

"If she rushes us," Jim wonders, "can I hit her?"

It is the age-old question that hunters and politicians alike have asked through time. If they challenge me, can I respond? Do I have the guts, the answers? Am I man enough?

Suddenly the female turns and bounds away into the brush. Jim's head sinks to his chest; so does Webster's. Both men are rattled, perplexed by the suddenness of events and the gun's stunning blast. Neither speaks. The lioness, after all, might appear again, even from behind; she could still charge out of the bush, although neither believes she will.

The male is dead, his mane ragged and worn. An old hunter. A tough guy. The king of his tiny corner of Africa.

The male is dead, and it is close to dark in Tanzania. Webster rests his heavy rifle against a bush.

"Are you a good shot with that?" Jim asks. "If she had charged, could you have stopped her?"

"Well, I'll be honest," his guide replies. "Ninety-nine times out of a hundred, when we fire these rifles, it's like a stick of dynamite going off, and the animal changes course or turns and runs. We don't hit them if we can help it."

These were the most words Jim Barcia heard his professional speak at one time on the entire safari.

Jamie in Two Worlds

2010

Chapter 19

Is the elk shot by me any more or less a necessary death than these or that of the thousands of rabbits and mice inadvertently destroyed in the process of growing and harvesting my organic, all natural, oat bran breakfast cereal?

Bloodties[1]
Ted Kerasote

Jamie Wilson has been a professional hunter since 1987. Big-game hunting is all he ever truly thought about doing. He also leads photographic safaris in Mozambique, Zambia, and South Africa.

Bob Eastman, who has hunted leopard and other species with Wilson three times, says, "He's a great walker, a woodsman, and a bird expert, too.

"We were driving through the bush one year, and there was this little parrot sitting in the track that wouldn't fly as we got close. Jamie had the driver stop, and he jumped out and caught it in his hands. It was a young bird and was hurt for some reason. In camp, Jamie fed it evaporated milk, and to this day it's still part of his family."

Something Dies, Something Is Born

Jamie Wilson was born, raised, and schooled in Zambia. He was a child of English parents. His wife, Eveline, is of Dutch extraction. Although they look homeward, toward their European roots, and spend their winters in the Netherlands, they are otherwise firmly African.

[1]Page 240.

Bob Eastman has hunted with guide Jamie Wilson on several occasions. Jamie has a Zambian passport and is a citizen of that African nation. Although he does not regret his choice to become a professional hunter, Jamie believes that it is, regrettably, "a dying profession."

The vast movement of peoples across the earth is the signature of the twenty-first century: Mexican immigrants flooding into the Southwest region of the United States, Haitians and Cubans into Florida, Indians into England, North Africans into southern Europe, and Chinese into Australia. It is a fluid world, moving from poverty and totalitarianism toward relative prosperity and democratic institutions. People are not lining up to enter Russia or China or Burma or Zimbabwe, all ruled by repressive dictators at this writing.

Today, Jamie is a citizen of Zambia and has a Zambian passport. Andrew, his father, was not at all convinced that following game was a good way for the boy to make his way in the world and would probably have preferred that Jamie become a doctor or a lawyer. Still, the father and the father's friends were all hunters, and their treks through the bush and the resulting gunfire and smell of gunpowder were exciting, even romantic.

Jamie gained a great deal of experience while hunting with his father and started working in the safari business as a teenager. His first jobs were guiding photographers. Only later did he apprentice himself to become a hunting guide, which is the PH near the peak of prestige—if not a position of high income, security, or longevity—in the African guiding and tourism hierarchy.

"I loved the bush," Jamie says, "still do. I did some photographic safaris, but they just weren't very exciting. I was always thinking about the crack of the rifles and the smell of gunpowder and remembered making biltong[2] with my dad."

Although he does not regret choosing to become a professional hunter, Jamie believes that it is, regrettably, "a dying profession."

Jamie uses the term "regrettably" not just because the occupation fills his life with travel and adventure and acquaintances around the world, although that is true. He says he does not regret the decline of the profession simply because it suggests coming changes, the need to adapt and learn new skills, the requirement to run harder simply to stay in one place.

The passing of the professional hunter and the traditional safari, as the world has known them for more than a century, indicates that the

[2]Biltong is the quintessential African bush meat. Jamie Wilson says biltong is never smoked but simply dried in the shade, perhaps hung over a line or the branches of a bush. Drying takes two to five days, depending on the temperature and humidity. Jamie's favorite meat is eland, wildebeest, or kudu, but he says that actually "beef is the best due to its fat content. It's tastier. Our game does not have much fat at all. Zebras and pigs carry some fat, as well as hippos, which is actually not bad biltong if you eat it before it gets too dry and too hard!"

Surrounded by trophies of the hunt, Bob Eastman says that hunting in Africa has been his lifelong passion. Yet on each trip, he carries a briefcase filled with business books. He studies in the evening around the campfire and while eating lunch in the shade of a miombo *tree.*

African continent is losing its wild way of life. It is gradually losing its colorful costumes, its tribal heritage, and its multiplicity of languages and customs. Africa is becoming international. Cosmopolitan. Tame.

Soon the cultural practice of ritual scarification may go the way of headhunting and female circumcision, of wearing plates in the lips and stacks of rings to stretch the neck, although one can argue that is a good thing. Soon the international blue business suit may entirely displace mud-cloth robes, while the legal brief and the AK-47 displace the council of elders and the panga. New tyrants to displace the old tyrants.

While working as an apprentice PH, Jamie realized an opportunity in the safari industry. Zambia had recently changed its laws to allow only Zambian citizens to own and operate safari companies. When an African nation (or perhaps any nation) passes such legislation, its jurists and politicians find ways to interpret the law to favor their particular constituencies, but this unexpected event gave Jamie an edge.

Jamie formed Mogambo Safaris with partner Grant Cumings, and they acquired a hunting lease in the Luangwa Valley. Later, they expanded their initial property to include three additional zones, one of which was the fertile Kafue region. It was fertile because of the rich alluvial soil (locally referred to as "black cotton" soil), but plant or animal agriculture was cursed because of the presence of the tsetse fly. Through this venture Jamie became an outfitter before he earned his license as a professional hunter.

By 1987, he had successfully apprenticed for five years and qualified for his professional hunter's license and membership in the Zambian Professional Hunters Association. No sooner was Jamie rising from the party-induced hangover, however, than the politicians again changed

Bob Eastman celebrates his most recent leopard trophy, shot with his recurve bow. "Now is the time to go to Africa," Bob maintains. "The game is still plentiful and the cost of the trip, while expensive for the flights and outfitters and trophy fees, has to be reckoned over the course of a lifetime."

the prerequisites for owning a safari company. Mogambo Safaris and many others lost their concession rights.

Curiously, Jamie Wilson was not deterred from his outdoor and wildlife way of life by this second bureaucratic move, and he continued to work as a hired PH within the industry, strengthening his résumé and his reputation as a fine guide. He could manage the crew and locate game; perhaps more important, clients were happy to book with him.

During this time he relocated his home from Lusaka, the capital city of Zambia, to Johannesburg, South Africa. Chafing under the business management and leadership of others, seeing the profits of his hard work make others rich, Jamie was eager to build his own company. He earned a South African professional hunter's license and, by spending time in Mozambique, qualified to guide there as well. Eventually, he moved permanently to northern Mozambique.

To make his guiding services even more versatile and valuable, he obtained his private pilot's license and purchased an airplane. Ultimately, with thousands of hours flying across the continent, he acquired his commercial and instrument licenses. His Piper PA-31-325 Navajo is fitted with twin turbocharged engines with counter-rotating propellers. With a maximum takeoff weight of sixty-five hundred pounds, it can carry up to seven passengers and their gear.

The airplane and commercial license have been extremely valuable in the normal course of Jamie's work as a big-game outfitter.

"In 2005 a client of mine took a one-hundred-and-ten-pound elephant in Mozambique, and I flew him and those teeth out of the bush together," he says. "I've flown many others as well: men with gunshot wounds, snakebites, crocodile bites."

Today, Jamie Wilson concentrates his safaris in the Niassa Reserve of Mozambique and the Luangwa Valley of Zambia. He has taken more than one hundred and twenty lions and leopards, two hundred and fifty buffaloes, several elephants, and even rhinos. He speaks English, Spanish, and Portuguese and several indigenous languages. When the season is completed, the bills have been paid, and the scratches, bruises, and bites have healed, he resides in the Netherlands, and this, being African and European, allows him to enjoy the best of both worlds.

Perhaps it is in working with his native assistants that Jamie Wilson excels. Asked how he recruits and trains his crew, he replies, "From villages around the concession. For trackers I try to employ the ex-poachers . . . or current poachers. They know what they are doing and where the game and the water is.

"Your average white PH can follow a blood trail, but for trackers, you've got to have natives. I've worked with some of these fellows who can track across rock and bare ground at a trot, and when they stop and point, you'd better be ready to shoot."

As much as he loves his work and recognizes that Africa is becoming more "civilized" and bureaucratic, it is those very trends that he finds frustrating.

"The worst thing that ever happened," he says, "is once, when I was young and inexperienced, I picked up a client at an airport. We were supposed to hunt elephants in a special area. Somehow, we were met at the airport by my contact, the man who helped me arrange the hunt, and he was with a bunch of government officials. Guess what they all wanted? Right. Money. I gave it to them, and then they disappeared, leaving me in a foreign country, almost broke and stranded with a client! *Asante sana* to you too. (Thank you very much.)

"It's always like that when dealing with officials. The ones that really make my blood boil are the government game scouts who try to get bribes from clients. Makes me want to chuck it all sometimes. Do something else. Not a librarian or an accountant, though, and even being a pilot gets boring."

So the life of the professional is not all guns and roses. A bush camp is lonely, and there is the persistent fly and malaria. Like many PHs, Jamie has malaria and suffers from an outbreak every year.

"I don't take antimalaria medication because it's not good for you to take it all the time," he says. "I carry the cure with me all the time, though. I use the Chinese herbal medication artesunate[3] and normally shake it in two days because I try to recognize it early. On a hunt with Bob Eastman last year in November, I got it but carried on hunting."

Reflections

All of Jamie Wilson's complaints disappear when a client arrives and they shake the noise and confusion of the cities, the officials and their paperwork, and enter the vast silence of the bush.

"Leopard is normally the easiest of the Big Five," Jamie says, "and Bob Eastman is a good hunter. He's patient and doesn't make noise and move around in the blind. Still, I remember the first hunt didn't turn out so well.

"His leopard got into the tree and noticed something it didn't like. Maybe a reflection from Bob's broadhead, because since then Bob has always used a black marker to darken them and make sure they don't shine.

"I especially remember a leopard hunt with Bob when about twenty elephants came through! We got out of there fast, as elephants generally don't like me. They've even been known to tramp through our camp in the middle of the night.

"Then, when we went back to that blind, a couple of lions came in, and one enormous black-mane fellow jumped up onto the bait, which was several baboons. Bob wanted to shoot, but I didn't have a tag for lion.

[3]The drug artesunate is extracted from the Chinese herb *Artemisia annua.* Manufacturers say it is presently the only medicine that the malaria *Plasmodium* strains has not developed a resistance to.

"After the lion fed on the bait, it came over to the blind to investigate us, and believe me, that was nerve-racking. We walked out in the dark back to back, and I'm pretty sure the big male followed us. At times like that my .458—I usually carry a .375—feels reassuring, but I kept trying not to think that the guy at my back that night only had a bow and arrow.

"We got out of there quickly, only to find out that the driver hadn't heard our radio call signal. He and the truck were still miles away; there were hungry lions nearby, and it was pitch black."

Although he has a touch of the African PH's reluctance about archery, Jamie says, "Usually, bow hunters do very well with us on leopards or lions. The cat hunting is quite good, but plains game is more challenging in this area. There is plenty of game, it's just tougher for a bow hunter to hunt it."

Jamie enjoys bow hunters and appreciates the fact that they demonstrate a greater commitment to their skill and to the hunt than some of his gun-toting clients.

"I enjoy using the bow on the big cats. But good bow hunters like to get out and walk and stalk, and that's OK in a controlled environment, but so many things out there are willing to stalk back. These animals are just too smart to be stalked like North American game, and the only way to take a good sampling of plains game in my areas is to sit at a water hole and let them come to you."

* * *

Jamie Wilson is not optimistic about the future of hunting.

"It's going to disappear in Africa, maybe worldwide. With so many people and so much pressure on the land, it's just inevitable. Here, it's viewed as a rich white man's sport, and even if that's no longer true, it isn't held in high esteem."

What the Wife Knew Addendum

Married only two years, Ann Eastman accompanied her husband, Bob, on his first safari to Africa in 1968.

"It was very exciting," she recalls.

A speech therapist and substitute teacher, she felt there was little balance between the Los Angeles school systems and the primitive wilderness of the Lost Continent. The L.A. school board had offered her full-time employment, but it turned out that this was an offer she could refuse. She preferred Mozambique to the Watts District the year following the murderous race riots in that urban neighborhood.

In memory, the petite Michigan blonde still envisions the herds of buffaloes, the giraffes and zebras, the wildebeests and impalas that took her breath away in those days before she had children and grandchildren, before she had a permanent home and glasses and acquired all the pleasures and bruises of growing up and holding her brilliant, scrappy family together.

Ann had never seen such animals except in books or in zoos, or perhaps on early black-and-white television shows such as *Zoo Parade* or *Wild Kingdom* with Marlin Perkins. And she was the only woman in the bush camp, a fact that could have been troublesome except that everyone—from the professional hunters to the lowliest skinners—treated her gently and with patience. They explained. They demonstrated. They experienced her not as an outsider but as one of the group. They did not view her as a helpless woman because she was not a hunter or a rugged and knowledgeable outdoors person. They did not condescend, and that made all the difference in her ability to enjoy or simply be present during the adventure.

"I'm not a hunter and never have been," Ann says. "I'm just personally not interested in killing an animal, and yet I don't have any qualms about others hunting and shooting. I don't even mind watching, and I understand when someone makes a good shot and a game animal dies and is recovered quickly."

All this is just fine for the spouse of a single-minded bow hunter, a man with the time and ability to make it happen in Africa or Alaska, a hard worker, a student of "the game." Ann became a student as well, preferring her breakfast of impala steaks medium rare, if the bush chef asked, but he didn't, and so most of them turned out well done, if not crispy, and she ate them and did not complain.

"My main job was to hang onto Bob's belt so he wouldn't fall out of the Jeep," she says, recalling the heat and the dry bush outback, the preposterously bouncing truck equipped for riflemen and only adapted for bow hunters because those 1968 clients refused to hunt with guns.

The hunt itself was not her first encounter with Africa, though.

Prior to joining Bob in Mozambique, Ann flew to the William Holden Safari Lodge in Kenya. Today it is the Mount Kenya Safari Club, near the high slopes of Africa's second-highest mountain, Mount Kenya, which straddles the equator. The club was founded in 1959 by the late film star William Holden, eccentric American Ray Ryan, and Swiss financier Carl Hirschmann, and its luxurious buildings and grounds are maintained in a style reminiscent of colonial-era splendor.

Ann's brief stay at Holden's Mount Kenya Safari Lodge was intoxicating, but it was the flight from Nairobi to Lourenço Marques (now Maputo) that she recalls most vividly . . . because it almost didn't happen. At the airport in Nairobi, airline officials told her they had sold her reserved seat.

"Sorry, but you can book a seat on the next available flight."

Ann had also booked her flight from Lourenço Marques into the bush, so any delay would not only be inconvenient, but it would also be terribly expensive. Theoretically, the hunt was to happen the very next day; therefore, the flight was nonrefundable. A true hunter's spouse, an organizer and improviser at heart, Ann began to negotiate, and although she felt a trickle of inner panic, her exterior remained calm, she says, even cool.

Faced with this exasperating American woman who would simply not go away and come back later as instructed, an airline official finally asked, "If we can get you on this airplane, do you care where you ride?"

Without hesitation, Ann answered firmly, "Fine," and she flew for the first time in the cockpit of a commercial airliner. The seat for the pilot-in-training was not altogether comfortable, she remembers, but the crewmen took pains to point out the sights.

In just such a stumbling and hesitating manner, often dancing along the edge of disaster, are unforgettable memories made.

Of course, the flight to Mozambique's capital was not the only memory of that trip more than forty years ago. There were also the hours sitting alone in a Jeep while the men disappeared behind a screen of acacia to track a wounded buffalo into deep grass on the edge of the veld.

"What were they thinking, leaving me alone in that Jeep? Anything could have happened!"

And yet, nothing happened except the heat and the flies and the waiting, and in this manner Ann perhaps became a hunter as well. She was proud.

"It was nerve-racking," she says, but you can almost hear her smile at the memory.

Perhaps waiting in that open Jeep did not require her to be physically tough or especially keen of eye, or quick to draw her bow, aim, and loose an arrow, but she was alone, in the bush, in Africa, and she is right that anything could have happened. And if something had happened, one can imagine her arguing, cajoling, facing the problem, overcoming it. She was indomitable. And later, when the men returned, and asked in their manliest and perhaps most patronizing manner, "How was your day, dear?" she would put down her book, take off her sunglasses, brush back her bangs, and point to the dead mamba or the lion tracks or the dent in the fender from the charging rhino and respond with that special momlike sweetness she brings to adventure at home or abroad, "Oh, fine. Did you find your buffalo?"

In the coming years, Ann Eastman made several trips to Africa with Bob and several as a member of a tour group. Each trip had its own flavor. The pyramids. The Kasbahs of Morocco. A wild flight through the mountains of Zimbabwe, watching as game animals fled from the beating blades of the South African military chopper: "Hey, mates! Send your wives over and we'll take 'em for a ride."

Be careful what you ask for, boys. This little blonde may not be a hunter or a shooter, but she's tougher than she looks.

Eastman's Africa, A Half-Century of Bowhunting Addendum

We inhabit a universe in restless motion, and thus all things change continually. The electrons in rocks and flowers vibrate at velocities near the speed of light. Discarded plastic bottles and the thick hair from an elephant's tail may require centuries to degrade, but they do eventually disintegrate.

Africa, perhaps more than any other place on earth, has changed dramatically during the past hundred years. A century ago, the massive continent was still being fought over, exploited, and colonized by European foreign powers.

Today, Africa's independent nation-states appear to be spiraling downward into technocratic black holes of tribalism in the Christian zones, into medievalism and fanaticism in the Muslim zones. This devolution is being supervised—indeed, driven—by expanding and rapacious Asian economies.

Swarming with hungry humans and burgeoning, poverty-stricken cities, Africa's magnificent animal resources are almost certainly doomed. Except in isolated and heavily protected pockets, they cannot survive the twenty-first century in their natural condition.

The spiraling arc of Africa's rise and subsequent disintegration—the revolutions overtaking its outback and the animals and people who live there—have been documented continuously by men and women who have visited to hunt its big game. Sub-Saharan Africa, for instance, entered the twentieth century with colossal elephant herds and great elephant hunters: Bell, Sutherland, Neumann, and others. And most of those hunters wrote about their years of experience chasing elephants and managing commercial safaris in "the bush."

Addendum: Eastman's Africa

Whether the ultimate goal of a safari is ivory or a hunting client's satisfaction, the trek itself—the journey from today to yesterday, from comfort to hazard, from packaged food to blood on one's hands—has become a permanent romantic ingredient in African and hunting lore. In spite of every on-the-ground reality, this image has not changed.

The old-fashioned safari system—white tents, cocktails by starlight, files of native porters carrying canvas-wrapped bundles of food and tools, and danger on the plains or in the rain forest—remains the standard by which we imagine and measure an African expedition. Ernest Hemingway, Karen Blixen, Robert Ruark, Peter Capstick, and many other writers—the "others" doubtless presenting more straightforward and less imaginative accounts—have immortalized the safari and safari guides.

For more than a century, kings, princes, and commercial magnates from all over the world have been transfixed by the safari image. Rich enough to afford its romance, they have shipped countless hunting trophies home. Now the safari era is over, however, smothered by a tsunami of historical change that even the romantic writers of the West have been ill-equipped to resist. But the news may not all be sad.

One way passes and another appears. To the surprise of many of today's observers, hunting in Africa is actually thriving. Hardships and international pressures notwithstanding, hunting in the sub-Saharan states has become, for want of a better term, "democratized."

Hunters by the thousands now travel to Africa with gun and bow because entrepreneurs have developed big-game opportunities that preserve otherwise threatened species and provide sustainable hunting at affordable prices.

Most governments recognize that the bow and arrow are effective for harvesting most, if not all, big game—certainly the antelope and plains species and at least five of the classic Big Six: elephant, rhinoceros, hippopotamus, lion, leopard, and Cape buffalo. Rhino is another question altogether.

Correspondingly, the nature of professional hunters, Africa's legendary guides, has also changed. One could argue that they have at last become truly "professional" and that, in the twenty-first century, they have developed greater foresight and a wider range of abilities and concerns. Client safety and the well-placed shot remain paramount, but there is also a deeper understanding of the fragile African ecosystem and appreciation for preserving it. Many of today's professional hunters are employed by ranchers, owners, or tenants of vast tracts of land, and a PH's time is split between guiding hunters, photographers, and sightseers and monitoring the health of game populations living within high fences.

One could also argue that today's PH has more book learning but less bush savvy, more time in the classroom but less time in the field. One could argue that he has less practical experience than old-school guides, who learned their craft through arduous apprenticeships—driving, tracking, and skinning—rather than through written examinations. In the old days, becoming a professional hunter was not an option for men of color, so perhaps the occupation of guiding has also become democratized.

* * *

Robert Eastman's half-century hunting career spans the African transition between the era of luxury safaris and the present. With twenty-four hunting trips to the sub-Sahara, he has experienced the rich pleasures of wild game dinners by candlelight and of roaring lions prowling just outside a thorny *boma*. Bob has hunted bongos in a never-ending misery of mud and rain in fly-infested tropical forests. He has hunted elephants in a land so parched that one cannot comprehend how it supports life.

Having taken practically every game species in Africa with a bow, and having hunted in just about every sub-Saharan country and in half-a-dozen countries north of the equator, some on numerous occasions, Bob Eastman has experienced the changes overtaking that dynamic continent. He is an archer, a bow hunter in the classical sense. He is deeply concerned about the populations of game he hunts, and though he is aware that his tools of choice saddle him with limitations and responsibilities, he is nevertheless passionate and focused on his objective.

Bob's professional hunters have been competent and knowledgeable men. Some of them learned bushcraft working for old-time PHs when the law was loosely enforced. Others are the new breed, cautiously optimistic about the future and working to preserve Africa's biological diversity. It is these younger PHs especially who understand the forces loosed upon the continent and who work with zoos (zoological gardens) and preserves, offer photo safaris, and recognize the power of distant animal welfare organizations. They also realize that a footloose way of life may not be for the faint of heart and is surely not permanent or secure.

Speaking of the older breed of African hunter, this book contains a number of fresh interviews with this scarred and musty professional. These are men who have rarely spoken of their safari experiences and have never written about them. By and large, they have kept to themselves their tales of tracking wounded buffaloes through high reeds at twilight, of dealing with native mutiny and murder, and of clients with trembling hands at the moment when one must shoot well or die hard.

It was the old PHs who saved African hunting, for it was they who fought poachers, tribal savageries, and the new national bureaucratic classes to preserve a wild opportunity. Paradoxically, their way of life changed in the process of saving it. Today, the African adventure is available—and will be in the near future—to hunters of lesser financial means but of no lesser passion, especially to hunters with archery gear.

This book is bush and camp, starlight unobscured by neon glare, and hippos grunting at dawn, all re-imagined through Bob Eastman's eyes and experiences. To the man with nothing more than a slender recurve bow, hunting is no different today than it was the evening the first Maasai warrior confronted a black-mane lion with only a spear, a shield, and his courage. It is at once a lament for things lost and an eager portal to Africa in the twenty-first century.

Rick Sapp
Gainesville, Florida
May 2012

Bibliography

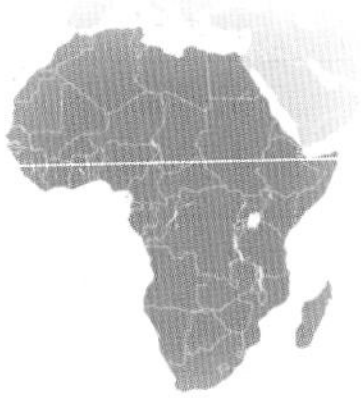

Anonymous. *History of the Bosjesmans, or Bush People; The Aborigines of Southern Africa—with Copious Extracts from the Best Authors, Showing the Habits and Disposition of the Above-Named Extraordinary Race of Human Beings.* London: Chapman, Elcoate, and Company, 1847.

Aurelius, Marcus. *"Meditations," in Marcus Aurelius and His Times.* Roslyn, New York: Walter J. Black, Inc., 1945.

Bakker, Robert T. *Raptor Red.* New York: Bantam Books, 1995.

Bear, Fred. *Fred Bear's Field Notes.* New York: Doubleday & Co., 1976.

Capstick, Peter Hathaway. *The Last Ivory Hunter: The Saga of Wally Johnson.* New York: St. Martin's Press, 1988.

Caputo, Philip. *Ghosts of Tsavo: Stalking the Mystery Lions of East Africa.* Washington, D.C.: National Geographic Society, 2002.

Corbett, Jim. *The Man-eating Leopard of Rudraprayag* in *The Jim Corbett Omnibus.* New Delhi: Oxford University Press, 1947.

Creel, Scott and Nancy M. Creel. "Lion Density and Population Structure in the Selous Game Reserve: Evaluation of Hunting Quotas and Offtake," in *African Journal of Ecology* (Selous Wild Dog Project, Frankfurt Zoological Society, c/o Selous Conservation Programme, Box 1519 Dar es Salaam, Tanzania), vol 35, issue 2, pages 83–93, June 1997. First published online 17 December 2003.

Cervantes, Miguel de. *Don Quixote.* New York: HarperCollins, 2003.

Durant, Will and Ariel. *The Lessons of History.* New York: Simon & Schuster, 1968.

Gladwell, Malcolm. *Blink: The Power of Thinking without Thinking.* New York: Back Bay Books, 2005.

Bibliography

Hemingway, Ernest. *Green Hills of Africa.* New York: Charles Scribner's Sons, 1935.

—. *True at First Light.* New York: Scribner, 1999.

—. *The Short Happy Life of Francis Macomber* in *The Snows of Kilimanjaro and Other Stories.* New York: Charles Scribner's Sons, 1927.

Herne, Brian. *White Hunters: The Golden Age of African Safaris.* New York: Henry Holt, 1999.

Hunter, J. A. *Hunter.* New York: Harper & Brothers, 1952.

Kerasote, Ted. *Bloodties: Nature, Culture, and the Hunt.* New York: Random House, 1993.

LeGuin, Ursula. *The Left Hand of Darkness* New York: Ace Books, 1969.

Leopold, Aldo. *A Sand County Almanac.* New York: Oxford University Press, 1949.

Marsh, Brian. *The Last Trophy.* New York: St. Martin's Press, 1982.

Marsh, Brian. *Baron in Africa: The Remarkable Adventures of Werner von Alvensleben.* Long Beach: Safari Press, 1997.

Neumann, Arthur H. *Elephant Hunting in East Equatorial Africa,* in *Library of African Adventure,* Vol. 3. New York: St. Martin's Press, 1994.

Ortega y Gasset, José. *Meditations on Hunting.* New York: Charles Scribner's Sons, 1972.

Ruark, Robert. *Uhuru: A Novel of Africa Today.* New York: McGraw-Hill, 1962.

—. *The Honey Badger.* New York: McGraw-Hill, 1938.

—. *The Old Man and the Boy.* New York: Henry Holt, 1953.

Russell, Franklin. *Watchers at the Pond.* New York: Alfred A. Knopf, 1961.

—. *The Hunting Animal.* New York: Harper & Row, 1983.

Sandburg, Carl. *The People, Yes,* in *Harvest Poems*: 1910–1960. New York: Harcourt, Brace & World, 1960.

Serling, Rod. *Requiem for a Heavyweight,* a teleplay written in 1956.